Housing Policy and Rented Housing in Europe

Housing Policy and Rented Housing in Europe

Michael Oxley

Avebury Professor of Housing

and

Jacqueline Smith

Research Fellow
De Montfort University
Leicester and Milton Keynes, UK

This book is based partly on work financed by Avebury International,
Milton Keynes

E & FN SPON
An Imprint of Chapman & Hall

London · Glasgow · Weinheim · New York · Tokyo · Melbourne · Madras

Published by E & FN Spon, an imprint of Chapman & Hall,
2–6 Boundary Row, London SE1 8HN, UK

Chapman & Hall, 2–6 Boundary Row, London SE1 8HN, UK

Blackie Academic & Professional, Wester Cleddens Road, Bishopbriggs, Glasgow G64 2NZ, UK

Chapman & Hall GmbH, Pappelallee 3, 69469 Weinheim, Germany

Chapman & Hall USA, 115 Fifth Avenue, New York, NY 10003, USA

Chapman & Hall Japan, ITP-Japan, Kyowa Building, 3F, 2-2-1 Hirakawacho, Chiyoda-ku, Tokyo 102, Japan

Chapman & Hall Australia, 102 Dodds Street, South Melbourne, Victoria 3205, Australia

Chapman & Hall India, R. Seshadri, 32 Second Main Road, CIT East, Madras 600 035, India

First edition 1996

© 1996 Michael Oxley and Jacqueline Smith

Typeset in Times 10/12pt by Saxon Graphics Ltd, Derby
Printed in Great Britain by Page Brothers, Norwich

ISBN 0 419 20720 1

A catalogue record for this book is available from the British Library

Library of Congress Catalog Card Number: 95-71378

♾ Printed on permanent acid-free text paper, manufactured in accordance with ANSI/NISO Z39.48-1992 and ANSI/NISO Z39.48-1984 (Permanence of Paper).

To our families

Contents

List of tables

List of figures

Acknowledgements

Much of the material in this book has been assembled in the course of a wider research project on housing investment in Europe. This project has been financed by Avebury International, Milton Keynes. Avebury International provide project management, construction management, business consultancy and other services to social housing providers. Their support is gratefully acknowledged.

A large number of people throughout Europe have provided information; we express our gratitude to them all. The long list includes: Thierry Lacroix and colleagues at INSEE; Laurent Ghékiere and colleagues at UNFOHLM; Bruno Lefebvre, Université Paris; Laurence Bertrand, Laboratoire Logement; Franz Hubert, Freie Universität Berlin; Frau Imming, Frau Eipart and many colleagues at Statistisches Bundesamt; Dr Brenke and Markus Kelle at Bundesministerium, Bonn; Dr Bernd Bartholmai at Deutsches Institut für Wirtschaftsforschung; Mme Sirota and colleagues at Ministére du Logement; Patrick de la Morvonnais at Bureau d'Information et de Previsions Economique; Sako Musterd, University of Amsterdam; Hugo Priemus, Peter Boelhouwer and colleagues at OTB, University of Delft; André Thomsen, University of Delft; Tineke Zuidervaart and Michael Tuvil at Nationale Woningraad, Almere; Drs M. van Oostrom and Rob Ligterink at Dutch Ministry of Housing; Mr H. Schippers and colleagues at Central Bureau of Statistics, Netherlands; Mr M. Nacinovic and colleagues at the European Commission; Brian Stewart at the DOE; Scottish Homes; and the Northern Ireland Housing Executive. Special thanks are due to those people who took time out to talk to us and provide information for the book on visits to France, Germany, the Netherlands and Portugal, and to those individuals who read through drafts of the text relating to France, Germany and the Netherlands. The work on this book has benefited from the parallel research on housing development in Europe, conducted by Andrew Golland at De Montfort University.

Thanks are due to our colleagues who suffered, tolerated and cajoled us, and to students who raised questions and provided some answers.

The production of the manuscript was the result of much diligence and efficiency from Pauline Bennett who made sense of a mixture of scribbling, dictation, unedited discs and lots of alterations. We are most grateful for her help.The diagrams and tables have been put together by an extremely patient Neil Summerfield; his skills were much appreciated. Neil also produced the initial design for the cover.

Finally, to our families and friends who endured and encouraged us, a very big thank you indeed.

Introduction

1

This is a book about housing policy and rented housing in the countries of the European Union. The more detailed material concentrates on the provision of rented housing in France, Germany, the Netherlands and the UK. An addition to the literature on housing policy and international comparisons presents many challenges given that both the significance of policy analysis and the value of international comparisons have been called into question in academic debate.

1.1 POLICY AND COMPARISONS

The arguments about 'policy' have been largely about the significance of policy in explaining housing provision when set against broader social, economic and institutional factors that are at work in shaping housing systems (Harloe, 1985; Ball *et al.*, 1988). Critics of comparative housing studies have argued variously that:

1. They are dominated by a 'liberal interventionist' approach and exhibit a 'lack of analysis of structures of housing provision' (Ball *et al.*, 1988).
2. They are highly descriptive and lacking in social scientific analysis (a criticism advanced by one of the current authors, Oxley, 1991a).
3. Particularly regarding renting, studies are heavily influenced by the specific British experience and there is an 'Anglo-Saxon bias in comparative rental research' (Kemeny, 1995).

This book does not claim to address and resolve these arguments but it is written with an awareness of, if not a submission to, these critiques. In relation to policy, we are not claiming that current housing conditions, the tenure pattern, access to housing, and the quantity and quality of housing available are simply a function of policy decisions. Housing is, of course, influenced by a wide range of forces in society operating over long time periods. The way such forces, whether they be termed economic, social, demographic or institutional, work and their consequences must be understood if we are to advance complete explanations of current housing provision, or of how we perceive this provision. An analysis of such forces is not, however, the aim of this book. It is rather to examine what housing policy can do about housing provision. This means that the role of government in setting policy objectives and using policy instruments to achieve these objectives is our central concern. Thus we assume that policy does matter and it can make a difference to housing conditions in a country and, furthermore, differences between countries are partly a function of policy decisions, while also being influenced significantly by the wider forces in society.

We are concerned with the interaction between government and market forces in both the formulation and execution of housing policy. The role of government is not, however, seen simply as one of 'intervention' but more broadly one which is a necessary precondition for, as well as a crucial influence on, market forces. In examining the options open to government we consider the varying institutional arrangements governing the management, allocation and financing of different types of renting in several countries. Description is inevitable in order that differences may be displayed. The structure of the descriptions does, however, promote some understanding and analysis of the various systems that are in place. There is a good deal of data in the book which is intended both to enhance descriptions and to assist analysis.

We are not testing a narrow hypothesis but are advancing the broad hypothesis that differences between countries in the policy instruments used have important consequences for the allocation, consumption and production of housing. In examining this proposition we have tried to limit the bias that comes from seeing things through British eyes but, of course, the ultimate avoidance of such bias is not possible. The tenure specific approach that is a function of such bias, and in particular the use of a taxonomy which daubs renting 'private' or 'social', is acknowledged to be potentially misleading given the blurring of the distinction in many countries (Oxley, 1995). However, we do cautiously, and with sensitivity to the arguments against, use this division in setting out much of the information on the systems of renting which exist in particular countries. Such a division when used critically does in fact expose both the weakness of the private/social boundary and reveal potential policy options which may, in a British context, influence both the operation of rented housing and the nature of the private/social boundary.

1.2 GOVERNMENTS, MARKETS AND HOUSING

We are not assuming that housing provision is in the hands of either 'the state' or 'the market'. This is a false dichotomy. Markets are mechanisms for trading property rights. The state plays an essential role in defining, protecting and underwriting these property rights. The trading of property rights is subject to terms which the state influences. Governments from time to time redefine and moderate property rights and change the terms on which they can be traded. It is this process of influence over property rights in housing which has significant effects on the production, distribution, pricing, financing and profitability of housing (Oxley, 1995).

When we do refer to a more market-orientated provision, or more being left to market forces within a country, we are describing a situation not in which government has withdrawn or decided to do nothing but rather one in which it has decided to do something different. It has in this situation decided to leave more to atomistic and less to centralized decision making and it has allowed more to depend on demand and supply decisions taken on the basis of commercial criteria.

As we examine housing provision in Europe we find varying ways in which governments influence property rights and varying degrees of freedom which are granted to housing suppliers with respect to the decisions that they make. We also find governments influencing these decisions by mixtures of controls, subsidies and taxes.

The 'government' is assumed throughout the book to be the source of policy decisions. Why and how governments come to make policy decisions is not our topic; it is rather an examination of the instruments that governments can use to influence housing provision. The 'government' being considered is usually the 'central' government of a particular country but it is recognized in specific cases that lower tiers of government may be significant so that important decisions may be left to regional or municipal authorities. We also acknowledge, as explained in Section 1.7, that there may be some influence from supranational government through the apparatus of the European Union.

1.3 AN ECONOMICS APPROACH

As we are concerned with resource allocation we are inevitably dealing with economic issues. The theoretical framework that is set out in the early chapters is one that will be familiar to economists but hopefully understandable and useful to those who do not have a background in economics. This means that we do use concepts like 'demand' and 'supply' and 'market failure'. There is much concern with policy instruments which influence housing demand and housing supply. The role of prices in allocating housing is considered alongside administrative measures. The distinction between 'need' and 'demand' is essential to the analysis which is pursued. The concept of subsidy is analysed in some detail as are the different sorts of housing subsidy in use in Europe. There is a consideration of public expenditure on housing and housing finance mechanisms are examined.

1.4 RENTED HOUSING

In order to narrow the policy focus, and to be able in the space available to provide some detailed contrasts, we concentrate on rented housing. To put rented housing in context within a housing system it is necessary to give some consideration to the policy instruments applied to home ownership as well as those applied to renting. We make some comments on this in Chapter 4. We are not, however, attempting to explain differences in the volume of renting and owner-occupation between countries. This has been done elsewhere (see, e.g. Oxley, 1984; Matznetter, 1994).

We examine the wide range of ways in which government influences the terms on which rented housing is supplied and is priced and allocated. The various institutional arrangements surrounding housing, the different types of landlord, and the different financial arrangements for the development and provision of rented housing are set out. The organization of rented housing is examined with respect to varying structures of ownership and control.

We do not consider the many different types of 'mixed tenure' arrangements that exist, usually in a minor form, in some countries. Thus 'shared ownership', condominium provision and the various types of co-operative organizations are not given detailed consideration. The emphasis is thus on the major providers of rented housing, and their management, financing and allocative procedures.

1.5 THE WIDER CONTEXT

In order to set the rented housing systems in the broad context of the economic, demographic and housing situations in Europe, we consider in Chapter 5 sets of data which summarize the background against which rented housing policies can be examined. This information assists in the explanation of housing problems and the attempts at ameliorating these problems through policy action.

1.6 THE COUNTRIES CONSIDERED

Our geographical dimension is, at the broadest scale, that of the countries of the European Union. Some of the data in Chapter 5 covers all the countries which were members in 1995. However, we have not in the course of our investigations actively considered Sweden, Finland and Austria which entered the European Union in January 1995.

The detailed consideration of rented housing structures and policy approaches covers France, Germany, the Netherlands and the UK. Most of the information and the data provided for Germany relates, in fact, to the territory of the former West Germany. However, in Chapters 6 and 8 there is an explicit examination of the housing issues and the provision of rented housing in the 'new Bundesländern' of the old East Germany. The problems of integration of the two housing systems are considered.

The choice of countries allows us to consider some variety in both the structures of housing systems, especially the varying forms of subsidized rented housing, different sorts of landlords and different policy instruments. This choice obviously influences the issues which are highlighted. If there had, for example, been more emphasis on Portugal, Spain or Greece the problems associated with housing at different levels of economic development and urbanization as well as the policy priorities in countries with very low levels of social rented housing provision would have been more important issues.

Although some of the policy conclusions which are drawn are orientated towards the case for reconsidering housing policy in the UK, many of the policy implications are wider and relate to all the countries considered.

1.7 HOUSING AND THE EUROPEAN UNION

Whilst our main concern is the role of national governments as policy makers, the consequences of the European Union for housing systems and housing policy is a matter which has attracted increasing attention. There is a growing literature on the 'Impact of Europe' on housing. There are, for example, publications such as *Housing Associations and 1992: The Impact of The Single European Market* (Drake, 1991), *Europe and 1992: A Handbook for Local Housing Authorities* (Drake, 1992), *Scottish Housing and Europe* (Chapman *et al.*, 1994) and *The Housing Issue at European Level* (Alegre, 1990). There has also been a study of the consequences of the Maastrict Treaty for national housing policies (Priemus *et al.*, 1994).

A common theme of these publications is that the European Union has no competence in relation to housing and that the responsibility for housing policy remains with national governments. Housing is thus subject to the principle of 'subsidiarity', whereby political decisions are taken at the lowest possible level and responsibility rests with the European Union only when it can be more effective than the member states acting independently.

Housing organizations are, however, inevitably affected by those rules, directives and procedures which govern them as purchasers and suppliers of goods and services, employers of labour, and users of capital. Thus directives on such topics as public procurement, mutual recognition of qualifications, consumer protection, the environment, health and safety, construction, and financing are all of relevance to the providers of rented housing.

There has also been discussion of 'leakage' whereby housing organizations can benefit indirectly from European provisions which have primarily another objective such as urban regeneration or employment creation. The prospects of some 'leaked' funding is something which organizations have been encouraged to explore (Drake, 1991, pp. 29–37; 1992, pp. 53–74).

The most significant consequences of the European Union for housing are not likely, however, to come about as a result of the direct impact of European directives and funding programmes but as a result of the indirect consequences of closer political and economic integration. It has been argued that the 'Maastrict Treaty will have important implications for housing through several channels: factor mobility, competition policy and liberalization of markets, economic growth, lower inflation, cuts in government spending, tax harmonization and issues of citizenship and social justice' (Priemus *et al.*, 1994, p. 163).

The extent to which any of these effects occurs is at this stage inevitably a matter for speculation. It does, however, clearly seem illogical for the European Union to be addressing such problems as the mobility of labour and the alleviation of poverty without being concerned about housing. This is to some extent recognized by the establishment of an interest in housing by the European Commission's Directorate-General V whose designated field is 'Employment, Industrial Relations and Social Affairs'. There have, consequently, been European Commission publications on housing statistics and on the impact of European legislation on housing. There is also a directory of institutions, professions and advisory boards concerned with housing (European Commission, 1993, 1994a, 1994b).

Several housing networks have been established to promote housing at a European level. They include:

- CECODHAS: Le Comité Européen de Coordination de l'Habitat Social (The European Liaison Committee for Social Housing). Its members are social housing organizations. It is recognized by the European Commission and it is trying to press for a European housing policy; it is campaigning for a 'right to housing' to be recognized in the European Union.
- FEANTSA: La Fédération Européenne des Associations Nationales Travaillant avec les Sans-abri (The European Federation of National Organizations working with Homeless People).
- COFACE: La Confédération des Organisations Familiales de la Communauté Européenne (Confederation of Family Organizations in the European Community). This has a strong interest in housing.

More information on European housing organizations and networks is given in Drake (1991, 1992).

Although there may be political and economic convergence in Europe it does not follow that there will be housing policy convergence. Any attempt at the 'harmonization' of housing policies, given the great diversity of institutional arrangements and policy instruments described in this book, would be fraught with problems. The introduction of a common currency would be easier than the introduction of a common housing policy and probably a lot more useful. This does not mean that some European Union competence in housing will not eventually develop nor indeed that there will not be, at some point in the future, explicit European expenditure on housing. Neither possibility will require harmonization.

1.8 THE AGENDA

Further discussion of the Europeanization of housing policy is not part of our agenda, which involves, instead, an examination of the rich diversity of housing systems which exist in Europe.

Chapter 2 examines the aims of housing policy, utilizing the theoretical constructs of welfare economics and probing the policy objectives proclaimed in official statements.

Chapter 3 considers the policy instruments which, in principle, may be used in an attempt to match housing need, demand and supply. Chapter 4 examines the policy options adopted in practice in our main countries. This chapter also illustrates the difficulties of trying to measure the extent of government activity with respect to housing.

Chapter 5 sets out, with the aid of official data, contextual material on the housing situation in the various countries.

Chapters 6 and 7 then consider in detail the systems of social housing provision. This includes an examination of the organizational frameworks and the management and financing issues involved as well as a discussion of the policy problems.

Chapters 8 and 9 repeat this process for the private rented sectors, with some emphasis on the reasons for the relatively small sector in the UK and the policy options for growth suggested by European comparisons.

Chapter 10 provides an overview of a recurring theme, that of 'affordability'. The meaning of the term is examined, the changing pattern of affordability in different countries is explored and policy approaches to affordability are contrasted.

Conclusions on the varying policy approaches and the need for policy reform are set out in Chapter 11.

<table>
<tr><td>2</td><td></td></tr>
</table>

The reasons for housing policies

An analysis of rented housing in Europe inevitably involves a consideration of the role of government in housing provision. Governments could leave housing to free market forces but in practice they do not. They have policies which influence markets. Throughout Europe for over 100 years governments have concluded that housing is not something that can be supplied purely according to commercial criteria. They have not, however, decided to eliminate commercial criteria entirely and take housing completely out of the market place. Policies emanating from varying political regimes have been directed at influencing the supply of and the demand for housing. Intervention in housing markets has been the norm. This chapter considers the reasons for such intervention. The possible and actual means of intervention will be considered in Chapters 3 and 4.

2.1 A 'FREE MARKET'

For a market in any item to exist there must be property rights which can be traded. A property right is an enforceable entitlement to possess, use and exchange something. In a society where there is an acceptance that access to goods and services shall not be by physical force, government has a role in protecting and underwriting property rights. If there was a total reliance on atomistic market trading, property rights would rest mainly with individuals and firms. Thus, individuals would have rights to housing which allowed them to occupy housing or to allow others to occupy and these rights could be bought and sold. We might say all housing would be 'privately' owned and some would possibly be 'privately' rented. In this situation the production of housing would be by firms who were motivated by a desire to make profits. Individuals would buy, sell and rent housing in order to maximize individual satisfaction or utility.

A version of a free market which receives much attention in introductory economics texts is a perfectly competitive market (see Begg *et al.*, 1994, Chapters 9 and 15). In such a market there are many buyers and sellers, no individual consumer or firm exercises power over prices, decisions are made on the basis of perfect information and buyers and sellers have freedom of entry to and exit from the market.

A perfectly competitive economy, where all markets operate as per the requirements of the perfectly competitive model, has been viewed by some economists as an ideal which provides the most efficient allocation of resources. This thinking has its roots in the 'Invisible Hand Doctrine' of Adam Smith who in his *Wealth Of Nations* in 1776 argued that a freely competitive economy would automatically maximize satisfaction (Rowley and Peacock, 1975, p. 25).

The correspondence between perfect competition and an efficient allocation of resources has further foundations in the work of an Italian economist, Vilfredo Pareto (Nath, 1969, Chapter 2; Rowley and Peacock, 1975, Chapter 1) who demonstrated the symmetry between the conditions for an efficient allocation of resources and the equilibrium conditions of perfect competition. With a 'Pareto-efficient' allocation of resources, no one can be made better off without making someone else worse off (for more discussion, see Oxley, 1975; Begg *et al.*, 1994, pp. 258–261).

2.2 MARKET FAILURE

It would seem if the disciples of Smith and Pareto are correct, that the best option for governments would be to promote competition in all markets, including housing, for this would lead to an efficient allocation of resources. In practice, governments in Europe, as in most of the world, do not do this. Instead they have policies to directly affect the production and the distribution of housing. Why is this?

One set of reasons come, broadly, under the heading of market failure. Where the conditions necessary for a market efficient allocation do not exist there is a market failure. There are many reasons for market failure and it is not appropriate to rehearse them all here but see, e.g. Begg (1994, pp. 264–277), Brown and Jackson (1990, pp. 28–57) and Oxley (1975). One of the most significant reasons which is of relevance to housing is the existence of 'externalities'.

2.3 EXTERNALITIES

An externality arises when the decisions of firms and households affect the production and consumption of others in ways which do not involve trading in the market place. Externalities may create 'external costs' or 'external benefits'. In the production and consumption of housing there are widespread externalities which a perfectly competitive market system with minimal government intervention will not take into consideration. If, for example, a householder builds an extension to a house which blocks out the light coming into the windows of his neighbour's house, an external cost is imposed on the neighbour. All European governments have planning controls which are intended to prevent such externalities (although the strength and effectiveness of the controls varies a good deal). If the extension is poorly constructed it may be unsafe and present a danger to passers-by. Thus there is another type of external cost which building regulations are intended to minimize.

Poorly maintained housing may affect the values of housing throughout a neighbourhood, having an adverse effect even on the values of those houses which are well maintained. Faced with the question 'should I improve my house or not?' an individual may decide not to improve because the individual benefit is insufficient. However, if all the houses in a neighbourhood were improved the benefits to all householders might be considerable. The issue here is the merits of individual or 'atomistic' decision making compared with those of collective decision making. A perfectly competitive market works on the basis of atomistic decision making where individual assessments of costs and benefits determine the outcomes. The improvement of housing throughout a neighbourhood may require collective decision making and government may have a role in promoting such collective decisions. Governments may promote external benefits from housing improvement which would not otherwise be realized.

More broadly, the physical characteristics of housing resulting from its design and maintenance may influence the health of the inhabitants and in turn the well-being of a wider community. The quality of housing may thus be of significance for society as a whole. Good quality housing is likely to bring external benefits in the form of positive consequences for the health of the community. The relationships between housing and health were one of the prime reasons for governments in 19th century Europe showing an interest in housing conditions. In several countries, including the UK, housing policy was once a responsibility of health departments. In Britain, environmental health officers continue to exercise powers to enforce housing improvements on the grounds of an effect on health. It has been argued that housing design and lay-out may have consequences for both physical and mental health (Ineichen, 1993). The connection between health and housing has in recent years been the subject of renewed research and interest by policy makers throughout the European Union. It has been argued that the lack of decent affordable housing is a public health issue and a shortage of high quality affordable housing is damaging to the health of a nation (Arblaster and Hawtin, 1994). Where health expenditure is met mainly from public funds, there may be a case simply in terms of reducing public expenditure for putting public money into improving housing conditions. This is the case if there is a proven cause and effect relationship between health and housing quality, and housing expenditure is 'efficient' in the sense of reducing public expenditure elsewhere.

The nature and extent of this connection continues to be a matter for empirical investigation and political argument. The same is true of two additional areas where there may be significant housing externalities. These are education and crime. If improvements in housing conditions can have beneficial effects on educational attainment and on crime rates there would, again, be positive external effects associated with 'better' rather than 'worse' housing. The evidence for the connections and the degree of the cause and effect involved is not always straightforward. There may be a suspicion that the real cause of a problem lies in another area, in income levels, for example. Housing and health, education or crime might all be areas in which there is a manifestation of wider social and economic phenomena. If, notwithstanding these wider issues, significant externalities are suspected of being associated with housing, the desire to promote the external benefits of good quality housing and minimize the external costs of poor quality housing are likely to be powerful incentives for governments to influence housing provision.

2.4 MERIT GOOD

Merit goods are goods which society believes individuals should have but which some individuals decide not to purchase. Consumers decide not to purchase, or not to purchase in sufficient quantities, even though they could afford to do so. If governments decide to encourage the consumption of merit goods they reject the sovereignty of the consumer which is essential in the perfectly competitive world of Pareto optimality. The converse of merit goods is merit bads, such as harmful drugs, where similarly a government might reject individual preferences and adopt a paternalistic stance.

Good quality housing can be viewed as a merit good which will bring benefits to individuals over and above those which individuals perceive. According to some economists, education and health provision can also be seen as merit goods. There is a case for governments encouraging the provision of merit goods which will inevitably be under-provided in a market system.

A merit good view of housing is not accepted by all governments. It is a controversial view because it places the wishes of the government above those of individuals. Libertarian governments with a strong preference for individual decision making will be unimpressed by merit good arguments.

2.5 EQUITY

Even if markets work well they can only be expected to provide an efficient allocation of resources and not necessarily a fair allocation. Governments will be concerned with *efficiency* but they will also be concerned with *equity*. The latter concept involves considerations of fairness in the distribution of resources. Thus value judgements about what is and is not acceptable are an essential element of equity considerations. If governments make a value judgement that a very unequal distribution of housing is unacceptable they may wish to influence allocation to improve equity.

Inequities may be associated with some households living in very high quality housing while others have only housing of a basic or unacceptably low standard. The distribution of housing is likely to be associated, in any country which relies mainly on a market economy, with the distribution of income and the distribution of wealth. There is likely to be a high degree of correlation between housing conditions and income levels.

In such circumstances governments may be especially concerned about the low quality of housing occupied by low income households. This may be a market outcome which they seek to alter by redistributing resources, either in income or kind, towards low income households. The inability of some households to occupy housing of an adequate standard is a prime reason for western European governments intervening in housing provision. The value judgements which are involved in formulating such a policy stance involve not only decisions on distributional fairness but also on housing standards. A decision on what constitutes an adequate standard of housing is essential if such a policy is to operate satisfactorily. In practice, governments do enforce minimum standards in new construction by the use of building regulations. They also have standards of fitness for existing housing. Housing which falls below a minimum standard may be deemed unfit for occupation. However, above such an absolute minimum standard there will be a desire to improve conditions. These conditions might relate to more than the physical standards of individual dwellings and embrace the quality of neighbourhoods. The association of low income groups with particular neighbourhoods, and with 'problem estates' that have physical and social problems, will cause some governments to redistribute resources to such locations on grounds of equity.

2.6 DEMAND AND NEED

Distributional arguments for government activity are closely tied to the concepts of housing demand and housing need. In a market system the housing which a household gets will be determined by the household's housing demand. This is the quantity and quality bundle of housing services which a household is willing and able to pay for. This, in turn, will depend on financial factors such as the price of housing and the household's income. The price of rented housing can be taken to be the weekly or monthly rent of the accommodation.

Housing need, however, is a measure of the quantity of housing required to ensure that all households have accommodation of an agreed minimum standard. The number of separate units required is dependent only on the number of separate households. It is independent of ability to pay. Markets in housing operate on the basis of demand not need. If housing supply is insufficient to meet need governments may wish to intervene to ensure adequate supply.

2.7 MACRO-ECONOMIC POLICIES

Governments sometimes intervene in housing markets for reasons which are quite separate from a desire to promote efficiency and equity in housing provision. In particular, the management of the macro-economy can influence governments' actions with respect to housing. Housing markets sometimes feel the effects of wider policies designed to reduce unemployment, control inflation, increase economic growth or achieve a balance of payments in foreign trade. For example, cuts in public expenditure designed to control inflation can result in less support for public sector housebuilding, and higher interest rates can mean more expensive borrowing costs for housebuilders and landlords and thus higher housing costs. Rents have sometimes been controlled in several European countries as part of a wider anti-inflation strategy.

In each of the above examples governments have intervened in housing provision primarily for what we might term 'non-housing' reasons. In practice such action can provide the strongest impact that governments have on housing provision. A growing recognition of the connections has meant that the relationships between housing and the macro-economic circumstances of countries has been the subject of much discussion and research (see, e.g. Ermisch, 1990; Muellbauer, 1990).

2.8 DISEQUILIBRIUM

It is only when the equilibrium conditions of perfect competition are achieved that there is a presumption of efficiency (Nath, 1969, p. 31). In general equilibrium there will be a balance between demand and supply in all markets. Thus there would be a balance in the demand and supply of housing and in the factors of production used to produce housing. If such balance did not exist in practice, governments might be content for markets to adjust to a new equilibrium of their own accord. However, such adjustment might take some time. Thus if there is an increase in demand for rented housing it might be many months before landlords are able to increase supply. The extra supply might have to come from conversions or from new building. In the interim the shortages may mean that people are badly housed or homeless. Rather than waiting for market forces to take their time, governments can be tempted to take action to speed-up the process of adjustment to a new equilibrium. Thus, incentives to increase supply quickly by means of subsidies to suppliers could be introduced.

A different approach could lead governments to react against the rent rises that would result from higher demand without more supply by controlling rents. Such intervention could in fact slow down or even prevent adjustment to equilibrium but a government's political timetable may be so short that this is not a significant consideration even if they are aware of the possibility of such an effect.

2.9 GOVERNMENT FAILURE

The fact that governments decide to modify or replace market mechanisms does not mean that they will be successful. The modern apostles of Adam Smith continue to argue that government interventions may do more harm than good. Besides the literature on market failure, a literature on 'government failure' has developed. In summary it has been stated that 'The government failure literature discards the notion of the benevolent omniscient economic planner serving the public interest and replaces it with a muddling, imperfect, endogenous state that serves the interests of powerful lobby groups and the private interests of politicians and bureaucrats' (Brown and Jackson, 1990, p. 58).

At a minimum the concept of government failure should alert us to the problem of weighing the costs of government activity in markets against the benefits. It should not, however, lead us to assume that governments inevitably do worse than markets. Nor should it trap us into accepting a dichotomy between 'markets' and 'government' for, as argued in Section 2.1, markets require governments and the interactions between markets and governments take many forms. Useful policy analysis should lead us to examine these forms and, if market failure is the way a problem is perceived, to find means of correcting market failures without being overwhelmed by the pitfalls of inequitable and inefficient interventions.

2.10 POLICY OBJECTIVES

It is possible, as the discussion has suggested, to rationlize governments' reasons for not leaving housing provision to market forces in terms of a desire to correct for market failure, to redistribute resources on equity grounds, to achieve macro-economic objectives or to compensate for disequilibrium in the market. In practice all of these reasons can be found in western Europe. In addition, however, the reasons for intervention have included an ideological desire to promote one form of housing tenure rather than another and to undo the policies of a previous regime because of an expected political advantage.

In some countries the right to decent housing is written into the constitution. For example, section 47 of the Spanish constitution establishes the right of all Spanish citizens to decent and adequate housing and requires public authorities to create the necessary conditions and issue appropriate regulations to ensure that this right can be implemented (see Netherlands Ministry of Housing, Physical Planning and The Environment, 1992b). Section 22 of the Dutch constitution states 'It is the government's responsibility to see that sufficient housing is available' (quoted in Netherlands Ministry of Housing Physical Planning and The Environment, 1989). Article 65 of the Portuguese constitution states that 'Everyone has the right, for himself or for his family, to appropriate housing from the point of view of health and comfort, preserving personal privacy and private family life' (quoted in Laurent and Jacques, 1990).

The 'Loi Besson', passed in 1990, gives a 'right to housing' for all households in France. It attempts to ensure access to housing by all groups and each département is obliged to draw up a housing plan which includes action for the housing of disadvantaged groups (Power, 1993, p. 59). More information on the right to housing, as given in the constitutions and laws of the countries of the European Union, is provided in Daly (1994).

European governments since 1945 have proclaimed their intention to ensure that all households have access to decent housing. For example, in the UK governments of varying political complexions have repeated statements such as 'The government believe that all families should be able to obtain a decent home at a price within their means' (HMSO, 1977, p. 1). Sometimes governments acknowledge that there may be resource constraints on the provision of adequate housing, e.g. 'The basic aim of the government's housing policy is to ensure that, as far as the resources of the economy permit, every family can obtain a dwelling of a good standard located in an acceptable environment, at a price or rent they can afford' (DOE, Ireland, 1991).

Some statements suggest that there is an emphasis on lower income households. In Denmark it has been stated that the aim of housing policy is 'to ensure the provision of adequate housing for those on low incomes and other disadvantaged groups in society' (Danish Ministry of Housing and Building, 1984, p. 16; Boelhouwer and Heijden, 1992, p. 153).

These general statements of intent typically express a desire that a minimum number of dwellings (let this be N) of an acceptable minimum standard (let this be Q) should be available at a 'satisfactory' price (let this be P).

Minimum implicit values are attached to N and Q, and P has an implicit maximum value. No trade-offs are acknowledged. There is no suggestion, for example, that less than N will be accepted as long as Q and P hold. Few attempts are made to specify values for N, Q and P in any detail. In particular, there is typically no attempt to define quality. Some elaboration of such terms as 'decent', 'good standard' and 'adequate' might be sought by examining the interpretation of 'sub-standard' in government surveys of the housing stock or in legislation which requires minimum standards, but wide variations in interpretation are possible. Quality is inevitably an imprecise term, and therefore quality is difficult to quantify, but it is an essential ingredient of policy and comprehensive policy analysis must make use of quality indicators.

The price/rent variable, P, is rarely defined precisely. A 'price within their means' or a 'price or rent they can afford' might mean:

1. What individuals decide can be afforded (let this be P_c).
2. What the government deems a household ought to pay or ought to be able to afford (let this be P_g).

A definite commitment to P_c would imply an open-ended subsidy system if P_c always purchased quantities and/or quality less than N and/or Q. Some governments have defined a 'P-type value' with respect to a particular housing sector or section of the population by defining P as a maximum proportion of income to be paid by households, the difference between this and cost being made up by the state. This is an element of various housing allowance schemes. More generally, the issues involved here are part of the wider 'affordability' debate to which we return in Chapter 10.

2.11 POLICY COMMITMENT

Although much of the earlier discussion assumes, implicitly, that governments recognize housing problems and react to them, in practice the strength of government commitment to housing policy objectives varies greatly from country to country. The pressures to act might not be commensurate with the severity of the problem. Public opinion may be more muted on housing issues in some countries than in others. In Portugal, for example, despite the right to 'appropriate housing' stated in the constitution, the government's response to large housing shortages has been muted, and there is little political and media pressure to tackle the considerable qualitative housing deficiencies (Magalhães, 1995). The contrast with the extent to which housing is a political issue and the subject of important pressure group activities in many of the other European Union countries, such as France, the Netherlands, Germany and the UK, is striking.

2.12 MORE DETAILED POLICY AIMS

Governments committed to housing policy sometimes go beyond the generality of claiming they want decent housing for all households and identify more specific aims. The following aims have been proclaimed at various times in the last 50 years in most of the countries of the European Union.

1. The construction of new dwellings.
2. The improvement of the existing stock.
3. A reduction in specific shortages identified either
   a. with respect to particular locations, or
   b. as experienced by particular social or economic groups.
4. Promotion of the mobility of tenants.
5. Achievement of equity in the treatment of different tenure groups.
6. Encouragement of the supply of 'non-profit' or 'public' housing.
7. Promotion of an increase in the proportion of households in owner-occupied accommodation.

2.12.1 New housing

After the Second World War, the principal aim of housing policy throughout Europe was to increase the rate of production of new houses. Governments typically assessed current housing 'needs' by forecasting the number of households and surveying the stock to determine the number of habitable dwellings. The excess of households over dwellings determined the 'crude housing shortage'. Building new houses to reduce this shortage was seen as the key to success in housing policy. In the 1950s and 1960s many governments set annual dwelling production targets and became heavily involved in subsidy programmes designed to help meet these targets. In general election campaigns in the UK political parties attempted to outbid one another in pledges to build so many thousand houses in the subsequent 5 years.

The rate of house building increased steadily from the mid-1950s and 'peaked' in most countries sometime between 1968 and 1973. After this the typical experience was a fall in annual output as costs escalated rapidly and the policy emphasis switched to improvement.

Production targets in more recent years have usually been stated in less unequivocal terms. In some cases they have been replaced by statements of 'requirements' or more general acknowledgements that new building must continue.

All governments continue to accept that new building is necessary but they state that it must be compatible with macro-economic policy objectives. Additionally, a recurring theme in official statements is that concern with quantity has been moderated by concern with quality.

2.12.2 Improvement

Policy statements from the 1970s onwards argue for an increasing emphasis on improving the housing stock, on modernization, and on increasing standards by installing basic facilities such as inside WCs and fixed baths or showers in more houses. In many cases the emphasis is not merely on physical structures but on neighbourhoods as well, with combined programmes for dwelling and environmental improvements. The Dutch government (Netherlands Ministry of Housing and Physical Planning, 1975) was typical in taking the view that with the quantitative housing shortage, which had existed since the war, eliminated, policy makers' attention and resources should turn to improving existing dwellings and their environments. French governments have been especially concerned about housing quality with the housing census and the 'Nora Report' (Nora and Eveno, 1975) revealing large proportions of the stock 'unfit' or in need of basic amenities.

The Danish government argued in the 1970s that, with much new housing having been built in the 1960s, now 'the more pressing demand is for more urban renewal on a scale hitherto unknown'. There are, however, in this case, both housing and 'non-housing' reasons for the shift of emphasis from quantity to quality. The Danish government claimed that 'urban renewal creates more jobs per unit of investment, and repair and maintenance is more labour intensive and less of a strain on foreign reserves than new building' (Danish Ministry of Housing, Ministry of the Environment, 1977, p. 3).

In 1979 the West German government stated that a principal aim of Federal government housing policy was 'preservation of the housing stock worth preserving while at the same time implementing suitable modernization and renewal measures to improve the neighbourhood environment' (German Ministry for Regional Planning, Building and Urban Development, and Federal Ministry for Economics, 1979, p. 3).

2.12.3 Specific shortages

A recurring theme in policy statements from the 1970s onwards was that an excess of dwellings over households had produced a situation in which there was no longer an 'overall' housing shortage but rather 'specific' shortages; specific to particular locations or certain social or income groups.

The 'social groups' and 'geographic' dimensions to specific shortages combine to comprise part of the 'inner city problem' identified not only in British cities but in many large conurbations in western Europe. The correspondence between housing policy and urban planning policy has led governments to argue that housing policy can be viewed as part of a process via which wider 'planning' goals are pursued.

The UK's 'Housing Policy Green Paper' acknowledged the case for a more 'selective' approach to policy which gave special help to specific groups and locations. It was argued that 'a national approach can draw attention and resources away from the areas with the most pressing needs' (HMSO, 1977, p. 7). Inner city areas were seen as having particularly severe housing problems. The groups facing special housing difficulties were identified as low income households, homeless people, one-parent families, battered women, the physically handicapped, the mentally ill and mentally handicapped, old people, single people, mobile workers, and ethnic minorities. While it was argued that any national housing policy is likely to be judged by how far it helps those facing the most pressing problems, in practice, policy action in the UK has been characterized by a comparatively non-selective approach and 'blanket' policy instruments have predominated.

2.12.4 Tenant mobility

There are both equity and efficiency motives associated with attempts by governments to encourage greater mobility within the private and public rented sectors. The equity aspect has typically involved arguments about tenants on high incomes living in low rent accommodation. In the Netherlands there have been specific measures to promote a more equitable relationship between income levels and the size and quality of dwelling occupied, and to reduce the immobility associated with those on relatively high incomes staying put in subsidized dwellings, thereby not releasing this accommodation for those on lower incomes.

The analysis of this issue has been very similar in Denmark where 'Housing Pacts' between the major political parties have demonstrated the political desire to encourage greater mobility within the housing stock by 'rent harmonization' and the use of individual subsidies for tenants. In both countries, rents have been related to historic building costs and thus older cheaper accommodation has proved attractive to occupants who perhaps gained a tenancy some years ago, when their incomes were lower.

So important has this 'rent-gap' issue been in the Netherlands, Denmark and Germany, that it is tempting to identify the wish to close the rent-gap as a separate aim of policy. However, the ultimate aim is to improve mobility and to obtain a more equitable and efficient use of the stock, including ensuring that large amounts of new accommodation are not left vacant because of high rents.

An efficiency aspect of tenant mobility is a desire to ensure that poor access to housing does not impede industrial and geographical mobility of labour. This is one of the reasons advanced for promoting an increased surplus of dwellings over households; some surplus in the system being viewed as a necessary condition for mobility. The British 'Green Paper' expressed concern for the relationship between housing and labour market mobility: 'We must increase the scope for mobility in housing. It is essential,

in a period of industrial change, that workers should be able to move house
to change their job' (HMSO, 1977, p. 8).

2.12.5 Equity between tenure groups

The virtues of allowing consumers free choice between different types of
housing and of government adopting an 'even handed' approach to alternative tenures have been expressed most explicitly in the Netherlands and
Denmark. The Dutch, for instance, have argued that 'The point whether one
prefers to live in a rented dwelling or in a privately owned dwelling is not
essential for the government. The policy aims to encourage the building of
sound housing in the proper places and at acceptable prices without any other
distinction being made' (Netherlands Ministry of Housing and Physical
Planning, 1975, p. 8) and 'The government endeavours to create choice
between rental and ownership housing without any unjustified difference of
treatment' (Netherlands Ministry of Housing and Physical Planning, 1977, p.
6).

In Denmark there have been attempts to bring the proportion of income
spent on housing by owner-occupiers more into line with that spent by
tenants, which has amounted to seeking to increase the proportion of income
spent on housing by owner-occupiers. The issue of equity between non-profit
housing association tenants and owner-occupiers has been particularly
important because of the arguments voiced by the politically significant
federation of non-profit tenants. The federation has claimed that owner-occupiers receive unfairly beneficial treatment largely as a consequence of mortgage interest tax relief.

In relation to housing policy four aspects of equity can be identified:

1. *An equitable relationship between the incentives given by government
   towards housing consumption: a concern not to give more incentive to
   one tenure than another.* This conflicts directly with the objective of
   encouraging owner-occupation unless there is evidence that owner-occupation has previously been 'under-subsidized'.
2. *An equitable relationship between the payments for different units of
   accommodation.* This amounts to a desire that rent levels or prices
   adequately reflect the size and quality of accommodation. A particular
   concern with a pattern of relationships between rents and the quality of
   accommodation has led some countries to introduce 'rent harmonization
   policies'.
3. *An equitable relationship between the proportion of income spent on
   housing by different households.* This particular perceived inequity is that
   of low income households paying a high proportion of income for accommodation while higher income households are devoting a lower proportion of income to housing. This issue has been tackled in some countries
   by housing allowance schemes.

4. *An equitable physical distribution of the housing stock.* This amounts primarily to a concern with the relationship between household size and dwelling size and quality: an issue which, again, has been tackled in some countries by housing allowances which effectively give extra resources to larger (and lower income) households to enable them to acquire 'reasonable accommodation'.

In operational terms, each of these notions of equity is vague. In practice, governments have introduced measures which have hindered supply in certain tenures and encouraged supply and reduced price in others. It is difficult to reconcile propositions of equity between tenures with the attempts to encourage owner-occupation. This may be defended in terms of 'giving people what they want' but no choice is made independently of the incentives which favour that choice.

2.12.6 Encouragement of the supply of 'non-profit' or 'public' housing

In most, but not all, European Union countries, the state has been committed in supplementing the market supply of rented accommodation by low rent 'non-profit' or 'public' housing. The variations between countries and some details on how such housing is supported are given in Chapter 6.

In general there is now less commitment to public housing than there was and the purpose of such housing has been increasingly under review. A major issue is whether public housing is primarily for lower income groups. In the Netherlands and Denmark there has been much support for the notion that a wide cross-section of households should have access to such housing, while the French tradition is more allied to the view that public housing is for those unable to afford the alternatives.

In both Ireland and the UK, sales of council houses have been encouraged and public expenditure limitations have reversed the growth of this sector. In Germany, the Netherlands, Denmark and France a principal focus of attention is whether aid should go mainly to households in an income-related fashion or constitute capital and rent subsidies. This is the 'subject' versus 'object' subsidies debate which will be taken up in Chapters 3, 4 and 7. With housing allowance schemes gaining strength in each country, the subject subsidy approach has gained much ground. This is viewed by non-profit housing movements with some apprehension as it threatens the level of direct support for their dwellings. As an aim of policy, the provision of public housing is now granted less emphasis in several countries than in the past. There has been a marked switch towards policies to promote owner-occupation.

2.12.7 Promoting owner-occupation

The promotion of owner-occupation is currently a most significant aim of policy. Many European countries have policies designed specifically to increase the proportion of the housing stock held by owner-occupiers. Statements of support for owner-occupation abound in the literature produced by each government, although in Denmark, for example, there are strong views of dissent from supporters of non-profit housing who consider the aid to owner-occupation too strong. The Germans and the Dutch are concerned about their levels of home ownership being lower than in other European countries. German policy statements in the 1980s and 1990s have emphasized increasing the opportunities for more citizens to become home owners while recognizing that there is a continuing need to build social housing to meet specific shortages (Bundesministerium, 1990, pp. 259–260).

The British government issued a white paper in 1987 which set out its housing policy objectives (HMSO, 1987). The commitment to encourage the spread of home ownership was confirmed but the government wanted to promote rented housing partly by making private renting more viable. The role of local authorities as providers of housing was gradually to diminish.

2.13 CONCLUSIONS

All governments pay lip service to the general objective of helping households obtain decent accommodation at a reasonable price, together with the other aims set out above. The emphasis on specific aims varies, of course, between countries but one could not claim that the aims of housing policy are startlingly different in any of the European countries. The position might be summarized by stating that all countries have:

1. A supply objective, related to the size and quality of the stock.
2. Equity objectives related to the distribution of the stock, the relative prices paid for housing services from different parts of the stock and the payments made for housing services by households in differing personal circumstances.

There have, over time, been changes in the emphasis given to particular aims. After the Second World War, and in the 1950s, there was great emphasis on house building and increasing the number of houses completed each year. In the 1960s and 1970s more emphasis was gradually attached to improving the quality of the stock, and many governments decided to try and do this by subsidizing renovation of existing housing. In all the countries there was, in the 1970s, an increased emphasis on achieving a distribution of housing subsidies that concentrates assistance on those households that are deemed to be in greatest need. Another aim of policy, which became increasingly significant in the 1970s and 1980s, was that of increasing owner-occupation. In the 1980s and 1990s more market-orientated policies have developed in many countries and public expenditure reductions have moderated housing policies. Changes in the political complexion of the government in power obviously brought about some changes in the emphasis given to particular aims. Some governments have, for example, been more inclined to declare their support for non-profit housing than others, but it has been changes in emphasis rather than the outright rejection of any of the aims that have characterized the housing policy goals of specific administrations.

Government statements of aims and objectives are vague. Terms like 'quality of accommodation' and 'a price within a household's means' are always left ill-defined. The aims are not usually susceptible to quantitative appraisal. Governments tend not to set themselves operational targets now that specific house building aims are rarely declared.

Housing policy is always subject to constraints imposed by other policy objectives. Within housing policy, many goals are pursued simultaneously. There is thus scope for conflict between housing policy and other policy goals and for conflicts within housing policy.

Housing policy in the 1990s has become the subject of deeper questioning in the light of several sets of factors. These are:

1. The belief that major quantitative shortages of housing no longer exist.
2. Pressure to cut public expenditure generally as monetarist views of macro-economic policy have gained favour.
3. A political decision to expose housing more to market forces.
4. A questioning of the effectiveness of supply-side subsidies which have promoted the provision of social rented housing.
5. An ideological desire to promote higher levels of home ownership.
6. A desire to 'target' assistance to where it is most needed.

These factors have combined in many countries in the European Union to reduce levels of direct public expenditure on housing. Much of this expenditure had supported investment in new social rented housing. The support for home ownership has meant more indirect support for housing in the form of tax reliefs for mortgages and for capital appreciation in owner-occupied housing.

The position of rented housing is problematic in circumstances where governments wish to see a larger proportion of householders as home owners. Governments do not explicitly state in such situations that they want fewer households to rent. They do often suggest that more rented housing should be supplied by commercial landlords. Even where governments acknowledge a continuing significant role for public sector providers of rented housing, they are requiring that more money for development be raised in the private sector money markets and that rents be raised to more 'market' levels. The difficulty in both these circumstances is the gap between the rents that landlords require and what households can pay.

We have seen that welfare economics provides, in principle, market failure reasons for government intervention in housing markets, and in particular the external costs of poor quality housing and the external benefits of high quality housing give a rationale for housing policy. The relationship between the ability to pay of low income households and the high rents of decent quality housing gives a significant reason for government action to promote access to housing of an acceptable standard.

The aim of decent housing for all households at a price they can afford has been espoused by governments throughout Europe. In practice, however, this generalized aim is supplemented by specific objectives related, for example, to encouraging particular tenures and reducing shortages for particular groups in society. The aims of housing policy are often secondary to those of macro-economic policy. Public expenditure reductions to achieve anti-inflation goals have often reduced the vigour with which housing aims have been pursued. The strength of commitments to housing policy vary. Nowhere in Europe, however, have governments concluded that housing can be left totally to market forces. They have opted for various forms of intervention. The instruments of intervention are examined in the next chapter.

Policy instruments

If governments decide that they wish to influence the provision of housing then they may do so by the use of a range of subsidies, taxes, regulations and controls. They may decide to deregulate or de-control. The precise instruments that they use will depend, if a logical approach is adopted, on the exact aims of housing policy and the perceptions of the causes of the housing problems to which policy is directed. The choice and application of instruments will be further conditioned by the institutional framework and the administrative structures in a country and the extent to which a government decides to work with, as opposed to reforming, the framework and structures. In this chapter we consider what instruments in principle are available to governments. In Chapter 4 we discuss the actual policy options that have been taken in the European Union.

3.1 REGULATORY FRAMEWORK

Measures to promote positive externalities in the location and building of housing, and to minimize the associated negative externalities, are likely to be part of a broader set of regulations relating to the physical aspects of real estate in general. Thus these measures will be similar to those relating to all buildings. Planning regulations can separate incompatible activities, keeping the smoky factory chimney away from the residential neighbourhood, and encouraging the development of schools and shops near to houses.

The safety of the construction can be influenced by controls on the building method and materials. These planning and building regulations can be viewed not as part of housing policy but as part of a wider planning policy. Energy conservation and environmental policies will influence the standard of insulation and the heating systems used in housing but again these are not strictly part of housing policy.

There are, however, means by which planning systems might favour one sort of housing rather than another. Preference might be given to social housing or social housing encouraged as part of granting permission for a wider development proposal. Various forms of planning concessions combined with a variety of land supply arrangements (Section 3.10) in Europe give varying degrees of promotion to specific housing forms as we shall see in Chapter 4.

3.2 NEED, DEMAND AND SUBSIDIES

If a government's aim is a decent house for all households at a price within their means (Section 2.10) then it is inevitably concerned with housing need. The concepts of housing need and demand were introduced in Chapter 2 (Section 2.6). Housing need has been formally defined as 'the quantity of housing that is required to provide accommodation of an agreed minimum standard and above for a population given its size, household composition, age distribution, etc., *without taking into account the individual household's ability to pay for the housing assigned to it*' (Robinson, 1979, pp. 55–56). Housing demand is the quantity of housing that a household can afford.

Housing need is not dependent on household income nor is it a function of rent levels or the price of housing, but housing demand depends on both of these. The level of total housing need in a country is equal to the total number of separate households. Thus, in Figure 3.1, if the total number of separate households is equal to On, the level of housing need is On. This is the number of separate dwellings of an acceptable standard that is required to house the population of a country. The acceptable standard for 'decent housing' is something which is normatively determined. The level at which the standard is set is very important. The lower the standard, the greater is the potential for the housing in an existing stock to count as 'decent'. The number of separate households that are recognized by the government affects the position of On. If only existing households identified in a census are recognized, the number will be smaller than if 'potential' households, who would form a separate living unit if circumstances permitted, are recognized.

With the position of On determined, Figure 3.1 can give an indication of the broad range of policy options open to a government. As with all demand and supply diagrams there is a simplification of reality rather than a full description of the real world. We need to assume that all units of 'decent housing' are identical in order to utilize this approach. The great real world diversity of units of accommodation complicates the picture but does not invalidate the broad conclusions about the policy options which are revealed.

If housing is subject to market forces, the demand curve D_0 shows the initial level of demand and the supply curve S_0 the initial level of supply of decent housing. In equilibrium, rents will be at Or and the quantity of

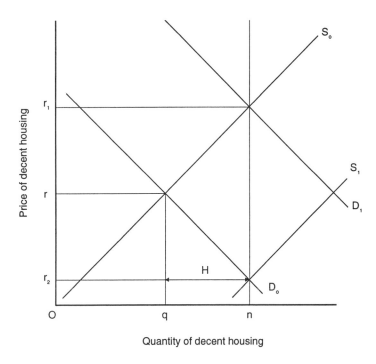

Figure 3.1 Housing need and housing demand.

housing demanded and supplied each month will be Oq. Housing need will not be met in total. There will be a gap between housing need and the housing demanded and supplied in the market place. The gap is equal to On minus Oq. This housing shortage (H) will have to be eliminated if need is to be satisfied. To eliminate H several policy options are possible. They are:

1. Shift the demand curve from D_0 to D_1. This increase in demand could be achieved by measures which subsidize consumers. These would be 'demand-side subsidies'. Equilibrium rents will increase to Or_1. Suppliers will be encouraged by higher rents to expand supply to On.
2. Shift the supply curve from S_0 to S_1.This increase in supply could be achieved by measures which promote more efficiency in supply and/or measures which subsidize suppliers. The latter would be 'supply-side subsidies'. Equilibrium rents will fall to Or_2. Households will be encouraged by lower rents to extend demand to On.
3. Government could supply, either directly or through a government sponsored agency, a quantity of housing equal to H. This housing would be made available to those households who do not successfully compete in the market for Oq. We assume that the government will not decide to supply all of On.

4. Some combination of elements of (1) – (3).

More cynically, government could reduce its quality standard so that the number of units of accommodation deemed to be of an acceptable standard rises.

In practice, governments in Europe have adopted policies which can best be characterized by option (4). These will be examined in Chapter 4.

3.3 SUBSIDIES AND INCIDENCE

The efficient use of subsidies to achieve policy goals requires understanding and prediction of the consequences of the subsidies. The way that the market responds to subsidies depends, in part, on the price elasticities of demand and supply, i.e. the responsiveness of demand and supply to price changes. This influences the incidence of subsidies or who effectively benefits from the subsidy.

Demand-side subsidies will, in a competitive market, raise rents. The extent of the rent increase depends on the elasticity of supply.

With a fairly inelastic supply curve, for any increase in rents the proportionate increase in quantity supplied is less than the proportionate change in rents. In these circumstances the effect of a demand subsidy is larger proportionate rent than quantity increases and much of the benefit of the subsidy goes to landlords; the incidence of the subsidy falls more on landlords than tenants. If, in the longer run, any higher profits which result encourage an expansion of supply the position might eventually be more favourable to output and to tenants.

A supply-side subsidy will, in a competitive market, reduce rents and increase supply. The extent of the changes will depend on the elasticity of demand. If demand is price inelastic the subsidy will bring about relatively large rent reductions and relatively small increases in quantity. With a more elastic demand curve the incidence of a supply-side subsidy falls more on landlords and less on tenants.

It is thus clear that although a subsidy may be paid to a household, some of the benefits end up with landlords and if a subsidy is paid to a landlord, tenants can get some of the benefit. The conditions in the housing market will determine the relative shares of the benefits.

The analysis can be complicated by a number of additional considerations in that some of the benefit of the subsidy may be further passed on to builders and to landowners. Also, in practice, the subsidies may discriminate between different types of tenants in different income and social groups, and between different types of landlord. They might, furthermore, vary with, for example, rent levels or the physical characteristics of dwellings. The subsidies may also have conditions attached which modify their price and quantity effects. We shall return to these points later.

3.4 DEMAND-SIDE SUBSIDIES

Demand-side subsidies increase demand. They make it cheaper for households to rent housing. Such subsidies are sometimes called 'subject' subsidies and can be divided into two sub-categories: 'unconditional subject subsidies' and 'conditional subject subsidies' (Oxley, 1987).

The former are income supplements which are not related to housing circumstances. A general increase in household income could be achieved by means of, for example, an income tax reduction or by cash payments. The higher level of disposable income would lead to higher demand for housing generally and more demand for rented housing as long as rented housing is a 'normal good'. This means there is a positive income elasticity of demand. The size of the increase in demand will be related to the income elasticity. The greater the income elasticity of demand, the greater the increase in demand for a given increase in incomes.

The income supplements might discriminate in terms of such factors as income level and household size. Larger supplements might be given to lower income and larger households. Again, the effect will be dependent on income elasticities which may vary between socio-economic groups. Income supplements may be part of wider welfare policy. They leave a large element of choice with households who may decide to spend their extra resources on items other than housing. Income supplements might lead to higher demand levels but because they are not targeted at housing they might not in practice be labelled a housing policy instrument.

Conditional subject subsidies have specific conditions attached to their receipt which link their provision to the consumption of housing. The nature and details of the conditions are potentially extremely varied. In practice the major conditions relate to rent levels paid and household size. Such conditions are attached to the major form of conditional subject subsidy: housing allowances. The money value of a housing allowance is typically a positive function of rent and household size, and a negative function of income. Allowances can also be tied to the consumption of housing of a specified minimum standard.

A household has to find acceptable housing before an allowance can be paid and thus those who are literally homeless do not benefit. The maximum value of the allowance is typically limited by an upper limit to eligible rents and incomes. For administrative reasons, and sometimes also to ensure that the allowance really is used for housing, payment might be made to landlords who reduce, accordingly, the payments they require from their tenants.

Housing allowances are intended to increase the quality of housing consumed and also to reduce the proportion of household income devoted to housing. The relative weight given to these two objectives varies from system to system. If only the second objective is achieved the extent to which the measure is truly a housing policy instrument, as opposed to a more general welfare measure, can be questioned.

Critics of housing allowances claim that many households who are eligible do not claim because of ignorance or administrative barriers. Thus the 'take-up' can be low. As allowance payments fall as income increases their withdrawal can be viewed as a sort of 'negative tax' which can impede work incentives. This is related to the concept of the 'poverty trap' whereby earning more can result in a disproportionate reduction in benefits. As, in practice, many recipients are not active participants in the labour market this criticism is somewhat blunted. More significant might be the argument, advanced in Section 3.3, that with inelastic supply in the housing market much of the benefit goes in the form of higher rents to landlords.

Home owners also benefit from demand-side subsidies in the form of tax concessions or so called 'tax expenditures'. These are fiscal privileges which reduce the tax which a home owner would otherwise have to pay. The principal type of tax expenditure involves interest payments on loans for house purchase. These are typically deductible from the tax payer's gross income thus reducing the volume of income on which tax is charged. There may also be capital gains tax concessions. The details and generosity of these arrangements vary considerably from country to country but a common feature is that, in contrast to housing allowances for tenants, the largest benefits tend to go to those with the most expensive houses who are in receipt of the largest incomes.

3.5 SUPPLY-SIDE SUBSIDIES

Supply-side subsidies increase supply. They make it cheaper for builders and landlords to provide housing. The subsidy can be a cash payment to providers of housing or it can take the form of a fiscal concession which reduces tax payments. A supply-side subsidy may assist the building of new housing, the improvement of existing housing or simply the continuing provision of housing. When targeted at quality improvements, the subsidy may be linked to neighbourhood and environmental enhancement.

Supply-side subsidies, because they are related to objects, in the form of buildings, are sometimes called object subsidies. Pure object subsidies are paid to increase housing output without any discrimination as to who occupies the dwellings. In practice most supply-side subsidies in Europe have been 'conditional object subsidies'. Such subsidies have been a highly significant means for supporting social rented housing which is intended for lower income groups. The details of the conditions attached to the receipt of subsidy vary considerably but include agreements to keep rents within specified limits and let properties to households with incomes below given levels. Usually the eligible dwellings have to be of a minimum physical quality.

Among the many possible forms of supply-side subsidies the following are the most significant:

1. Grants: either lump sum or periodic.
2. Loans at low rates of interest.
3. Contributions to loan repayments.
4. Loan guarantees.
5. Cheap land.
6. Tax concessions.

Lump sum grants may be given for the development of blocks or groups of dwellings or even for individual houses. Given to developers they effectively reduce construction costs and to landlords they may reduce the costs of acquisition or property retention. They might be expected both to increase the quality of housing supplied and to reduce rents.

Periodic grants might effectively be contributions to maintenance and management costs which are intended, again, to have both quantity and price or rent effects.

Much supply-side subsidization is linked to the provision of finance for development. Loans may be provided directly by government or a government agency. The funds lent to housing providers will have been raised from taxation or public sector borrowing. The subsidy element is the difference between the rate of interest charged to housing organizations and the prevailing market rate.

Rather than raise funds itself government may encourage housing suppliers to raise funds in the open market. It might then make on-going contributions to the amortization or interest payments on the loan. Only these contributions rather than the whole loan will count as public expenditure.

Another possibility is that government underwrites the loan, thus reducing the risk from the lender's point of view. This should mean that housing organizations are charged a lower rate of interest. The cost reduction associated with this lower rate is effectively the subsidy received.

Local or central government can provide or procure land at sub-market rates for the use of housing developers. Housing organizations can be given the land at reduced prices or even for free.

The tax status of a housing provider may confer several concessions. Some organizations have charitable status which either exempts them from particular taxes or reduces their liability. These measures may give one-off benefits where there is, for example, a capital gains or property tax exemption or there may be on-going benefits such as income or profits tax exemptions.

An object subsidy may be designed to overcome a 'front-loading' problem. This is the problem which arises when the costs of a housing development are heavy at the initiation of a project and in the early years but fall over time. To address this issue subsidies may be degressive. Thus they are most generous in the first year of a development and fall gradually over time until they are eventually phased out. When costs fall in real terms over time but incomes increase degressive subsidies can be strategically linked to rising rents.

The period of time for which a subsidy is granted and the certainty of its continuance are likely to be factors which significantly influence the effective value of a subsidy and the supply-side response to its provision. Subsidies which are guaranteed for many years will have more significant effects than short-term measures.

The implementation of subsidies and debates about the various forms of subsidy tried throughout Europe will be discussed in Chapter 4, but it is worth stressing at this stage that arguments against supply-side subsidies and in favour of demand-side subsidies have gained strength in recent decades. Supply-side subsidies have been very costly and governments looking for public expenditure cuts have often decided to concentrate reductions in this area.

3.6 SUBSIDIZE INCOMES OR RENTS?

The theory of consumer choice, utilizing budget line and indifference curve analysis, has been used to examine the relative merits of subsidizing incomes or rents or providing low cost housing (see, e.g. Stafford, 1978, pp. 68–69; Richardson, 1978, pp. 352–355; Robinson, 1979, pp. 117–120). The properties of budget lines and indifference curves are set out in, for example, Begg *et al.* (1994, pp. 75–94) and Samuelson and Nordhaus (1992, pp. 97–102).

In Figure 3.2 the budget line, AB, shows the combinations of two goods, 'housing' and 'other goods and services', that can be purchased by a household given a limited income and the relative prices of the options. Indifference curve i_1 shows different bundles of the two goods which give the household equal satisfaction. Points to the right of AB represent unattainable combinations given the household's resources and to the left of AB some income is left unused. The tangency between AB and i_1 at q gives a point of optimum satisfaction.

Higher indifference curves such as i_2, i_3 and i_4 give higher levels of utility. Indifference curves, representing the tastes of households, are drawn on the assumption that consumers can rank combinations of goods according to the utility they provide, that more is always preferred to less and that households have a diminishing marginal rate of substitution, so that to hold utility constant diminishing quantities of one good must be sacrificed to

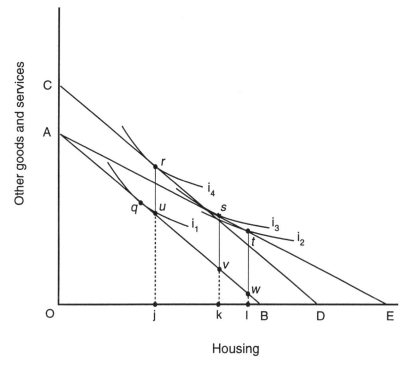

Figure 3.2 Housing policy instruments and utility.

obtain equal successive increases in the quantities of the other goods. The properties of indifference curves ensure that they slope downwards, become flatter as they approach each axis and they never cross (Begg *et al.*, 1994, pp. 78–79). If the government subsidizes household income, the budget line shifts outwards. With a new budget line at CD the household can reach indifference curve i_4 and obtain a new equilibrium at *r*.

Measures which subsidize rents reduce the relative price of housing and alter the slope of the budget line. AE shows a new combination which is open to the household with the original income level but lower rents. The maximum attainable level of satisfaction is, in this case, on indifference curve i_3 at point *s*. It has been argued that income supplements are superior in welfare terms to rent reductions because the consumer has a higher level of satisfaction at *r* than at *s*. Furthermore, the exchequer cost of the income subsidy which, measured in terms of other goods and services is equal to *ru*, is less than the cost of the rent subsidy which is *sv*. There is thus an argument that 'income supplements are best' because they give greater utility for equal or less public expenditure.

If the household not only has a rent subsidy but is additionally allocated rented housing according to an administratively determined criterion of need the amount allocated might be Ol in Figure 3.2 in which case the household is in disequilibrium at t on a lower indifference curve, i_2, than at s or r. This option has an exchequer cost equal to tw. Thus the administratively allocated public or social housing option can be argued to be inferior to both the income supplement and rent subsidy options on grounds of consumer satisfaction and public expenditure. This rank order of policy options, with income supplements preferred to rent subsidies which are in turn preferred to public housing, is however open to several fundamental challenges which we will now consider.

If the purpose of government intervention is not the maximization of consumer satisfaction but more housing consumption, then the order of preference is reversed with only Oj being consumed with the income supplement but Ok with the rent subsidy and Ol with public provision or allocation. If government is intervening for externality or merit good reasons (Sections 2.3 and 2.4) it will wish to override the outcomes of individual preferences.

The welfare analysis is set in a partial equilibrium framework. In particular, it assumes that after an income supplement is paid the relative prices of housing and non-housing remain unaltered. Budget line and indifference curve analysis shows preferred positions. The final combination of housing and non-housing consumption consequent upon any price or income change is partly dependent on supply-side adjustments. Supply inelasticity will limit the ability of consumers to obtain additional units of housing as demand increases after housing allowances or income subsidies are received. If increased incomes result in more housing demand and the price of housing services increases relative to all other prices, a simple shift of the budget line will not accurately reflect the final outcome of an increase in income. Some changes in the slope will be apparent. Economic welfare is dependent on satisfactions obtained from consuming bundles of goods. The final consumption bundle depends on a series of demand and supply adjustments. Without explicitly allowing for these adjustments one cannot make a judgement as to the relative merits of price reductions or income subsidies.

The welfare analysis assumes that there are no restrictions on the supply of accommodation and households can make a free choice about how much housing they consume. Some households will be better able to bid themselves into situations of greater utility and/or greater housing consumption than others. Any sort of discrimination or entry conditions set by public or private sector landlords work against the reality of this assumption.

Although the diagram relates to an individual household, the analysis is sometimes used in an attempt to support the general proposition that current housing payments are not relevant in assessing how much assistance to give any household. Implicitly this assumes that equal increases in income give equal increases in utility for any household at a given income level, and income supplements therefore satisfy the conditions for horizontal equity. This will only be the case if the relative prices of housing and non-housing are the same before subsidy for all households who are to receive assistance. In practice this will not be the case and the slope of the initial budget line will vary from household to household because housing services are available at different prices to different households. Rents vary, for example, with the age of properties and location. If housing services are not priced on a consistent basis, income supplements of equivalent size have different consequences both for utility and housing consumption for households with equivalent incomes who face differing prices per unit of housing.

The income supplement and rent subsidy options are usually assumed (Richardson, 1978, pp. 352–355) to operate in a situation where supply is market determined and the subsidies modify consumer choice but consumer sovereignty retains an ideological supremacy over state decisions. A preference for an allocation which gives a household Ol in Figure 3.2 can be advanced by rejecting the consumer sovereignty proposition and by challenging the assumptions about the operation of the supply side of the housing market. If, in a given set of market and institutional arrangements, it is seen to be likely that inefficiencies in market provision will occur, governments might opt not for tackling these inefficiencies but for creating other mechanisms for provision.

3.7 RENT CONTROLS

Governments have a variety of means at their disposal to control or influence the rents which are charged for housing. As we shall see in Chapters 4, 6 and 8, the means which are adopted are limited by the institutional arrangements governing the types of rented housing available.

If rented housing is provided by private sector landlords motivated by profits and operating in competitive markets, rents will be determined by demand and supply and, in equilibrium, rents will be at a level where quantity demanded equals quantity supplied. If governments control rents below market equilibrium this will increase quantity demanded and decrease the quantity supplied, thus creating excess demand. Many economists have argued that rent controls are inevitably undesirable (e.g. Brenner and Franklin, 1978; Stafford, 1978). Rent controls are blamed for creating shortages, reducing the quality of the rented stock, encouraging disrepair and promoting black markets as measures are sought to circumvent controls (Stafford, 1978, p. 104).

Conclusions about the adverse effects of rents controls are usually based on simple demand and supply models in a comparative static equilibrium framework. The assumption, typically, is that rent controls are equivalent to fixing a price per unit of housing below the market equilibrium.

In practice the controlled rent level may not be fixed. It might increase over time with changes in inflation and possibly changes in the quality of the dwelling. What happens depends on the specifics of the control measures. The level of profit enjoyed by landlords before and after controls will also be significant. If, before control, landlords received excess profits, that is over and above the 'normal' profit required to ensure supply, controls may decrease profit without any effect on the quantity of housing supplied.

Rent controls have usually been accompanied by legislative provisions which give security of tenure to tenants so that landlords are not able to simply evict the current tenants and either get new tenants at higher rents or sell the dwelling with vacant possession. These measures limit the supply-reducing consequences of controls. They may also complicate the consequences of the subsequent lifting of rent controls and security of tenure provisions. Whilst simple economic theory may predict an increase in quantity supplied as a result of the removal of rent ceilings, a concomitant freedom to sell with vacant possession may reduce supply.

Over time many factors which change the positions of the demand and supply curves of rented housing can take effect: changes in incomes and increased availability of credit may shift demand in favour of home ownership, alternative forms of tenure may become available and new attractive non-housing investment alternatives for landlords may develop. Such circumstances may decrease the quantity of private rented housing supplied quite separately from any rent control effects. The controls can erroneously be 'blamed' for the reduction through the application of the *post hoc ergo propter hoc* fallacy (after the event therefore because of the event).

3.8 RENT POOLING, CROSS-SUBSIDIZATION AND COST-PRICE RENTS

Governments may influence rents not just by rent control 'edicts' but by the conditions that they attach to supply-side subsidies, the level of financial support they give landlords and, more generally, the rent setting policies they adopt which will give varying degrees of freedom to landlords. All of these measures may affect only public or social housing or all rented housing depending on the arrangements in force.

Several principles can be illustrated in a stylized fashion with the aid of Figure 3.3. This is not meant to depict the actual circumstances in any country but, as we shall see in Chapter 4, the arrangements in particular countries can be examined with respect to specific elements of the diagram. The current accounting cost of providing a dwelling will be a function of construction costs, the financing arrangements including the borrowing costs and the period of time over which any loans have to be repaid, the maintenance costs, and the management costs. Given that construction costs have been lower in money terms in the past and that much of the money borrowed to build dwellings several years ago may have been repaid, the current financing costs associated

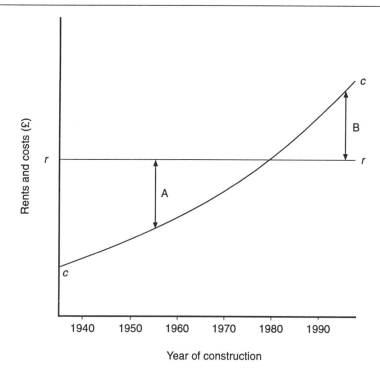

Figure 3.3 Rent pooling and cost-price rents.

with newer dwellings tend to be greater than those associated with older dwellings. As financing costs are usually a substantial proportion of total costs, even though maintenance costs may be higher for older than for newer buildings, the current accounting cost of older dwellings is likely to be less than for newer dwellings. Thus, cc, representing these costs in Figure 3.3 has lower values for dwellings constructed some years ago than for those built more recently.

In a rent regime where rents are set to coincide with the level of cc there would be historic cost pricing. The rents of older dwellings would be lower than for newer dwellings. Such rent setting has been a requirement for certain forms of social rented housing in several countries. This has created a problem of 'rent-gaps' with the higher rents for newer dwellings, which do not reflect market values or services provided, creating inefficiencies and inequities.

Instead of cost-price rents, governments might allow, or even promote, 'rent pooling' within a landlord's housing stock. Rent pooling allows accounting cost surpluses on older dwellings to contribute to reducing, or possibly eliminating, deficits related to newer dwellings. In fact, with rent pooling these surpluses and deficits become only nominal for the financing of the whole of a given stock is amalgamated in a single account. Rents are set according to a consistent set of principles but the cost of provision and the age of the dwelling are not relevant factors. Rents might be set according to market values, or a points system for particular facilities or some other administratively determined criteria. Thus rents may be at a level shown by *rr* in Figure 3.3. Surpluses such as 'A' contribute to deficits such as 'B'.

It might be argued that rent pooling results in a sort of cross-subsidization from the tenants of older to the tenants of newer housing. Nominal surpluses such as 'A' are 'transferred' to help cover nominal deficits such as 'B'. This cross-subsidization is a significant potential benefit, the size of which is dependent on the age and related cost structure of the stock as well as the number of dwellings included in the pool. The pooled stock could be at various scales. Thus it might be, for example, a single estate, the whole stock of a particular landlord or even all the rented stock within a country.

The positioning of *rr* is a matter for government policy. If it is such that values like 'A' are large and values like 'B' are small an overall surplus from the rented stock can be made. It might be argued that with total rental income exceeding total accounting costs a 'profit' has been made. However, the exact definition of profit is a matter for debate. Compared with the opportunity cost of provision, which takes account of the costs implied in employing resources in rented housing rather than another use, the rental income may not yield any surplus or profit.

If *cc* in Figure 3.3 depicts the accounting costs to be met by the landlord, one can envisage various forms of supply-side subsidies from the government shifting the position of *cc*. The specifics of the subsidy system will determine the way in which *cc* shifts. A per unit subsidy, which did not discriminate in terms of costs or the age of dwelling, would move *cc* downwards in a parallel fashion increasing type 'A' surpluses and reducing type 'B' deficits. If the subsidy discriminates by age of dwellings or covers a proportion of costs, or is in some other way positively related to the size of the financing costs of dwellings, *cc* may be shifted downwards more for newer than for older dwellings. We will return to the possibilities in Chapter 4 in the light of what options have actually been tried in Europe.

3.9 TENURE, ALLOCATION AND POLICY INSTRUMENTS

In devising a housing policy a government might broadly accept the existing institutional arrangements, and implement controls and subsidies within this framework or, more radically, it might attempt to change the existing institutional arrangements. We will now consider the possibility of such changes relating, in turn, to tenure, land supply and capital markets.

For the sake of a convenient working taxonomy we make a distinction in later chapters between private and social rented housing. However, the division between these two categories is blurred in several European countries and tenure categories defined by who owns the housing may be less important than considerations of how the housing is allocated and how rents are set (Oxley, 1995). Many sorts of classifications involving various groupings and sub-groupings are possible. One survey of tenures in nine European countries identified 42 kinds of tenure including several types of owner-occupation (Siksiö, 1990).

Governments can work with existing suppliers of rented housing using subsidies and controls in an attempt to achieve policy objectives or they can promote new forms of tenure. They might promote the development of local authority housing, housing associations and co-operatives with grants and tax concessions. The allocation of such housing will be subject to varying degrees of influence by the state. Whilst there has been a movement away from support for certain forms of social housing in Europe, there has also been a search for new forms of provision including arrangements which are not restrained by public expenditure limitations. Some governments espouse the aim of 'tenure neutrality' and thus do not want to favour one form of tenure rather than another. Although discussion of housing finance and subsidy measures which might be tenure neutral abounds in academic literature (see, e.g. Barr, 1987, pp. 365–367; Hills, 1992, pp. 286–291) a mix of policy instruments which promotes only free choice by households in the determination of whether one owns or rents or rents from one type of landlord rather than other, has proved elusive in practice. As the discussion in Chapter 2 showed, some governments in Europe have in recent years explicitly stated that they reject tenure neutrality and wish to promote particular tenure forms, especially owner-occupation.

3.10 LAND SUPPLY

The mechanisms by which land is made available for housing development and the price at which it is provided can have important consequences for the volume of investment in housing and, in the case of rented housing, can have a significant impact on rents and the allocation process for the completed dwellings. Any subsidies paid to landlords and tenants could, as indicated in Section 3.3, give some benefits to land owners. The extent of the benefits is dependent on the land supply process. If a market in housing land is characterized by competing buyers and sellers, and land is seen as a factor of production, neo-classical rent theory predicts that land values will be residually determined (for elaboration and discussion see, e.g. Alonso, 1964; Ball, 1985). In these circumstances the demand for housing land is derived from the demand for new housing and the maximum bid from a developer is a function of expected revenue from sales or rents minus costs including normal profit. The relative power of developers and land owners in the market will determine the price actually paid.

Governments may intervene in these market processes by land use planning controls and by subsidies and taxation. By such means they may influence the use to which land is put and the price at which deals in land are transacted, using if desired a mix of measures which favour housing generally or particular types of housing.

In more wide-ranging forms of intervention in the land market, governments can invest themselves or their agents with powers to buy and sell land. Thus, municipalities might acquire land and pass it on to housing providers at a market or a subsidized price. The land might even be given free of charge to a preferred housing developer or landlord. The range and complexity of institutional arrangements that are possible in the land market are reflected in the great variety that there is, in practice, in the cost and conditions attached to the acquisition of land by Europe's housing developers.

3.11 CAPITAL MARKETS

The terms on which finance for housing development is available will have significant consequences for the costs of the housing services provided and, depending on rent policies, possibly a major effect on what tenants pay for their housing.

The supply of housing finance takes a variety of forms in Europe with varying mixtures of specialist and non-specialist housing finance institutions. In principle, governments could allow the cost of finance to be determined commercially. In practice, subsidizing this cost has been a major form of intervention in Europe.

Government can go further and either promote the development of specialist housing finance institutions by subsidies, taxes and preferential regulations or it can create state-managed institutions which allocate funds in accordance with government policy. The way in which these institutions obtain their funds can vary from direct provision from the proceeds of taxation or government borrowing to borrowing in the open market. Once governments become active in manipulating, persuading and managing the price and cost of housing funding, the options open to them for subsidizing housing, and effecting the nature and terms of housing provision, are multiplied many times.

3.12 SUBSIDIES AND PUBLIC EXPENDITURE

If we define a housing subsidy as an explicit or implicit flow of funds initiated by government activity which reduces the relative cost of housing production or consumption below what it otherwise would have been, two propositions follow:

1. Measuring the value of subsidies will be very difficult in practice.
2. Public expenditure on housing will be neither a measure of housing subsidy nor an indication of the degree of intervention in the housing market.

We have seen that housing subsidies may involve direct payments or they might include various tax concessions or privileges resulting from preferential regulations. The money value of these concessions, especially where they relate to the land and capital markets, may be very large but difficult to determine, for no money changes hands.

When we say that a subsidy reduces cost 'below what it otherwise would have been', we have the problem of identifying this benchmark. Ascertaining what would have been the position without intervention will require some modelling of the interactions involved and some empirically determined estimation of quantitative changes. In practice this will be very complex.

If we are interested in the degree to which rented housing is subsidized we will have to compare it with something else. For this purpose do we treat it as a consumption good and compare it with food or clothing or as an investment good and compare it with a factory or a shop? Comparing the comparative taxation and subsidy arrangements in a quantitative fashion could result in a conclusion that housing is more or less subsidized in one country than another but the assumptions involved and the data used should make us very suspicious of the results. Establishing with great accuracy the fiscal neutrality position for rented housing and measuring deviations from this will be close to impossible. This does not deny, however, the merits of examining alternative means of intervention in practice and questioning their consequences, as we will do in Chapter 4. We should also be cautious about the significance of estimates of the value of subsidies as indicators of government activity because governments may pass laws which regulate housing and have very strong influences over access to housing without any subsidy being involved.

The public expenditure on housing identified in governments' budgets will consist partly of money which effectively replaces funds from other sources and partly of funds which complement such sources. Not all of it will reduce housing costs. Not all of it will be a subsidy. Conversely, as the argument above shows, many subsidies involve no public expenditure at all.

3.13 CONCLUSIONS

Governments have a range of policy instruments at their disposal to influence the terms on which housing is provided, the amount of housing available, the rents charged and access to accommodation. Governments may choose to set a general regulatory framework and work mainly with market forces, modifying their impact by the use of demand- and supply-side subsidies. If they do, they should be aware of arguments about the relative merits of object and subject subsidies and the effective incidence of subsidies.

More fundamental intervention will challenge existing forms of provision and promote new institutional arrangements. This might, for example, promote alternative tenure forms and create new land and capital market institutions.

Whilst the degree of intervention is difficult to measure exactly there has been much debate about the extent to which housing provision should be 'left to the market' and what form government activity should take. Although this debate is steered throughout Europe by the aims of housing policy and the perceptions of the causes of housing problems it has also been shaped by wider debates about the role of the state. As the next chapter will show, the actual choice of policy options has been influenced not just by housing policy considerations but also by other policy objectives particularly those related to the management of the macro-economy.

Policy options in practice | 4

In this chapter we consider the policy instruments that govern-
ments in France, Germany, the Netherlands and the UK have
used with respect to housing, and to rented housing in particu-
lar. Differences between countries in the strength of the distinc-
tion between private and social renting will be apparent. The
changing balance between object and subject subsidies will be
demonstrated.

Some information on public expenditure on housing will be
presented and the problems of quantifying the extent of housing
subsidies and, more broadly, the degree of intervention in hous-
ing markets, will be shown. The complications provided by
cross-subsidization, tax concessions and land market subsidies
will be illustrated. Comments on the growing significance of
income related housing assistance are complemented by some
information on the operation of housing allowance schemes in
the four countries.

4.1 POLICY STANCE

It would be possible to identify examples in Europe of each of the policy
instruments set out in Chapter 3. However, we do not find in practice
governments carefully examining their housing objectives and choosing the
mix of instruments to most efficiently achieve their goals. Rather housing
objectives become mixed with, and often subsumed in, wider political and
economic agendas.

Throughout Europe the sort of unmet housing need identified in Figure
3.1 persists despite many years of subsidization and control. To characterize
policies towards rental housing in terms of an ideal of increasing supply to
meet needs has become less representative than a view which sees policy
geared to reducing public expenditure and shifting the costs and the risks of

new provision from the public to the private sector. We must be careful, however, not to jump from this to generalizations about more private and less social provision. As the data in Table 6.1 (Chapter 6) shows, although social rented dwellings accounted for a lower proportion of dwellings completed in 1993 than in 1980, in some countries, e.g. the UK and the Netherlands, they comprised a larger proportion of output in others such as Denmark and France.

Although some subsidization of additional production continues in the Netherlands much of the support for rented housing was until 1995 a consequence of on-going commitments from earlier government decisions especially those under the dynamic cost-price rent system (Section 6.6.2(d)). These commitments have now been cancelled in exchange for writing off the housing associations' debts with the government. The objectives of policy relate largely to redistributional measures designed to ensure that the better off pay more and mobility is promoted both within the rented stock and between renting and owning.

In the UK policy has also focused on measures to achieve less direct expenditure on rented housing and to switch assistance towards households and away from buildings. Higher rents are designed as much with expenditure reduction objectives as housing objectives in mind. A major policy aim in the 1980s was to reduce the amount of council housing by means of the 'Right to Buy'.

Often governments do not produce explicit statements about their aims for rented housing. Rather their policy objectives have to be inferred from a combination of statements on housing policy in general and from their action towards renting in particular.

4.2 PRIVATE AND SOCIAL RENTING

In comparing policies between countries significant differences exist in the extent to which the measures adopted have been tenure orientated. Tenure neutral policy, as explained in Chapter 2, would not discriminate between renting and owning or between different forms of renting. The degree of tenure bias in UK policy sets it aside from the rest of Europe. In relation to social renting the policy measures adopted since 1979 have quite clearly been designed to reduce the size of the local authority owned sector and increase home ownership. Council tenants have been encouraged both to buy their houses and to transfer their dwellings to other landlords. Meanwhile increasing the size of the private rented sector has been an explicit aim. Policies in other countries have not showed a similar discrimination with respect to tenure. Indeed in some countries, e.g. France and Germany, the distinction between private and social renting is much more blurred and many incentives apply equally whether the landlord is a private company or a social housing supplier.

Given the problems of distinctions between tenures, several comparative housing studies have been critical of a tenure-orientated approach. Barlow and Duncan (1988), for example, question the usefulness of tenure, viewing it as a typology which provides few useful insights into the promotion and use of housing. Ruonavaara (1993) reviews several academic critiques of tenure and argues that cross-national comparisons are difficult because what is meant by tenure types such as 'private' or 'social' renting varies between countries. Kemeny (1995) challenges the approach to tenure adopted in English language comparative research and suggests that different forms of renting exist irrespective of ownership.

The wide variety of owners of rental housing is apparent from the accounts in Chapters 6 and 8. A summary of the ownership of rented housing in the four countries is provided in Table 5.11 (Chapter 5). Here, for the sake of a working division and, in order to make some contrasts between the UK and other countries, we *do* use a private/social renting split but are aware that the significance of this division varies between countries (for further elaboration, see Oxley, 1995).

The differences in the degree of distinction between 'private' and 'social' rented housing in different countries is related to institutional structures and political decisions made over long time periods. There is a difference between countries in the extent to which governments accept, and by their policies even accentuate this distinction, as is the case in the UK, and the extent to which governments are keen to promote production, and to influence rents and allocation, independent of who owns the dwellings, as is more the case in Germany.

4.3 DEMAND- AND SUPPLY-SIDE SUPPORT: QUANTIFICATION

In the 1950s and 1960s throughout Europe there was an acknowledgement that there was a housing shortage. The key issue was housing production and supply-side subsidies were used to promote output. Much of these subsidies were geared to the building of houses to rent. As housing shortages were reduced there was a reduction in supply-side subsidies and an increase in demand-side subsidies in the form of tax concessions to home ownership and housing allowances mainly to tenants. While the shift in emphasis was justified in terms of 'concentrating help where it was most needed' by subsidizing people rather than bricks and mortar it was also driven by a desire to cut direct public expenditure on housing, with property subsidies involving direct expenditures but home ownership being supported largely by forgone fiscal income which does not always show up directly in public accounts. Given the differences between countries in ways of defining housing expenditure, in identifying subsidies and measuring the value of housing assistance, comparisons of the levels of housing expenditures, and the composition of this expenditure between countries, is difficult. However, by using a variety of sources it is possible to observe certain common trends over time in the different countries. The continuing shift away from supply-side support in the 1980s and 1990s is apparent from an examination of the data for each country.

In Table 4.1 we can see that in France construction-orientated state expenditure fell in relation to other assistance from 28 to 12% of the total from 1978 to 1992. In 1992 about 32% of this 'aides à la pierre' (aid to 'bricks') consisted of subsidies associated with loans for social rented construction and improvement. The remainder took the form of grants and loan related assistance for the construction and improvement of owner-occupied and private rented dwellings. Two other items, together with the 'aides à la pierre' constitute the direct housing expenditure identified in the French budgetary statements. These are:

1. The housing savings subsidies (primes épargne logement) which are intended to encourage savings for housing investment.
2. The cost to the state of land tax concessions to housebuilders.

While these so called 'direct expenditures' constituted 38% of the Table 4.1 total in 1978 they were down to 19% by 1992 and expected to fall further by 1997. The housing allowance schemes (APL, ALS and ALF; see Section

Table 4.1 Distribution of public expenditure on housing (%): France, 1978–1997

	1978	*1980*	*1990*	*1992*[1]	*1997*[2]
Construction-related expenditure	28	25	13	12	11
Housing savings grants	3	7	8	6	6
Land tax concessions	7	6	2	1	1
Housing allowances	22	24	42	46	50
Expenditure from employers' schemes	10	10	7	6	6
Tax expenditures	30	28	28	29	26
Total (FF billions)	38.19	52.08	121.51	128.04	144.99

[1]Estimate, [2]Forecast.

Source: adapted from Geindre (1993a).

4.12) have grown in significance, from 22 to 46% of total housing expenditures by 1992, with further increases forecast. The switch from subsidizing buildings to subsidizing people is clearly an on-going process in France. The additional fiscal concessions (tax expenditures) in Table 4.1, which have not changed greatly in value in recent years, include incentives to home owners, landlords, savers and land owners.

In Table 4.2 the declining significance of interest rate subsidies and tax concessions for social housing construction in Germany between 1970 and 1992 is apparent. The relative importance of tax concessions for the construction of owner-occupied dwellings increased up to 1990. This contributed to a situation in which total housing construction support, including tax concessions for non-profit co-operatives and payments under modernization and energy saving programmes, actually rose from 66 to 74% of total housing support. There was, however, a fall to 65% by 1992. The major growth was in housing allowance payments (Wohngeld) which rose from 7 to 30% of the total from 1970 to 1992. Subsidies associated with housing savings schemes, whereby bonuses are paid to those who hold

Table 4.2 Distribution of public expenditure on housing (%): Germany, 1970–1992

	1970	1980	1990	1992
Social housing construction (including interest rate subsidies and tax concessions)	45	34	37	27
Tax concessions for owner-occupier construction	17	31	33	28
Tax exemptions for non-profit co-operatives	2	1	1	1
Modernization and energy saving subsidies	2	6	3	2
Länder-specific supplementary subsidies				7
Total housing construction subsidies	**66**	**72**	**74**	**65**
Construction savings subsidies	27	17	5	5
Housing allowances	7	11	21	30
Total	**100**	**100**	**100**	**100**
Total (DM billions)	7.04	17.57	17.35	24.22
Excluding construction savings subsidies:				
housing construction subsidies total	91	87	43	39
housing allowances	9	13	57	61
Total	**100**	**100**	**100**	**100**
Total (DM billions)	6.51	13.98	30.30	39.86

Source: calculated from data in Ulbrich (1992).

money on contractual terms in housing savings accounts, fell. The money
from these accounts allows potential buyers to accumulate capital and
borrowing potential with the housing finance institutions.

With the construction savings subsidies excluded from the totals, the
switch from construction to personal assistance is seen to be much more
dramatic. As the data at the foot of Table 4.2 shows, with this exclusion,
construction subsidies fell from 91 to 39% of expenditures from 1970 to
1992 and housing allowances rose from 9 to 61% of the total. The interpretation of the percentages in Table 4.2 must be tempered by the facts regarding
the significant increase in the total expenditures over the period as a whole
and particularly from 1990 to 1992 in the unified Germany. Furthermore, the
large variations between the Länder are important.

The data in Table 4.3 suggests that in the Netherlands property subsidies
fell relative to individual subsidies from 1975 to 1995, but they were still
more than 80% of the combined total in 1995. The fall was ameliorated by

Table 4.3 Distribution of public expenditure on housing (%): Netherlands,
1975–1995

	1975	1981	1987	1990	1995[1]
1. Property subsidies					
as % of 3	89	78	82	83	81
as % of 6	30	26	40	52	
2. Housing allowances					
as % of 3	11	22	18	17	19
as % of 6	4	7	8	10	
3. Total 1 + 2					
as % of 6	34	33	48	62	
4. Loans					
as % of 6	46	40	24	5	
5. Tax expenditures					
as % of 6	20	27	28	33	
6. Total					
3 + 4 + 5 (Dfl millions)	6 101	15 560	19 248	17 455	

[1] Forecast.

Source: Papa (1992, pp. 28–29) and own calculations.

the fact that much of the property subsidies were long-term obligations
established under legislation in the 1970s and were not supporting new
investment.

The decision by the government to cease direct loans to social housing
providers in 1988 explains the sharp reduction in the significance of government loan finance by 1990. An important and growing item has been fore-
gone fiscal income (tax expenditures). The figures for this item in Table 4.3

represent the difference in income from tax on imputed rent and taxation income lost from tax relief on the interest payments of home owners.

Table 4.4 shows that capital and operating subsidies declined considerably in the UK from 1976/77 to 1989/90. This was largely a consequence of cuts in capital expenditure programmes for local authority housing. The growth in the relative significance of housing benefits, rising from 12 to 30% of the Table 4.4 total, and tax reliefs rising from under 19 to over 46% are also quite clear consequences of policy decisions. The tax reliefs are associated

Table 4.4 Distribution of expenditure on housing (%): UK 1976/77–1989/90

	1976/77	*1979/80*	*1984/85*	*1989/90*
Capital and operating expenditures	69	68	40	24
Housing allowances	12	12	28	30
Tax expenditures	19	20	32	46
Total (£ billion)	18.3	15.7	13.6	14.0

Source: calculated from data in Hills (1992).

with income tax reductions for interest payments on home owners' mortgages. Given that the first two items in Table 4.4 support mainly tenants, the relative switch in support away from renting and in favour of home ownership is also illustrated by the data.

A modified approach to an analysis of housing expenditures is adopted in Table 4.5, where gross social housing investment in Great Britain is shown to fall relative to housing benefit and income support between 1980 and 1993. The gross social housing investment includes local authority and housing association commitments. The income support relates to home owners in mortgage difficulties as well as to tenants. While the relative significance of home owner tax reliefs is seen to increase up to 1989/90 they declined by 1992/93 as a result of new restrictions on the rates at which mortgage interest payments were deductible for tax purposes. Tables 4.1–4.5 have been based on studies of housing expenditure in each country which have adopted vary-

Table 4.5 Housing expenditure (%): Great Britain, 1980/81–1992/3

	1980/81	*1984/85*	*1989/90*	*1992/93*
Gross social housing investment	53	37	34	35
Housing benefits and income support	17	25	24	37
Mortgage interest tax relief	30	38	42	28
Total (£ billion)	6.3	12.2	16.5	18.8

Source: calculated from data in Wilcox (1993).

ing definitions and have categorized information in different ways. Thus, while they allow us to make comparisons over time within countries they do not provide an entirely satisfactory basis for comparisons of the relative importance of different sorts of housing expenditures between countries. These tables do allow us to confirm the increasing importance of housing allowances and thus 'subject' subsidies. This is a shift that has been well documented (see, e.g. Oxley, 1991b; Boelhouwer and Heijden, 1992). There remain, however, significant differences between countries in the relative importance of subsidies to housing demand and subsidies to housing supply. One study, by Papa (1992), has attempted to compare direct government expenditure and forgone fiscal income associated with housing on a consistent basis between certain European countries. The results for the four countries we are considering are shown in Table 4.6.

Table 4.6 Types of subsidy, relative significance: Netherlands, Germany, France and England, 1988

| | | Direct government expenditure and forgone fiscal income on housing: (a) as % of GDP and (b) individual items as % of total | | | |
		Property subsidies	Housing allowances	Forgone fiscal income	Total
Netherlands	(a)	1.91	0.40	1.23	3.54
	(b)	54.00	11.30	34.70	100.00
Germany	(a)	0.18	0.17	0.40	0.75
	(b)	24.00	22.70	53.30	100.00
France	(a)	0.45	0.32	0.55	1.32
	(b)	34.10	24.20	41.70	100.00
England	(a)	0.36	1.14	1.23	2.73
	(b)	13.00	42.00	45.00	100.00

Figures for England estimated in original source by apportionment of UK totals.

Source: calculated from Papa (1992, Table 10.8, p. 172).

As the data in Table 4.6 has been compiled using different definitions to Tables 4.1–4.5, the results are not the same. The direct budgetary costs of construction and improvement work are included as property subsidies. The full costs to central and local government of the various sorts of individual subsidies are included as housing allowances. Whilst property subsidies are clearly supply-side measures and housing allowances are demand-side measures, the status of 'Forgone Fiscal Income' in Table 4.6 is more complex. For England this is exclusively benefits for owner-occupiers and could be classed as demand-side subsidization. However, in the other countries some of the tax reliefs go to housing developers and thus the forgone fiscal income is partly supply-side support. This serves to reinforce the conclusion that supply-side support is proportionately small in England (and in the whole of the UK).

The reductions in direct support for the provision of housing have resulted in less support for the production of rented housing while increases in housing allowances have supported tenants. Supply-side support tends to be long term and its value known at the start of a housing construction project. Allowances are typically reviewed periodically (sometimes every year) and thus their future values are less certain. This has the effect of making new provision more risky. Housing providers have more difficulty in predicting future income when a large proportion of it is to come from housing allowance payments.

According to the estimates in Table 4.7 the distribution of subsidies between owner-occupiers and tenants varies between 49% of support going to tenants in the UK and 65% in Germany. These estimates need however to be treated with caution, as do all the estimates in this section, because

Table 4.7 Subsidy distribution between owners and tenants (%): Netherlands, Germany, France and UK, 1990

	Subsidies to owner-occupiers	Subsidies to tenants
Netherlands	40	60
Germany	35	65
France	50	50
UK	51	49

Source: based on data in BIPE (1991).

although there has been an attempt to take account of object subsidies, subject subsidies and additional tax expenditures, the apportionment to tenures requires some very generalized assumptions.

4.4 SUBSIDIZING TENURE CHANGE

Only in the UK have there been massive subsidies designed especially to change the tenure balance away from social housing and in favour of home ownership. The subsidies under the 'Right to Buy' scheme introduced in 1980 have been extensive but are not recorded as a public expenditure cost. Rather the proceeds from the sales have had a positive effect on the public accounts.

The rules regarding the discounts have been changed several times. A minimum tenancy period of 2 years for a house now gives a 'Right to Buy' at a 32% discount on the market value with an extra 1% for every year's tenancy up to a maximum discount of 60%. The discount on flats ranges from 40% to a maximum of 70% after 15 years. Over 1.5 million dwellings have been sold and the proceeds from sales are considerably greater than that of any other privatization programme (Wilcox, 1993, pp. 36–38). There are also important financial implications arising from the Large-Scale Voluntary

Transfers (LSVT) whereby local authorities transfer ownership of all their stock to a newly established housing association. Between 1988 and 1994, 150 000 dwellings had been transferred by this means. The new associations do not count as part of the public sector and are thus freed from investment constraints if they raise money privately. The transfers increase the housing benefit costs to the Treasury as housing associations unlike local authorities do not effectively make a contribution to these costs. To offset this, from 1993 the government imposed a 20% charge on capital receipts from LSVT (Aughton and Malpass, 1994, pp. 36–38).

4.5 CROSS-SUBSIDIZATION

As the information in Section 4.11 shows, cross-subsidization of housing development can occur as a result of land being transferred to housing organizations at less than market prices. In the UK an important form of cross-subsidization has also occurred within the council owned rented stock as a result of rent pooling. The rent pooling arrangements described in Section 3.8 have applied to British council housing since 1930s but rented housing suppliers elsewhere in Europe have not typically adopted rent pooling and so the cross-subsidy benefits are not apparent.

Given that cross-subsidies involve transfers which government is not directly a party to, they do not, by definition, appear in public expenditure statements. This further complicates the relationship between public expenditure on housing and the level of housing subsidies.

4.6 SOURCES OF HOUSING FUNDING

The exact sources of 'public' funding for housing varies between countries. In the UK and the Netherlands the relevant funds are raised mainly from the taxation and borrowing activities of government. In Germany the individual Länder put substantial funds into property subsidies. Indeed there are separate supplementary construction subsidy programmes devised by some Länder, and they can provide supplementary housing allowances.

In France the range of sources for the direct 'public' funding of housing is more complex. A summary is provided in Table 4.8. A falling proportion of the housing funding identified is coming from the central state: 66% in 1984 and 52% in 1992. A growing proportion is, however, being provided by the 'Régimes Sociaux' which are public funds fed by a variety of sources including subsidized savings accounts and national insurance contributions. The funds support housing with subsidized loans and grants. The importance of funds from employers under the '1% patronal scheme' is also growing. The details of the support given to social housing by these means are set out in Chapter 6. The funds are channelled into both property subsidies for social housing organizations and into housing allowance schemes. Given that the

'Régimes Sociaux' and '1% patronal' are a consequence of state activity, the distinction between these and central government funding may seem somewhat artificial. However, the exploitation of these funds is at 'arms length' from the government. The municipalities and départements provide supplementary funding equivalent to about 3% of the total 'public' funding.

Table 4.8 Sources of public funds for housing (%): France, 1984–1992

	1984	1990	1992
The central state	66	56	52
Régimes sociaux	28	34	35
Employers	4	7	10
Local authorities	2	3	3
Total (FF millions)	63 883	77 160	87 131

Source: French Housing Ministry (1994a, Table 311).

4.7 TAX CONCESSIONS

A source of funding not included in Table 4.8, but identified for each country in varying ways in Tables 4.1–4.6, is 'Forgone Fiscal Income'. This lost tax revenue as a result of concessions granted by central (and sometimes local) government is of growing significance. These 'tax expenditures', as identified in Chapter 3, are, however, extremely difficult to measure and compare (Wood, 1990). This is largely because the nature and value of the concessions are specific to the fiscal regime of the given country. Housing is treated for tax purposes in a variety of ways throughout Europe and, even where there are similarities in the types of tax levied, the rates are different. Where there are concessions the scope and the incidence of the concessions vary. Some comments on each country will illustrate the complexity of the issues. There is not an attempt here to describe taxation and reliefs in full detail. Further accounts can be found elsewhere (see Papa, 1992; Acosta and Renard, 1993; Dieterich et al., 1993; Haffner, 1993; Needham et al., 1993; Williams and Wood, 1994).

In France a variety of land and property taxes are in operation, some with variations from one municipality to another. These differences can in themselves influence housing costs. Real estate tax which is a recurrent tax related to property values is paid by the owners to the local authorities. Housing financed by the state-sponsored PAP and PLA loans (Chapter 6) is exempt from real estate tax for 10 years after completion. No capital gains tax is paid by landlords in the social sector. Capital and depreciation allowances reduce the tax bills of private sector landlords.

Purchasers of property must pay an acquisition tax, usually equal to 0.6% of the price for new dwellings and 4.2% for other dwellings. The rates are higher in some départements. VAT is levied on transactions in new but not old housing but property transfer taxes apply to the latter. There is no tax on imputed rents. Owner-occupiers can receive a tax rebate or tax credit equal to 25% of the interest paid on a loan subject to a ceiling of FF 15 000. The tax concession is for 5 years from the date of purchase and only those on incomes below specified limits related to family size are eligible (Papa 1992, p. 29).

In Germany tax concessions are a very important means by which government encourages investment in all types of housing. The principal concession takes the form of generous depreciation allowances which are available to investors in rented housing and to home owners. The details of the former are given in subsequent chapters. Home owners can claim a depreciation allowance equal to 5% of the price of a house plus 50% of the land value for 8 years from the point of acquisition, but only once in a lifetime. There are extra concessions for families with children. There is, however, no mortgage interest tax relief. There are generous deductibility arrangements for costs associated with energy saving and renovation. There is favourable tax treatment for all housing with only modest differences between tenures (Hills *et al.*, 1990). The annual property tax is low, estimated at 0.1% of open market value on average (Dieterich *et al.*, 1993). A property acquisition tax of 2% is payable. Imputed rents are not taxed and income from renting is free from VAT as are land and property deals generally.

In the Netherlands the rental of dwellings is exempt from VAT. The owners of social housing are exempt from the real estate transfer tax which is levied at 6%. The net income from rent is subject to corporation tax at 35% but social landlords are exempt. An annual property tax is levied by the municipalities and the rate varies considerably with location but a typical rate in 1990 was 0.5% of market value (Needham *et al.*, 1993, p. 68).

Owner-occupiers pay a tax on imputed rents equal to 3.5% of market value. This to some extent offsets the very regressive effect of the tax relief on mortgage interest. There is no limit on the amount which is deductible for income tax purposes. The larger the mortgage and the higher the income, the greater is the amount deductible. However, given that this concession applies to all forms of borrowing, and not just that for house purchase, the extent to which this is really a housing subsidy may be questioned. The questioning arises in relation to the definition of subsidy which views a housing subsidy as a measure which reduces the *relative* cost of housing. If it *is* counted as a housing subsidy it amounts to a very significant measure. It contributes considerably to a situation in which, on average, owner-occupiers appear to be subsidized more than tenants. Estimates for 1990 which include the affect of this measure suggests that tenants benefit on average by subsidies worth Dfl 1755 per annum and owner-occupiers Dfl 3150 per annum (Needham *et al.*, 1993, pp. 139–140).

In the UK the construction of dwellings is zero rated for VAT, allowing builders to reclaim VAT on inputs but not requiring them to tax sales. The

1% stamp duty is effectively a property transfer tax. Dwellings priced below £60 000 are exempt. Local authority housing is exempt from taxation which applies to private companies and those housing associations which are registered as charities enjoy the freedom from income tax and corporation tax compatible with their charitable status. The occupiers of housing are liable for council tax which is related to the value of the property but varies considerably between municipalities.

Home owners do not pay tax on the imputed rental income from their housing nor is capital gains tax payable on a principal residence, but given the size of the annual exemptions few home owners would be liable even if it did technically apply. The major tax concession to owner-occupiers is mortgage interest tax relief. The generosity of this measure has, however, been reduced considerably in recent years. Since a limit of £30 000 has been placed on the amount of borrowed money which is eligible for tax relief since 1983, the real value of this has declined with inflation. From 1988 money borrowed for improvements was no longer eligible and only one set of tax relief per dwelling was allowed. This stopped joint purchasers each claiming relief. In the 1990s the rate at which the relief has been paid has been gradually reduced so that from April 1995 the applicable rate is only 15%. This contrasts with the earlier situation where relief was calculated at the relevant marginal rate of income tax.

These comments on the four countries illustrate the diversity of arrangements between, and indeed within, countries. The extent to which any tax concession is really a subsidy, in that it creates a shift from a fiscal neutrality position either between tenures or between housing as a whole and other sectors of the economy, is a matter for on-going theoretical and empirical analysis. It is clear that tax concessions make it difficult to measure the degree of government subsidy to housing within any country and make comparisons between countries very complex. This needs to be borne in mind, together with the other comments about the relationships between subsidies and public expenditure in Section 3.12, in any interpretation of the earlier tables in this chapter.

4.8 GRANTS AND CONDITIONS

The object subsidies available to housing are often conditional. The nature of conditional object subsidies varies considerably across Europe. Conditions attach in varying forms to the rents that can be charged for subsidized properties, the income levels of occupants, allocation procedures and the quality of the accommodation provided. Again some examples from the four countries will make this clear.

In France the subsidized PLA loans are provided on the condition that rents are set according to a formula which takes account of the dwellings' size, location and facilities and allows for limited periodic increases. The incomes of tenants of subsidized social housing are to be below prescribed levels. There is an interesting linkage between object and subject subsidies in France whereby the provision of both PLA loans for construction and PALULOS improvement grants (Chapter 6) makes tenants eligible for consideration for the APL housing allowance.

The Germany subsidy system sets minimum standards in the rental sector and maximum standards in the home ownership sector. The federal government's social rent principles limit the rents of subsidized dwellings until public loans have been repaid. The incomes of the tenants of subsidized housing should be below prescribed ceilings.

Subsidies and rent levels were closely connected in the Netherlands until 1988. Since then there has been more freedom with respect to rent determination but new regulations have required both maximum rent increases and minimum growth rates for rental income. There are no formal income limits for the tenants of subsidized dwellings. In fact social sector tenants are estimated to have incomes only 10% lower than those in commercial rental dwellings where rents on average are about 16% higher (Priemus, 1995). The issue of tenants with above average incomes benefiting from state subsidies is, however, of concern for the government which is seeking to reduce the perceived 'mismatch' between rents and incomes. Grants to promote the construction of dwellings for owner-occupation have been tied to maximum income levels of the occupants.

While local authorities in the UK are theoretically free to set rents as they wish as long as they act 'reasonably', the government exercises considerable control over rental income by means of a subsidy system which assumes certain rent increases from year to year. Housing associations also have some nominal freedom in setting rents but the government expects rents to be 'affordable' for people in low paid work. With reducing grant levels this has been a major problem for associations (Aughton and Malpass, 1994, pp. 58–60). Unlike the situation in France and Germany, there are no formal income limits for access to subsidized housing but the 'Right to Buy' incentives, owner-occupier subsidies and the structure of the housing benefit system combine to provide strong incentives for those who can afford to leave subsidized rental housing to do so.

4.9 ALLOCATION MECHANISMS

It is clear that by the conditions they attach to object subsidies governments can have an important influence on the allocation of housing. Additionally regulations, or less severely guidelines, on who has preferential access to housing are operated in varying degrees.

In Chapter 6 the roles of allocation boards, including representatives of central and local government, in France, in the allocation of social housing, and the need for a certificate of entitlement to social housing obtained from the municipality, in Germany, are identified. In the Netherlands the considerable municipal control over the allocation of all housing which was possible under the Dwelling Space Act of 1947 has been modified by the Accommodation Act of 1993 which gives discretion to municipalities in the degree of freedom they grant to landlords in the allocation of dwellings below given rent levels. The Dutch Individual Rent Subsidies Act requires landlords to obtain municipal consent to the allocation of dwellings which require rent subsidies of more than Dfl 275 per month (Netherlands Ministry of Housing, 1993).

There are no means in Britain for government to intervene directly in the allocation of private sector dwellings. The Housing Act, 1985, does state that in selecting tenants local authorities must give 'reasonable preference' to persons who occupy insanitary or overcrowded houses, have large families, live in unsatisfactory conditions and are homeless. The term 'reasonable preference' is, however, subject to a wide interpretation and in practice councils have a very large degree of discretion and develop their own allocation systems. These typically involve waiting lists and points systems which endeavour to measure need.

4.10 FINANCE AND SUBSIDIES

Capital finance for the provision of rented housing is usually borrowed money. The money may be provided directly by the state, at either market or sub-market rates of interest, it may be provided by specialist financial institutions at sub-market rates because of special privileges granted by the state or it may be borrowed in the open market with or without some sort of state-sponsored guarantee. The four countries provide examples of all the options.

In France the cheap loans to finance social rented housing are issued by the CDC and CFF (Chapter 6). Given that low rates of interest, as a result of tax privileges, are paid on the savings which finance these loans, the advantage of sub-market rates can be passed on to the borrower.

In both France and Germany, as the data in Tables 4.1 and 4.2 suggests, housing savings grants or subsidies are significant parts of the state's overall support for housing. The 'special circuit' for housing finance that they create by encouraging savings in housing-specific schemes through tax concessions or state bonuses facilitates an additional flow of funds into housing investment at low rates of interest.

In Germany low interest loans of up to 85% of project costs are granted by the federal and Länder governments and the state can guarantee money raised from private sources thus lowering the interest rate.

Loans from the state plus loans from the private sector with guarantees from central and local government once provided 100% of the development funding for social housing investment in the Netherlands. However, since 1988 all loans have had to come from the private sector but they can be guaranteed by the Social House-Building Guarantee Fund (WSW) which in turn is backed by the Central Housing Fund (CFV) and ultimately underwritten by the state (Priemus, 1995). These arrangements are elaborated in Chapter 6. The CFV is fed by contributions from housing associations in accordance with their means. It can issue interest free loans to associations in need.

In the UK when local authorities engaged in significant housing development their borrowed funds, both from central government and from the private money markets, financed the construction. The privileged risk position of both central and local government allowed a local authority housing account to borrow below market rates. Now that local authority housing development has virtually ceased, social housing development relies on housing associations whose finance is coming increasingly from the private money markets. While some fully publicly funded development is still possible, consisting of grants and loans from the Housing Corporation and possibly local authorities, mixed funding, involving a large proportion of funding for projects being borrowed commercially, is increasing.

This new scale of commercial funding of housing associations has led to interest in the creation of a Dutch style guarantee scheme in the UK (*Social Housing*, 1991). A major problem for UK housing associations is that they are small by European standards. The average size of 287 units in 1993 compared with 2342 in the Netherlands and 4755 in France (European Commission, 1993, p. 38). Size constrains the asset base and limits borrowing potential. The need for some form of credit enhancement with new means of attracting private finance to housing associations is a continuing source of discussion (Pryke and Whitehead, 1991). With an increasing importance attached to private finance in several countries it may well be that in the future, with restrictions on credit flows between countries abandoned, there will be more cross-border financing of housing throughout Europe, with housing organizations borrowing from whichever international lender provides the best deal. The current risk associated with exchange fluctuations will disappear if the common currency option eventually comes to fruition.

4.11 LAND SUPPLY

The nature of the land use planning system within a country, the land taxation system and the availability of special mechanisms which influence the terms on which housing developers can acquire land, all have important consequences for the cost of supplying housing. Through such means many 'hidden subsidies' to housing, which do not appear in any public expenditure statements, can take effect. The market in housing land is controlled in a variety of ways in Europe (Barlow, 1993). The complexity of the arrangements and the differences between countries makes it impossible to give a comprehensive account here (for more information, see Acosta and Renard, 1993; Dieterich *et al.*, 1993; Needham *et al.*, 1993; Williams and Wood, 1994). A few comments on each country will, however, serve to illustrate the variety of means by which the state can influence housing provision through land supply and pricing mechanisms.

In France PLA subsidized loans for social housing can only be granted if the price of land is below a ceiling (which varies with location between FF 600 and 900/ m^2). Local authorities can provide special subsidies to bring the price down, but in Paris and other large cities the land price greatly exceeds the ceiling. The 'Delabarre Statute' in 1991 addressed this issue via a linkage mechanism whereby, subject to the requirements of local housing plans, private sector builders can be required to subsidize the supply of land for social housing (Acosta and Renard, 1993, pp. 29–30 and 66–67).

German municipalities are legally required to provide sufficient land for low cost housing. The provision of land from the municipalities can be at 50% or more below market prices (Dieterich *et al.*, 1993 pp. 96–97). The Bund and Länder as well as the municipalities sell land at sub-market prices for social housing developments.

The Dutch municipalities exercise a very strong influence on the supply of housing development land. Most land for development is acquired, and disposed of, by the municipalities. Disposal for social rented housing is linked to plot prices within certain guidelines set by central government. If there are good reasons for development in a high cost location, central government can subsidize costs so that plot prices for socially rented housing fall to the guideline level (Needham *et al.*, 1993, p. 70). Land prices in the Netherlands are strongly influenced by the planning system and by political decisions (Needham, 1992).

In the UK housing associations may be provided with low cost land by local authorities who, given expenditure constraints, are unable to exploit the land themselves. In a wider context there have been attempts via the planning system to increase the supply of land for 'affordable housing' (Barlow and Chambers, 1992; Barlow *et al.*, 1994). Since 1990 local authorities have been able to impose planning conditions requiring affordable housing. By this means private developers effectively subsidize social sector provision by promoting some low cost rented housing as part of a wider scheme. The establishment of planning obligations between a developer and a local authority can establish an agreement that affordable housing will be provided in the context of local planning objectives (Barlow, 1994).

There is a continuing debate about the desirability and effectiveness of such 'affordable housing' approaches which may be seen as a means of transferring potential 'planning gain' or betterment from a landowner or developer to social housing provision. A wide ranging *Inquiry into Planning for Housing* (Joseph Rowntree Foundation, 1994a), noting that the policy aim was to achieve a reduction in housing costs to compensate for inadequate levels of public funding, questioned whether it was appropriate for private developers and land owners to provide such cross-subsidy. It was suggested that free or cheap land was an inadequate substitute for more effective funding mechanisms.

Table 4.9 Land costs and housing costs: France, Germany, Netherlands and UK ,1992

	Land costs for social dwellings as % of total construction costs	Land costs as % of house prices
France	16.0	–
Germany	8.9	27.1
Netherlands	12.7	26.3
UK	25.0	36.2

Source: European Commission (1994) and Golland (1995).

The role of land costs in influencing housing supply and costs is an important consideration in housing policy. The data in Table 4.9 suggests that, in relation both to the costs of constructing social rented dwellings and to house prices, land costs are high in the UK. The use of policy instruments to address this issue is likely to be of continuing concern.

4.12 HOUSING ALLOWANCES

The increasing significance of housing allowances is apparent from the data in Tables 4.1–4.5. Both the volume of expenditure devoted to this form of assistance and the numbers of beneficiaries have been growing for over two decades. The reasons are associated with budgetary and distributional preferences by governments for subject rather than object subsidies (Oxley, 1987). They gained in favour as crude housing shortages were perceived to be eliminated, and with freer markets in housing, allowances were expected to help compensate for unequal distributions of income and cushion the effect of higher rent levels. They should also, in Germany and the Netherlands in particular, be seen in the context of a 'rent-gap' problem where, with rents related to historic costs, there have been higher rents for newer than for older dwellings. Housing allowances have been expected to ameliorate the effects of this 'inconsistent pricing' (there is more on the shift away from object subsidies in Section 7.3).

In the UK, as in the Netherlands, housing allowances are available only to tenants. In Germany and France home owners also can benefit. Comparisons of housing allowance systems are available elsewhere (Howenstine, 1986; Oxley, 1987; Kemp, 1990). Here some comments on each of the four countries illustrates the diversity of arrangements which are in operation.

In France housing allowances are available to help reduce the rent burden for low income households. In the case of APL, allowances can be paid directly to the landlord. Allowances take three forms:

- Allocation de Logement à caractére Familial (ALF) – family housing allowance.
- Allocation de Logement à caractére Social (ALS) – social housing allowance.
- Aide Personnalisée au Logement (APL) – personal housing allowance.

ALF was the original housing allowance initiated in 1948 to help families meet the increases in rent consequent upon rent liberalization. It is an income related allowance allocated to individuals or couples with responsibilities for children, infirm parents or other dependants. The ALF is paid out of a fund called the Fonds National des Prestations Familiales (FNPF) (National Fund for Family Allowances), which is supported by employers contributions.

ALS is awarded to those persons on low incomes who might not qualify for ALF but still need help with their housing costs, e.g. to those over the age of 65, the handicapped, workers younger than 25 years, long-term unemployed and beneficiaries of other social benefits. Funds for ALS are distributed by the FNAL – Fond National d'Aide au Logement (National Housing Aid Fund). The FNAL is financed partly by the state and partly by both employers' contributions and funds from the 1% housing scheme (Section 6.3.2).

APL was initiated in the 1977 financial reforms as part of the government's move away from financing the production of housing to subsidizing its consumption. To qualify for APL a beneficiary must live in a dwelling that is eligible as a result of state support. Although the occupants income is taken into account, APL is tied to the dwelling as well as the individual. Funds for APL come from a number of sources; contributions are made from the FNPF and the FNAL, and other social allowance budgets, and fed into the Fonds National Habitat (FNH); added to this are contributions from the housing ministry budget. To try to ease the budgetary burden of escalating housing allowance costs half of the funds from the employers' 1% scheme has been reallocated from social housing loans to housing allowances.

The 'Wohngeld' housing allowance system was introduced in Germany in 1965. It was set up with the aim of ensuring that decent homes were available to low income households during a time of rental decontrol in the housing market. Funds for housing allowances are derived 50% from the federal government and 50% from the Länder. The system stipulated that payment for adequate accommodation should not exceed 15–25% (or up to 30% for individuals) of the total spending of the household. The payments are always directed to the tenant, never the landlord. The main principle of the system is that the payment reduces rents and housing costs, and is therefore not treated as a general income supplement. The actual amounts of payments are calculated according to an extensive set of tables. If a household is receiving social benefits, all of its housing costs can be covered and rents can be subsidized 100% at the margin.

Eligibility for Wohngeld is dependent on the level of a household's income, the number of persons in the household and the amount of eligible housing expenditure.

A maximum income limit exists for Wohngeld, which will increase as the number of earners in a household, increases. Housing allowances are subject to a maximum rent level. This is adjusted every few years to take account of changing incomes and rents. Between 1965 and 1991 nine adjustments to this limit occurred (Bundesministerium, 1992a). The system is inherently problematic because, in the periods between adjustments, rents and incomes will be rising but the limits for Wohngeld qualification will remain the same. This leads to households gradually 'outgrowing' the system in these periods – possibly facing difficulties in meeting rents, and then re-qualifying when the limit is adjusted.

About 10% of all tenants receive housing allowances. Various additional housing allowances have been introduced in many Länder to help households experiencing difficulties due to the Wohngeld system. They only apply in the social sector. These schemes operate in a similar way to housing allowances and take a number of different forms: 'Härteausgleich' (a hardship compensation), 'Mietgarantie' (a rent guarantee) or 'Mietausgleich' (a rent compensation).

The housing allowance system operating in the Netherlands was established in 1975. There are three main conditions for eligibility to Individual Rent Subsidy (IHS). The applicant must be at least 18 years of age, be living in a self-contained rental dwelling and not have savings which are above a given limit. The exact amount of the subsidy will then depend on income and the rent level.

The IHS is granted on the basis of sets of tables which represent different age groups and household sizes. These are adjusted annually to account for increases in rents and incomes. Housing allowances are usually paid directly to the social landlord rather than the tenant, who will use it to lower the rent. In 1990, 29% of tenants qualified for IHS, and 95% of IHS went to the social sector (Netherlands Ministry of Housing, 1993).

While IHS does lower the rent burden for low income households it is still this group that devote the largest proportion of their income to rent. The average rent to income relationship in 1990 for low income groups was 20% and for average income groups 17%. For households with income two or three times the average, only 12% of income was devoted to rent (Netherlands Central Bureau of Statistics, 1992).

The IHS programme has become, as have housing allowances in a number of countries, an increasing burden on government expenditure. Changes were introduced to the system that initially lowered the rent ceilings to reduce the number of applicants and to cap the amount of monthly payments: 'By limiting the maximum monthly payments for newly allocated housing to Dfl 250 (some exceptions allowed), low income households are virtually barred from the newest and the best quality housing even in the social rented sector' (Van Weesep and Van Kempen, 1992a, p. 8). As higher income households are at the same time being encouraged to move out of social rented housing into more expensive accommodation there is increasing concern that social segregation in this sector may begin to be a problem.

In Britain a national housing allowance scheme was introduced in 1972. Before this some councils had their own personal assistance schemes. The Housing Benefit Scheme introduced in 1982 distinguished between 'standard' cases where rent rebates or allowances were payable and 'certified' cases where supplementary benefits applied to low income households. The two schemes led to much confusion.

The post-1988 system removes the 1982 distinctions and strives to treat all claimants on the basis of a common test of income and outgoings (Aughton and Malpass, 1994, pp. 74–82). Where household income is below an administratively determined adequate or 'applicable amount' 100% of eligible housing costs are covered by housing benefit. This is likely to be the full rent except where, for private tenants, a given rent is judged to be too high relative to others in the locality. Above the applicable amount housing benefit falls (tapers) at a rate of £0.65 for each extra £1 of income.

In 1993 in Great Britain 66% of council tenants received housing benefits, 51% of housing association tenants and 49% of private tenants. The cost of housing benefits are rising rapidly. By 1993/94 spending at £8.8 billion was double the 1989/90 levels. Higher rents are the main cause of the increase. The open ended nature of the commitment is a worry for the Treasury.

There is considerable concern about the relationship between the Housing Benefit System and the poverty trap whereby, when put in the context of welfare benefits as a whole and liability for tax and national insurance contributions, small increases in income lead to large reductions in benefits (Wilcox, 1993, pp. 18–19). A reduction in the housing benefit taper from the rate of 65%, which is steep by international standards, is one frequently mooted potential improvement to the system.

A broader comparison of income related support for housing costs would consider other means of welfare support, outside of the housing benefit system, and include more discussion of, for example, the additional help that the German social assistance, Sozialhilfe, provides for housing costs as well as the consequences of income support for home owners in the UK (see, e.g. Kemp, 1990; Joseph Rowntree Foundation, 1994b).

4.13 CONCLUSIONS

A wide range of policy instruments are used to influence housing provision. Support for rented housing has shifted away from object and towards subject subsidies. Public expenditure constraints are limiting supply-side grants and loans. In France and Germany several policy instruments apply equally to public and private sector landlords.

Tax expenditures provide a large and increasing form of support for housing. Much of this support is for home ownership. Valuing these concessions is difficult. This point, together with the effects of land market interventions, makes it difficult to measure both the consequences for public expenditure of varying housing market arrangements and the degree of subsidy that housing receives. The impact of government on rented housing provision is also a function of the nature of the conditions attached to object subsidies and the influences of the state on housing allocation.

The growth of housing allowances suggests that the view that the problems of rented housing provision have become less one of aggregate supply and more one of distribution and affordability has gained strength.

There are many differences in the details of the policy instruments in operation in Europe which stem not just from variations in objectives and ideology but also differences in institutional arrangements. While subsidiarity is the rule, the richness of the variety provides an environment in which there is much potential to learn from the experiences of others.

Housing policy context | 5

This chapter provides an overview of the housing situation within the member states of the European Union over the period 1970–1993. It will thus serve as a source of background information and a general introduction to the more detailed analysis of housing systems in the subsequent chapters. Initially some demographic and economic indicators are presented. There will be some discussion of the convergence of European economies in line with European and Monetary Union (EMU). There will then be some information on the relative size of dwelling stocks in the European Union, and levels of housing construction and investment. The division of the dwelling stocks by tenure type and ownership will be examined before issues of housing quality and homelessness are explored.

Information is given for all 15 European Union members as at 1 January 1995. However, most of the comments are related to the 12 countries who were members at the end of 1994. Data for Germany normally relates to the former West Germany unless otherwise indicated. The comparability of some of the data must be treated with caution due to varying definitions and statistical sources.

5.1 ECONOMIC AND DEMOGRAPHIC DEVELOPMENTS

The development of national economies and their population growth will both affect housing. Population growth and the number of households influence the level of housing need. Table 5.1 shows the population of countries in the European Union.

The data reveals a significant growth in population in a number of countries over the period 1970–1993. In particular Ireland, Greece, Portugal, Spain, the Netherlands and Luxembourg have all grown by over 15%. A number of these countries have also experienced net immigration,

Table 5.1 Population ('000s): European Union, 1970–1993

	1970	*1980*	*1990*	*1993*	*Growth 1970–1993 (%)*
Belgium	9651	9847	9993	10068	4.3
Denmark	4929	5125	5141	5181	5.1
France	50772	53880	56735	57530	13.3
Germany	60651	61566	63253	80975	4.3[1]
Greece	8793	9642	10140	10346	17.6
Ireland	2950	3401	3503	3563	20.8
Italy	53661	56416	57647	56960	6.1
Luxembourg	340	364	380	395	16.2
Netherlands	13039	14150	14951	15239	16.9
Portugal	8380	9272	9808	9860	17.7
Spain	33876	37386	38959	39117	15.5
UK	55632	56330	57411	58088	4.4
Austria	7467	7549	7718	7928	6.2
Finland	4606	4780	4986	5066	9.9
Sweden	8043	8311	8559	8692	8.1

[1]1970–1990

Source: OECD (1991) and European Commission (1994).

particularly Spain by 32 900 in 1992 and the Netherlands by 59 000 in 1992. The former West Germany was projected to experience a decline in population growth as its death rate continued to exceed its birth-rate. Population growth between 1970 and 1990 stood at only 4.3%. However, reunification has increased the population to over 80 million inhabitants with many ethnic Germans settling in the new German borders and future growth rates have been revised upwards.

Those countries experiencing the lowest rates of population growth included Belgium, Denmark and the UK. In Denmark deaths exceeded births from 1981 and therefore most of the population growth has been due to net immigration. In the UK the birth-rate has been somewhat higher and accounts for a larger proportion of population growth.

The number of households rather than population size reflects more accurately levels of housing need. Household data is given in Table 5.2.

The number of households across the Union have increased considerably since 1970. In the Netherlands this growth was over 50%. Household growth in France, Ireland, Portugal and Spain exceeded 30%. The growth

Table 5.2 Households ('000s): European Union, 1970–1991

	1970	1981	1986	1991	Growth 1970–1991 (%)	Average household size 1991
Belgium	3238	3608	3716	3953	22	2.5
Denmark	1796	2030	2148	2251	25	2.2
France	16407	19044	20657	21500	31	2.6
Germany	21991	25100	26739	28175	28	2.3
Greece	–	2974	3234	3344	12[5]	3.1
Ireland	726[1]	911	976	1029	42[7]	3.3
Italy	–	18632	20118	20600	11[5]	2.8
Luxembourg	–	128	134	145	13[5]	2.6
Netherlands	3986	5103	5711	6135	54	2.4
Portugal	2294	2924	3099	3176	38	3.1
Spain	8860	10665	11354	12040	36	3.3
UK	19687	20700	21600	22800	16	2.5
Austria	–	2764	2826	3013	9[5]	2.5
Finland	–	1782	1888	2066	16[5]	2.4
Sweden	–	3498[2]	3670[3]	3830[4]	9[6]	2.2[3]

[1]1971, [2]1980, [3]1985, [4]1990, [5]1981–1991, [6]1980–1990, [7]1971–1991.

Source: European Commission (1994) and national government sources.

in the number of households has everywhere been greater than the population growth, as there have been significant increases in household formation. This has been associated with increases in one-person households through young people leaving home and a growing number of divorces and separations. There has also been an increasing number of one-parent families.

Household size has consequently decreased. Between 1970 and 1987 the average household size in the Netherlands fell by 22%, with a decrease of 15% in Denmark, 14% in the UK and 13% in France (Boelhouwer and Heijden, 1992). The data in Table 5.2 shows that only four countries, Spain, Portugal, Ireland and Greece, have an average household size of more than three persons.

Table 5.3 shows Gross Domestic Product (GDP) per head and changes in the growth of GDP since 1970. Portugal and Greece are clearly the poorest countries in the European Union. Over time rates of economic growth have fallen considerably, particularly in France and Germany. Negative growth

Table 5.3 Growth of real GDP (% change on previous year): European Union, 1970–1993

	1970	1980	1991	1992	1993	GNP per head 1993[2]
Belgium	6.3	4.2	1.5	0.9	−1.3	15.8
Denmark	2.0	-0.4	1.0	1.2	1.4	20.5
France	5.7	1.6	1.3	1.4	−1.0	16.9
Germany[1]	5.0	1.0	3.1	1.1	−1.1	20.8
Greece	–	–	1.8	1.5	−0.1	5.6
Ireland	3.2	2.7	2.3	3.9	2.4	9.2
Italy	–	–	1.4	0.9	−0.7	15.9
Luxembourg	–	–	3.1	2.4	0.3	26.8
Netherlands	5.7	0.9	2.0	1.4	0.4	15.9
Portugal	–	–	2.2	1.1	−1.2	5.6
Spain	–	–	2.4	1.0	−1.0	10.8
UK	2.3	−1.7	−2.2	−0.4	2.0	14.1
Austria	–	–	3.1	1.5	−0.3	16.8
Finland	–	–	−6.4	−4.0	−2.0	–
Sweden	–	–	−1.8	−1.7	−2.1	22.2

[1]Figures after 1991 include new Bundesländer, [2]Thousands of ECU, current prices.

Source: OECD (1991), Barclays Bank (1995) and European Commission (1994).

rates, reflecting the recession of the early 1990s, were apparent in several countries in 1993. Recovery was, however, already underway in the UK. Ireland managed to maintain positive growth rates.

Higher rates of growth in an economy might be expected to increase housing investment by creating additional demand, higher incomes and additional resources. Statistical analysis of economic growth and housing investment levels has not, however, shown a significant relationship between the two factors. Furthermore, models which combined indicators of housing need and economic growth using demographic, GDP and housing stock variables contributed only a little to explanations of differences in housing investment and housebuilding rates between countries (for full details, see Oxley and Smith, 1994). If these factors together do not explain differences between countries, there are strong a priori reasons for believing that other factors, particularly policy variables, are important.

Table 5.4 Consumer prices and unemployment: European Union, 1989–1993

	Consumer prices (annual % price change)			Unemployment rate (as % of workforce)		
	1989	1991	1993	1989	1991	1993
Belgium	3.4	3.2	2.8	7.3[1]	7.1	9.6
Denmark	4.8	2.4	1.2	9.4	10.6	12.4
France	3.5	3.1	2.1	9.4	9.5	11.7
Germany	2.8	3.5	4.2	7.9	6.3	8.5
Greece	13.7	19.4	14.4	7.5	8.6	10.5
Ireland	4.1	3.2	1.5	17.9	14.8	16.8
Italy	6.6	6.4	4.2	12.1	11.0	11.5
Luxembourg	3.6	3.1	3.6	1.3[1]	1.4	2.1
Netherlands	1.1	3.9	2.6	8.3	7.1	8.8
Portugal	13.4	11.4	6.5	13.5	11.4	5.6
Spain	6.7	5.9	4.6	16.3	16.3	22.7
UK	9.3	4.5	1.9	6.3	8.1	10.5
Austria	–	3.3	3.6	5.0	5.8	6.8
Finland	6.7	4.2	2.1	3.4[1]	7.6	17.8
Sweden	–	9.4	4.7	1.5	3.0	5.6

[1] 1990.

Source: Barclays Bank (1994a,b, 1995).

Two further economic indicators, consumer prices and unemployment levels are shown in Table 5.4. Generally in Europe inflation has been converging in line with EMU requirements (see also Table 5.5). Some countries are, however, still experiencing high rates of consumer price increases. In Greece inflation has begun to slow from a peak of almost 23% in 1990, but still needs a further dramatic reduction to meet European Union requirements (Barclays Bank, 1994a). Portugal has continued to achieve lower rates of inflation each year from an average 12.1% between 1985 and 1992 to 6.5% in 1993 (Barclays Bank, 1994b). Other countries, particularly Denmark and the UK, have reduced inflation significantly since 1989. High unemployment levels in a number of countries are a continuing problem. The number of people out of work is particularly high in Spain and Ireland.

Table 5.5 illustrates more comprehensively projections of European Union convergence criteria in 1996. The four main criteria relate to government debt, budget deficit, inflation and interest rates.

Table 5.5 Projections of EMU convergence criteria in 1996

EU members	Government debt	Budget deficit	Inflation	Interest rates
Germany	✓	✓	✓	✓
Luxembourg	✓	✓	✓	✓
UK	✓	✓	✓	✓
Denmark	✗	✓	✓	✓
Finland	✓	✗	✓	✓
France	✓	✗	✓	✓
Ireland	✗	✓	✓	✓
Netherlands	✗	✓	✓	✓
Austria	✗	✗	✓	✓
Belgium	✗	✗	✓	✓
Spain	✗	✗	✓	✓
Italy	✗	✗	✓	✗
Sweden	✗	✗	✓	✗
Greece	✗	✗	✗	✗
Portugal	✗	✗	✗	✗

Convergence criteria: government debt, debt below 60% of GDP; budget deficit, deficit below 3% of GDP; inflation, less than 1.5% above average of three lowest inflation rates; interest rates, less than 2% above average of three lowest long-term rates.

Source: Lloyds Bank (1995).

Only three countries are forecast to meet the criteria by 1996: Germany, Luxembourg and the UK. Most countries will however meet inflation criteria (only Greece and Portugal will not) and four countries will be outside of the interest rate requirement. Moving to a single currency in 1997 requires a majority of countries to have met convergence criteria. Based on these projections this condition will not be in place which will mean further delays in the move to monetary union (Lloyds Bank, 1995). The adjustments in economic systems, particularly reductions in public expenditure as economies strive to meet the convergence criteria may have serious consequences for housing systems including cuts in housing expenditures (Priemus *et al.*, 1994).

5.2 HOUSING CONSTRUCTION AND TENURE

Table 5.6 gives information on dwelling stocks in Europe between 1970 and 1991.

Table 5.6 Dwelling stock ('000s at end of year): European Union, 1970–1991

	1970	1980	1990	1991	Dwelling stock per 1000 inhabitants 1991
Belgium	3434.9	3810.7	–	3748.0	395
Denmark	1743.0	2161.9	2353.2	2375.0	462
France	18263.0	24264.0[2]	26237.0	27011.0[5]	463[4]
Germany	20087.0	25406.0	26839.2	27139.1	421
Greece	–	3999.0[1]	–	4690.0	457
Ireland	–	892.1	1026.2	1039.0	286
Italy	–	21937.0	23232.0	–	404[3]
Luxembourg	–	125.6	–	134.7	351
Netherlands	3786.5	4848.7	5892.0	5965.0	393
Portugal	–	–	4165.1	4181.1	424
Spain	–	14726.1	17091.9	17154.3	441
UK	19203.0	21426.0	23440.0	23750.0	411
Austria	–	3052.0	–	3393.3	435
Finland	–	1838.1	2209.6	2249.7	449
Sweden	–	3670.0	4044.0	4106.0	475

[1] 1981, [2] 1983, [3] 1989, [4] 1990, [5] 1992.

Source: European Commission (1993, 1994) and national government sources.

The size of the dwelling stocks in France, the Netherlands and Spain have increased considerably in comparison to other countries. Growth in the stock has been particularly low in the UK and Belgium.

In 1991 France, Denmark, Greece, Spain and Sweden had the largest number of dwellings relative to population size. Those with the smallest stocks include Ireland, Luxembourg, the Netherlands and Belgium. In some countries a smaller dwelling stock is accounted for by the fact that households are generally larger. This, for example, might partly explain the situation in Ireland. Alternatively, a smaller dwelling stock per thousand inhabitants could be representative of a high level of need. Trends in growth of the dwelling stock can be examined in more detail by looking at data on dwelling construction. This is shown in Table 5.7.

The data shows a common tendency for construction rates to decline since 1970. In the early 1970s many countries were achieving some of their

Table 5.7 Dwelling construction ('000s new dwellings): European Union 1970–1993

	1970	1975	1980	1985	1990	1993	New dwellings completed per 1000 inhabitants 1993
Belgium	–	–	34.1	24.8	30.1	–	4.4
Denmark	50.6	35.5	30.3	22.6	27.2	14.0	2.7
France	456.3	514.3	378.3	257.0	256.5	245.3[1]	4.5
Germany	478.0	436.8	389.0	312.0	256.5	431.9	6.6
Greece	–	–	136.0	88.5	103.0[2]	–	10.0[2]
Ireland	13.9	26.9	27.8	24.0	19.5	21.4	6.1
Italy	–	–	287.0	200.8	182.6	–	3.6[2]
Luxembourg	–	–	2.0	1.3	2.7[2]	3.0[1]	7.5[1]
Netherlands	117.3	120.8	113.8	98.1	97.4	83.7	5.5
Portugal	27.9	32.0	38.2	35.5	62.1	–	6.7[3]
Spain	308.0	374.4	262.9	191.5	281.1	257.0	5.7
UK	362.2	322.0	242.0	207.7	200.3	182.0	3.1
Austria	–	–	–	41.2	40.4[2]	43.4	5.4
Finland	–	–	49.6	50.3	51.8[2]	30.4	6.0
Sweden	–	–	51.4	32.9	66.9[2]	35.1	4.0

[1]1992, [2]1991, [3]1990.

Source: European Commission (1993, 1994) and national government sources.

highest levels of housing production. The UK has experienced one of the biggest falls in dwelling output from 362 200 in 1970 to 182 000 in 1993.

The number of dwellings completed relative to population size was relatively high in Greece, Luxembourg, Portugal and Ireland. Germany, the Netherlands and Spain also had high construction rates due to the introduction of programmes to alleviate shortages. Those countries with a particularly low rate of construction include Denmark and the UK. However, at the same time Denmark had one of the largest dwelling stocks per thousand inhabitants in 1993. The dwelling stock in the UK was not so substantial relative to the population size.

Table 5.8 represents an attempt to estimate the construction of dwellings for renting. The estimates are calculated by adapting official data which classifies new construction not in relation to the type of investor or owner but rather in terms of a tenure split between owning and renting.

Table 5.8 Construction of dwellings intended for renting (% of total dwelling construction): Netherlands, France, Germany and UK

	1985	1993
Netherlands	56	37
Germany	42	36
France	21	25
UK	21	18

Source: Estimates from national data and European Commission (1994).

In 1980, 45% of housebuilding in the UK was for renting. The large reduction since 1980 in the proportion of new dwellings intended for renting in the UK has resulted in much lower levels of rented housing production than in the other countries. This is mainly a consequence of a large reliance on public sector output, and the collapse of this output with constraints on local authority housebuilding. About 15% of all production in the UK in 1993 was by housing associations.

Table 5.9 gives information on housing investment in Europe. The data gives an impression of the amount each country invests in housing as a percentage of GDP and as a percentage of total investment. The data gives an impression of the amount each country invests in housing as a percentage of total investment.

Table 5.9 Housing investment in Europe: averages, 1970–1992

	Housing investment (% GDP)	Rank	Housing investment (% total investment)	Rank
Belgium	4.83	9	24.6	6
Denmark	4.95	7	25.1	5
France	6.06	2	27.7	1
Germany	5.93	3	27.5	2
Greece	6.10	1	27.0	3
Ireland	4.95	7	21.8	8
Italy	5.56	4	NA	NA
Netherlands	5.43	5	25.9	4
Portugal	3.95	10	18.2	10
Spain	5.14	6	23.6	7
UK	3.50	11	19.4	9

Source: United Nations Economic Commission for Europe (1993) and own calculations.

France, Germany and Greece are ranked as the top three European countries for both indicators, with the Netherlands and Italy also ranked highly. The UK and Portugal have invested the least in housing. Over the period 1970–1992, the UK invested on average about half of the amount of France and Germany. Throughout Europe housing investment tended to increase slightly during the 1970s but decrease in the course of the 1980s.

Table 5.10 Housing stock by tenure (estimated % of stock in given tenure groups): European Union, *c*. 1990

Country	Owner-occupied	Social rented	Private rented	Other
Belgium	65	6	28	1
Denmark	52	24[1]	18	6
France	54	17	20	9
Germany	38	15	43	4
Greece	77	0	23	–
Ireland	81	11	8	–
Italy	67	7	21	5
Luxembourg	68	1	30	1
Netherlands	45	40	15	–
Portugal	58	4	35	3
Spain	78	2	16	4
UK	67	26	7	–
Austria	50	18	21	11
Finland	71	14	13	2
Sweden	43	36[2]	21	–

[1]Includes 7% of the stock managed by co-operatives, [2]includes 15% of the stock managed by co-operatives.

Source: estimated by the authors from a variety of sources including European Commission (1993), Ghékiere and Quilliot (1991) and other official data.

The distribution of the housing stock between different tenure types is shown in Table 5.10. Problems of classifying dwelling stocks in this way are discussed in Chapters 4, 6 and 8. The distinction between social and private renting is sharper in some countries (e.g. the UK) than others (e.g. Germany).

Over half of the 150 million dwellings in the European Union are owner-occupied. Only Germany, the Netherlands and Sweden have less than 50% owner-occupation. Ireland, Spain and Greece have the highest levels of home ownership. Over the last 20 years levels of owner-occupation have increased markedly. This has been at the expense of both the social and private rented sectors.

The size of the rental stocks are decreasing in many countries. This situation clearly has important implications for the mobility of households, tenure choice for low income and one-person households, and the availability of short-term easy access accommodation. High rates of owner-occupation have not always proved successful. During economic recession serious problems have been experienced in housing markets where owner-occupation accounts for a large proportion of the stock, e.g. in the UK.

Table 5.11 Ownership of rented dwellings: France, Germany, Netherlands and UK

France, 1992 (dwellings used as principal residence)	%	Germany, 1987	%
Private landlords	47.1	Private person/partnerships	65.0
HLM organizations	39.8	Co-ownerships (rented)	7.1
Other social landlords	6.6	Co-operative	7.0
Institutional investors	6.5	Non-profit landlords	17.5
		Other commercial landlords	3.4

Netherlands, 1992	%	United Kingdom, 1993	%
Housing associations	58	Local Authorities and New Town corporations	60.5
Municipal housing agencies	10		
Other non-profit institutions	9	Housing associations	11.0
Private landlords	13	Private landlords	28.5
Institutional investors	10		

French Housing Ministry (1994a), Hubert (1993), source: Netherlands Ministry of Housing, Physical Planning and Environment (1993) and DOE (1994).

In Table 5.11 the rented housing stock in France, Germany, the Netherlands and the UK is classified by ownership. The information shows that there is a diversity of landlords. In France and Germany private landlords or private persons and partnerships control the largest proportion of the rented stock, while in the Netherlands 58% of the stock is owned by housing associations and in the UK 60% is under local authority control. The many different forms of ownership illustrate the variety of institutional arrangements for rented housing.

5.3 HOUSING CONDITIONS

It is widely accepted that housing conditions in Europe have improved considerably in the last few decades. As governments switched from new production of dwellings to modernization and renovation of the existing stock, quality overall increased significantly. A problem with illustrating these improvements and making comparisons is the lack of data collected according to a common definition. This should be remembered when examining the information presented in Table 5.12. The statistics divide the dwelling stock according to its state of fitness or repair based on nationally determined criteria. Of the countries where data is available it is clearly the new European Union members, Austria, Finland and Sweden, who have the

Table 5.12 Condition of the dwelling stock (% of total stock): Europe, 1991

	Good dwellings	Dwellings lacking basic amenities	Unfit dwellings	Dwellings in serious disrepair
Belgium	57	28[1]	14[2]	–
Denmark[3]	88	12	–	–[4]
Spain[5]	49	40	11	–
Ireland	–	7	6	–
Italy	52	49	–	–
Luxembourg	80	11	9	–
Netherlands	80	——— 15 ———		–
Portugal[6]	77	16	1	6
UK[7]	86	1	7	9
Austria[3]	93	7	–	–
Finland[3]	90	17	–	–
Sweden	99	–[8]	–	–

[1]1982–1983, [2]1992, [3]1993, [4]approximately 250 thousand dwellings (=10%) are in need of urban renewal, [5]1990, [6]estimates, [7]data applies only to England, [8]practically all dwellings have all modern amenities.

Source: European Commission (1994).

highest quality dwelling stocks. All three countries have over 90% of their stock in the category 'good dwellings'. Four further countries have over 80% of their stock in this category, i.e. Denmark, the UK, the Netherlands and Luxembourg, while Italy and Spain have a relatively low proportion of 'good' dwellings. These latter two countries have correspondingly a large number of dwellings lacking basic amenities. While the UK does have a high proportion of good quality dwellings compared with other European countries, it has the largest proportion of dwellings classified as being in serious disrepair, which together with 'unfit dwellings' made up 16% of its stock in 1991.

Data for France and Germany is not given in Table 5.12. National sources however, report that in France 9.5% of the stock was lacking both WC and sanitation facilities in 1988 (a reduction from 48.6% in 1970) and 9% of households had declared themselves to be 'badly housed'. In 1990, 1.4 million dwellings were classified as 'very poor quality' (dwellings lacking at least one of the following three elements: water, WC, sanitation facilities). This stock is concentrated mainly in rural areas (French Housing Ministry, 1994a). In Germany, the 1987 census reported that only 1% of dwellings were lacking both WC and bath, while 73.4% of all dwellings contained bath, WC and heating facilities. This is a big improvement from the 29.8% of dwellings with these facilities when the previous census was taken in 1968.

Table 5.13 Age of the dwelling stock (%): European Union, 1981–1982

	Pre-1919	1919–1945	1945–1970	Post-1970	Total
Belgium	27	23	33	17	100
Denmark	23	23	36	18	100
France	29	14	31	26	100
Germany	20	13	49	18	100
Greece[1]	12	18	32	38	100
Ireland	29	17	28	26	100
Italy	18	12	49	21	100
Luxembourg	23	19	36	22	100
Netherlands	13	15	35	37	100
Portugal	26	19	30	25	100
Spain	15	12	46	27	100
UK	29	21	35	15	100
Austria	23	10	32	44	100
Finland	–	–	–	–	100
Sweden[1,2]	13	19	48	20	100

[1]1980, [2]3% unknown.
Source: European Commission (1994, p. 47).

Part of the explanation for the number of poor quality dwellings in countries such as the UK, France and Belgium is the age of their dwelling stocks. This is shown in Table 5.13.

France, the UK and Ireland had, at the beginning of the 1980s, 29% of their stock dating from before 1919. Belgium and Portugal also have a large proportion of older stock. While building activity was high from 1945 to 1970 in many countries, some countries have very low levels of stock dating from after 1970, in particular the UK and Belgium. Meanwhile countries such as Greece, the Netherlands and Austria have large numbers of post-1970 dwellings.

Table 5.14 Average useful floor space (m^2) per dwelling: European Union, 1993

	Total dwelling stock	*Newly built dwellings*
Belgium[1], [2]	86.3	131.4
Denmark[3]	107.0	83.0
France[6]	85.4	96.9
Germany BRD	86.7	89.4[3]
Germany DDR	64.4	94.9[3]
Greece[1]	79.6[4]	117.0[1,5]
Ireland[5,7]	88.0	87.0
Italy	92.3[8]	93.1[6]
Luxembourg[2]	107.0	135.0
Netherlands	98.6	81.0[9]
Portugal[6]	–	84.0
Spain[5]	86.6[1]	92.4
UK[9]	79.7	76.0[10]
Austria	85.3	97.0
Finland[3]	74.8	80.3
Sweden	92.0[1]	90.0[5,3]

[1]1991, [2]total floor space, [3]1993, [4]inhabited dwellings, [5]estimate, [6]occupied dwellings, [7]1990, [8]1985, [9]1988, [10]only subsidized rental and owner-occupied dwellings, [11]dwellings built between 1980 and 1991.

Source: European Commission (1994, p. 48).

Table 5.14 shows the relative size of dwellings in Europe. Data for the total dwelling stock and for newly built dwellings is presented. Denmark, Luxembourg and the Netherlands have the largest useful floorspace (around 100 m^2) per dwelling in their existing stock. The average size of dwellings in the UK is among the smallest in the European Union. The UK has the smallest useful floor space in newly built dwellings. Some countries in Europe have a minimum officially required size for new dwellings either in square metres or number of rooms. This however, is not the case in Germany, the UK, Sweden and Luxembourg (European Commission, 1994).

5.4 HOMELESSNESS

While the previous discussion has illustrated some specific problems of quality there have been considerable improvements in general housing conditions in Europe. Many households have benefited from improving conditions yet at the same time there has been an increase in housing shortages, which have affected particular sections of the population, and there has been an increase in recorded homelessness in many countries.

In several countries, organizations working with the homeless report that the numbers of homeless or 'near-homeless' has increased during the 1980s and early 1990s. There are difficulties, however, in estimating the actual numbers of homeless individuals and households. The main problem is the lack of clarity in defining households or individuals that are homeless. The absence of an accepted definition of homelessness causes problems within countries and makes comparisons between countries even more difficult. Data on homelessness is not usually collected in the official census. The reliability of the 'estimates' are debatable.

These problems were recognized by a number of national organizations, who joined together in 1989 to form FEANSTA (the European Federation of National Organizations working with the Homeless). This organization has examined the nature and extent of homelessness in the 12 pre-1995 European

Table 5.15 Extent of estimated homelessness: European Union, early 1990s

	Year/Data source	Population (millions)	Estimated number of homeless
Belgium	1993, users of services for year	10.0	26379
Denmark	1992, users of services on one day	5.1	2947
France	1992, estimate for year	57.5	627000
Germany[2]	1990, estimate for year	64.0	850000
Greece	1993, estimate for year	10.3	10000
Ireland	1993, estimate for year	3.5	5000
Italy	1992, estimate on the basis of survey	56.9	152000
Luxembourg	1992, users of one service in year	0.3	608
Netherlands	1990, estimate for an average day	15.2	30000
Portugal	1993, estimated from survey[1]	12.8	2870
Spain	1990, estimated users of service[1]	39.1	29659
UK	1992, estimate for year on the basis of information from official sources and service providers	57.9	642980

[1]Estimates made on the basis of the available information, [2]figures for Germany adjusted downwards, includes immigrants.

Source: Daly (1994, p.4).

Union countries. The data in Table 5.15 brings together statistics produced by FEANSTA.

These statistics define homelessness largely in terms of only 'those without a roof or house'. This was deemed the most reliable, although 'a very limited and conservative definition' of homelessness (Daly, 1994, pp. 2–5).

Although the estimates presented in Table 5.15 suggest approximately 2.5 million homeless people in Europe, FEANSTA notes that if data were available which embraced a more comprehensive and realistic definition of homelessness this total might be doubled (Daly, 1994, p. 6).

Three main groupings can be distinguished in the table:

1. The largest member states of France, Germany and the UK which experience the highest rates of recorded homelessness, with at least eight persons per 1000 of all inhabitants estimated to be homeless.
2. A second group, including Belgium, Italy and the Netherlands, has a much lower incidence of homelessness, of about two out of every 1000 inhabitants.
3. The six remaining countries, i.e. Denmark, Spain, Germany, Luxembourg, Ireland and Portugal, have the lowest levels of homelessness, estimated at about one in every 1000 persons.

Many of the problems encountered in the collection of these figures will contribute to underestimation. For example, those countries with a more extensive service provision for the homeless will be more easily able to estimate numbers. Indeed some countries will have a higher level of recorded homelessness simply because their data collection methods and provision for the homeless are superior. In many countries, particularly Portugal, Italy and Greece, homelessness and poor housing are widespread. There is however, a lack of formal procedures for recording homelessness.

The numbers also represent different types of estimation. Some statistics are collected over a year, while others give an estimate of the number of homeless on any single day. For a full discussion and an explanation of the problems of definition, see Daly (1994).

The homeless in many European countries are increasingly young single persons and young families who are often allocated short-term overcrowded accommodation. A large number of homeless persons remain 'hidden' – staying with friends or relatives. In the UK, Shelter estimated that around 1.2 million persons were included in this 'hidden homeless' category. A further section of the European Union population is estimated to be at risk or potentially homeless due to insecure accommodation or family difficulties relating to housing.

It can be argued that, because of the wide range of causes of homelessness, a comprehensive housing policy is needed to combat the rising trend: 'Because homelessness crosses the conventional boundaries of policy, it calls for innovative, integrated responses ... ranging from national and local government, through voluntary and other providers, to transnational initiatives' (Daly, 1994, p. 2).

Many groups working with the homeless emphasize the role of rented housing in combating shortages. In subsequent chapters we turn to an examination of social and private rented housing provision in Europe. We consider the existing frameworks which governments will have to either work with, or modify, to meet the levels of need which are apparent.

<table>
<tr><td>**6**</td><td># Social rented housing: systems of provision</td></tr>
</table>

This chapter will examine what is meant by social housing in different countries. It will show how much social housing exists in Europe and how much social housing is being built. It will then consider in detail the management and financing arrangements in the social sectors in France, Germany, the Netherlands and the UK, and explore areas of concern in these countries. Chapter 7 will go on to make some comparisons across Europe, and draw out some common issues and problems being experienced in the different countries.

6.1 WHAT IS SOCIAL HOUSING?

Social housing is usually perceived to be rented housing. Social housing has been defined as:

1. 'Housing whose construction and in consequence rents are subsidized from public funds' (Emms, 1990, p. 1).
2. Being differentiated from other forms of housing in three major respects:
   a. It is provided by landlords at a price which is not principally determined by considerations of profit.
   b. It is administratively allocated according to some concept of need.
   c. Political decision making has an important influence on the quantity, quality and terms of provision (Harloe, 1988).

The provision of social housing carries with it connotations of public subsidy to the supply of accommodation with such subsidy being intended to assist the less well off. Thus, social housing may be designed specifically for lower income groups and be provided with the aid of state assistance. Its provision is one way of recognizing that there will be some households in a market system who cannot afford housing of some sort of minimum standard. Social housing usually has minimum standards attached to its provision.

Sometimes social housing is referred to as 'non-profit housing'. This is on the understanding that it is outside of the market sector and no surpluses for commercial distribution should be made from its operation. However, in some European countries social housing can also be provided through housing companies which are entitled to make limited profits, so that the idea of social housing being entirely non-profit making is not accurate.

In several European countries the state subsidizes directly the provision of owner-occupied housing, in some cases intending the subsidized dwellings to be for lower income households. Such accommodation might well be considered social owner-occupied housing. The emphasis in this chapter will be on social rented housing.

The character of social housing in terms of its target groups, access, allocation, financing arrangements and construction varies to such a great extent that a universal definition is difficult to apply. Problems are encountered particularly when attempts are made to distinguish between social and private renting. These problems are discussed in more detail in Chapter 4.

We are concerned mainly with subsidized rented housing which is allocated with reference to need. This housing is supplied in Europe by a variety of landlords including municipalities, housing associations, other non-profit organizations and commercial enterprises.

6.2 THE SIZE OF SOCIAL SECTORS AND LEVELS OF SOCIAL HOUSING CONSTRUCTION IN EUROPE

The tenure data in Table 5.10 (Chapter 5) shows that the Netherlands has the largest social rented sector in the European Union, at 40% of the stock, with the UK second highest at 26%. The UK is the country with the largest municipal housing stock despite the operation of the 'Right to Buy' and various other stock transfer mechanisms.

Greece is the only country in the European Union not to have a social rented housing stock. There is, however, a subsidized 'social' owner-occupied sector. This is also the case in Spain, Portugal, Luxembourg, Belgium, the Netherlands, Italy and France, where there are social housing programmes which are aimed at making home ownership more accessible to low income families. The position becomes more complicated if one considers shared ownership and other 'mixed tenure' initiatives.

The contribution that social rented housing makes to the total volume of housing construction varies considerably between countries and has changed over time as the figures in Table 6.1 show.

The relative change has been particularly significant in the UK. In 1980 the UK had the highest rate of new social housing construction in the European Union, when nearly half of all new dwellings were constructed in the social rented sector. Since that time the levels of new construction in this

Table 6.1 Newly completed social rented dwellings (% of all dwellings completed): selected European countries, 1980–1993

	Belgium	Denmark	Germany	France	Ireland	Netherlands	Portugal	UK
1980	NA	24	11	15	22	34	NA	45
1991	1	42	16	19	9	27	2[1]	17
1993	23	34	12[2]	28	10	27	NA	21

[1]1990, [2]1992.

Source: European Commission (1993, 1994).

sector have been decreasing rapidly, so that by 1993 only 21% of new construction was devoted to social housing. While the significance of new social building was declining in the UK, and also in Ireland, in other countries building for the sector was expanding.

The data in Table 6.1 shows these changes. The significance of social rented construction increased between 1980 and 1991 in Germany and France, and particularly in Denmark. The figures in Table 6.1 partly reflect the varying state commitments to the subsidization of public sector production and, in particular, the increasing level of new construction in Danish social housing. However, the changing proportions over time are, in some circumstances, mainly a function of the relative levels of private sector construction. In the past social housing construction was used by the state, in some countries, in a counter-cyclical fashion in periods of low private sector development.

The rest of this chapter will examine the social housing sectors in France, Germany (including a discussion of housing in the former East Germany), the Netherlands and the UK, respectively. This will involve a consideration of organizational and management structures, access and allocation procedures. The role of government in monitoring social housing bodies, influencing the financial arrangements for construction and improvement work, and in rent setting will be discussed.

6.3 SOCIAL HOUSING IN FRANCE

The social housing sector in France includes both public and private bodies. Most social housing is within the Habitations à Loyer Modéré (HLM) (Housing at moderate rents) movement and can be constructed for rent and owner-occupation (the subsidized financing which is available for ownership will not be explored here). Together with the 'conventional' social rented sector, more recently an intermediate rented sector has emerged. This sector is also subsidized and caters for individuals who have slightly higher incomes than those in conventional social housing but cannot afford to rent in the private sector.

6.3.1 Social housing provision and management

About 90% of social housing in France is built and operated by HLM organizations. The main role of the HLM organizations is to construct and manage rented housing and to provide dwellings for social ownership. There are about 1000 HLM institutions with a total stock in 1992 of 4.6 million dwellings. Approximately 3.3 million of these have been constructed or financed for rent and the remaining 1.3 million for social ownership. Within the HLM movement there are both public and private providers of social housing. These can be further sub-divided into five main groups with various responsibilities for managing or constructing social housing, either for rent or ownership.

Offices publics d'HLM (OPHLMs) are non-profit organizations which are sponsored by local authorities at the municipality or département level. The main objective of the OPHLM is the construction and management of rented housing aimed at individuals on low incomes, and as a secondary role the promotion of social ownership. They also carry out rehabilitation work on existing properties and other urban development projects. The average size of their stock is about 6000 units. Although the OPHLMs were originally the most important providers of social housing, since the early 1980s their share of new construction has fallen considerably.

Offices publics d'Aménagement et de Construction (OPACs) were created in 1973 and operate under a mixture of private and public law. Like the OPHLM they are public bodies sponsored by a local authority promoting social housing, and the two organizations work closely together. The size of their stocks is generally much greater than the OPHLM and averages about 17 000 units. Their activities also tend to be much wider than those of the OPHLMs and they have the power to buy land and develop directly.

Sociétés anonymes d'HLM have legal status under legislation that generally applies to private joint stock companies and are permitted to make limited profits. They are usually sponsored by private sector firms, by chambers of commerce and industry, by the agents of the '1% patronal' scheme (of which they may be a sub-company), by the bodies who allocate family housing allowances, and sometimes by public enterprises and local authorities, with the main aim of providing low-cost housing for their employees. They are entitled to public financial support and also make use of funds from the '1% patronal' scheme. Their role is essentially in rented housing but they do also have some activities in social ownership. Since the 1977 financial reforms the sociétés anonymes have taken over as the main provider of social housing in France. In 1991, 58% of all new social housing starts were constructed by sociétés anonymes compared to 42% for both offices publics (OPHLMs and OPACs).

Sociétés anonymes de Crédit Immobilier (SACI) are subject to the same rules as the sociétés anonymes. Their main role is to provide loans (both subsidized and unsubsidized) for home ownership. The SACI are therefore subject to a banking law of 1984, which governs the operating rules of financial establishments.

Sociétés anonymes coopérative d'HLM are subject to private company law and laws applying to co-operative societies, but also operate as non-profit institutions under regulation from the HLM movement. Originally co-operatives played a substantial role in social housing provision but, in spite of an increase in the scope of their activities in 1983, many co-operatives have been dissolved.

HLM institutions are managed by a council consisting of members appointed by the département's préfet and other organizations. The presence of members of parliament on these councils can result in considerable political influence over HLM activities. The HLMs co-operate closely at the regional level and are united nationally in the Union Nationale des Fédérations d'Organismes d'HLM (UNFOHLM). This umbrella organization is well organized and can have considerable influence on government housing policy.

Around 10% of French social housing is run by Sociétés d'Économie Mixte (SEMs). These are joint ventures with funding partly from the private sector, but they also have access to loans only usually available to HLM organizations. SEMs are created under private company law and funded to a large extent by the state and are supported by the Caisse des Dépôts et Consignations (Section 6.3.2) or local authorities.

Central government's representative at the département level, the préfet, plays a supervisory role with respect to the HLM organizations. The central government has issued a number of directives to control HLM activity, although its chief influence is its power to grant subsidies and therefore influence the amount of new building.

The main criterion for access to French social housing is income. Income must be below a set level. Prospective tenants are then given 'entitlement' or the 'right of entry' to social housing. Whether a dwelling is actually allocated and subsequently taken up will depend upon the size of the stock in the surrounding area and the extent to which there are more urgent cases on an existing waiting list. Priority would be given, for example, to individuals living in poor conditions and the homeless.

Allocations to social housing are decided by an 'allocations board' within each HLM organization. This is made up of representatives from the local authorities, local employers, the local mayor, the préfet and other bodies involved in social housing. Each of these will have some percentage of nomination rights for specific dwellings and buildings depending on the financial contribution they have made to build them. The préfet has responsibility for ensuring that a proportion of dwellings are available for the homeless and households living in poor conditions.

To try to avoid concentrations of lower income households in some areas a new law was introduced in 1991, 'La Loi d'orientation pour la Ville'. To achieve a better balance of dwelling quality and dwelling type this law stipulates that any urban area with more than 350 000 inhabitants having less than 20% social housing must pay, in effect, a penalty tax. The taxes are paid annually to sections in the local authorities. This money is then allocated, under the direction of the préfet, to organizations involved in the purchase of land for, and the construction of, social housing (*HLM Aujourd'hui*, 1991, pp. 59–61).

Further pressure has been brought to bear on HLMs by the introduction in 1990 of the right to housing law, 'Droit au Logement'. This aims to give every French citizen the right to a dwelling and, although there are no definite requirements for the HLMs to act, it is expected that the allocations committees will respond to the law.

6.3.2 Financing and subsidies for social housing

a. Construction of social rented dwellings

Social housing in France is financed from a number of different sources. Major changes, which resulted in the current system of finance, were introduced in 1977. These reforms created subsidized loans to finance social rented housing construction, the Prêts Locatifs Aidés (PLAs). The PLAs constitute the largest proportion of funding for new construction. Several other sources are also used to supplement these loans. An explanation of the different financing channels is given in Figure 6.1.

The largest part of social housing finance for new construction comes from the Caisse des Dépôts et Consignations (CDC). This is a public funding agency for social housing which is financed through savings banks holding households' savings in 'Livret A' accounts. The CDC grants 'PLA' loans to HLM and SEM organizations over a 35 year period. The central government provides a construction subsidy to the borrower which reduces the repayments on the PLA loan. The proportion of total construction costs that the PLA will cover depends upon the organization carrying out the construction work, but will usually vary between 95 and 55%. To cover total costs various other loans are therefore required to top up PLA loans and government subsidies.

Further PLA loans can be granted by the Crédit Foncier France (CFF). Each loan is drawn from commodity or debenture holdings and a government subsidy which is paid directly to the CFF. The conditions attached are slightly different to the CDC–PLA loans. The builder or developer must

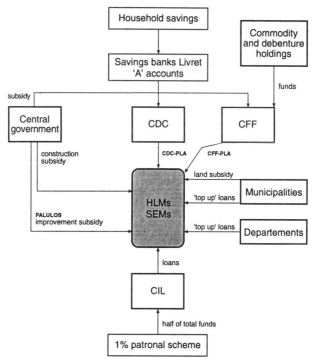

Figure 6.1 Social housing finance system: France. HLMs (Habitations à Loyer Modéré)(housing at moderate rents): includes both public and private providers of social housing with responsibility for construction and management. SEMs (Sociétés d'Economie Mixte): social housing providers and managers operating under company law and funded from public and private sources. CDCs (Caisse des Dépôts et Consignations): a public funding agency which is the main provider of loans for social housing construction. Financed through savings. CFF (Credit Foncier France): funded through its own holdings and government subsidy in its provision of loans for social housing construction. CIL (Comités Interprofessionels pour le Logement): one of the main agencies responsible for collecting funds from employers under the 1% patronal scheme and reallocating these funds for social housing loans and housing allowances.

cover at least 25% of the initial costs of construction and the CFF–PLA must not exceed 65% of a set development price. The loan may be at a fixed rate for 25 years or a variable rate for 30 years. These loans are awarded to private individuals as well as HLM institutions.

The granting of PLA loans and the respective government subsidies is subject to certain conditions including the signing of a contract between the developer and the government, which then gives the tenants the right to claim personal housing allowances, Aide Personnalisée au Logement (APL). The contract also fixes the rent at a maximum authorized level (Section

6.3.2(e)). PLAs can also be awarded to individuals provided that their income is below a fixed ceiling.

Additional loans from the CDC have been awarded to social housing bodies since 1990 to aid access to the social rented sector for certain disadvantaged households and to encourage social and economic integration in some inner city and suburban areas. A supplementary subsidy – the PLA d'insertion – can be granted by the CDC provided that conditions for a normal PLA loan and some further requirements relating to incomes and costs are met.

An additional form of financing for social housing construction that supplements PLA loans is the '1% patronal' scheme. Companies having a minimum of 10 workers make a compulsory contribution equal to 1% of gross wages. Before the 1980s, this contribution was collected entirely to finance building. However, since the 1980s, the total funds collected have been divided into two parts, with 0.53% allocated to the FNAL to help with housing allowance costs and only 0.47% going to the collection agencies to finance construction. The funds are collected by a number of agencies but mainly by the Comités Interprofessionnels pour le Logement (CIL), the chambers of commerce and by HLM organizations. Loans are available at very low rates but may make up only 25% of total costs. Further top up loans are sometimes available from local authorities and départements.

Another subsidy for HLMs is given in the form of land to build social housing. Local authorities may give land direct to HLMs, or where an HLM is obliged to buy land that is above a set limit for a particular area, a one-off subsidy is granted. Part of this will be awarded by the central government and part by the local authority.

The proportion of subsidy received from each source to finance social housing construction is likely to vary with each development. It may depend to a large extent on the quantity of funds available to the CDC from the Livret A savings accounts. The low interest rate of 4–5% attached to these savings means that households will often move their savings around if they can get a better return from other sources. This has caused problems as resources available from Livret A fell, due to a reduction in savings, by between 34 and 52 million francs between 1989 and 1992. However, at the same time the CDC has actually been able to increase its total resources available for social housing finance by drawing on other reserves.

b. Construction of dwellings for medium income renting

Organizations can qualify for loans to construct dwellings in the 'intermediate rented sector'. This sector aims to provide dwellings for those individuals whose incomes exceed the qualifying limit for social rented housing, but who still have difficulty in affording a rented property in the private sector. These loans, the Prêts Locatifs Intermédiaires (PLIs), are awarded to HLM and SEM organizations by the CDC, or to private individuals by the CFF.

Dwellings that are financed by PLI loans must be let for at least 9 years on the conditions that the rents do not exceed a given level and that tenants' incomes are not above a set ceiling.

c. Improvement subsidies for social housing

For the improvement of social rented dwellings, social organizations and individuals may qualify for a government subsidy – Prime à l'Amélioration de Logements à Usage Locatif et à Occupation Sociale (PALULOS). It is available for three main areas of improvement work:

1. For dwellings older than 15 years to be brought up to the 'normal minimum standard of habitation'.
2. To improve efficiency in energy provision.
3. Other improvement work which will extend the life of a dwelling.

The granting of PALULOS is subject, in a similar way to PLA loans, to the signing of a contract between the state and lessor which establishes the right of tenants to receive APL. The amount of subsidy awarded is limited to 20% of the total cost of improvement work, with a limit for the 'total cost' being set at FF 85 000 per dwelling (this percentage is sometimes increased to 30 or 40% in special circumstances). This government subsidy is given in instalments over the duration of the improvement work.

An organization in receipt of a PALULOS subsidy also has the right to receive a CDC–PLA loan for improvement work. The same conditions apply to this as with other CDC–PLA loans but they are usually limited to between 10 and 15 years, and may cover up to 50% of costs.

A second subsidy the 'aide à l'amélioration de la qualité de service', has been available to the same social housing organizations since 1988. This is a much smaller subsidy (with maximum payments of FF 3500) aimed at improving the living conditions for those in social dwellings.

d. Guarantees

When a social organization qualifies for a subsidized loan it is contracted into a guarantee system. This operates in the form of an 'insurance scheme' to cover the HLMs if they cannot meet all costs. The département and the HLM sign a contract under which the département accepts responsibility on behalf of the HLM if it defaults on payments. In return the HLM must pay regular premiums. These premiums are paid to the Caisse de Garantie du Logement Social (CGLS), the social housing guarantee bank, which is managed by the CDC under the control of an administrative council. The insurance scheme covers PLAs, PLA d'insertion and PALULOS loans, and the CGLS may also award one-off short-term loans or grants, with government aid, to HLMs in particular difficulty. The amount of the HLM contribution is a fixed percentage of its loan commitment, but does vary between the types of organizations.

e. Rents: setting and increases

Each HLM development is treated as an individual cost centre with no opportunity to cross-subsidize rents. Each project will have its initial rent determined individually. This will be calculated according to a number of factors, the main one being the cost of financing for the project. Rents for specific properties can also be determined according to a 'corrected' surface area which takes account of the size and the levels of amenities in a dwelling. The final decision on rent setting is left to the discretion of the HLM organization, but this must still fall within government set minimum and maximum levels. The government limits are reviewed annually and are adjusted by the current construction costs index. Because of the emphasis on the cost of financing in the calculation of rents, there is little correlation between the rent and the quality of the dwelling. In many areas, and particularly in Paris and other large cities, this has led to large rent differences between similar housing projects. Because of the desire of HLM bodies to select tenants on incomes high enough to support high rents, and with the demand for quality dwellings exceeding supply, tenant selection is a difficult process for HLMs and individuals on lower incomes can find it hard to secure accommodation.

Regulations for rent increases in the social sector have altered frequently. The main regulation laid down in the Code of Construction, is that increases, which can be made every 6 months, must not exceed 10% of the total rent. However, the government does still set an average guideline for rent increases which is closely related to the rate of inflation (this is separate to its guideline on initial rents mentioned above) and tries to ensure that the HLM organizations adhere to their social vocation. All rent increases are initially referred to the préfet, who has the power to refuse any increase which is considered unreasonable.

Recent trends in HLM rent policies, particularly the steepness of rent increases and the sharp differences between rents, have meant that this issue has become one of considerable concern. The government has set as a priority objective for HLM organizations the rationalization of rents (French Housing Ministry, 1993).

6.3.3 Evaluation

Many of the problems that are now facing the social rented stock in France are common both to other sectors, and to other European countries. Several changes that have come about are due to the deregulation of finance and its effect on housing (Lefebvre, 1992), in particular the switch from bricks and mortar subsidies to housing allowances (these changes are examined in more depth in Chapter 7).

The social rented sector is facing increasing pressures due to the effects of problems in other housing sectors. For example, while home ownership became increasingly popular in France throughout the 1980s access for those on low incomes has become more and more difficult. At the same time a recent sharp decline in the private rented sector, which has reduced supply and increased rents, has also forced many households on low incomes to rely on the social rented sector for accommodation.

While investment levels have been maintained in the sector, it has clearly not been enough to accommodate the increases in need that have been experienced. One solution is to find ways of increasing new construction in the sector. In the meantime, as a way of keeping the stock available for lower income groups, the income ceilings for right of entry to the stock have not been adjusted upwards for the past few years (Lefebvre, 1992). This has led to further problems of segregation and ghettoization in some parts of the stock, and increasing management problems for the organizations who are now expected to take on less privileged households.

HLM organizations are generally facing increasing financial difficulties and many are beginning to encourage sales of part of their stock to help with other costs. This has only recently begun to take place in France and is as yet very limited. Sales are coordinated by the landlord organization, but strongly monitored by local government and the préfet (Ghékiere, 1993). There are strict regulations concerning those able to buy their rented homes and on what terms. There is as yet no 'Right to Buy' as is the case in the UK.

6.4 SOCIAL HOUSING IN GERMANY

Social housing in Germany is a function of a method of financing housing and not of specific types of landlords. Since 1950 finance and subsidies for the provision of social housing have been available to any registered institution, private individual, company or institutional investor who agrees to adhere to a number of conditions. These concern rent levels and the income levels of the tenants they accept. There is thus an overlap between 'private' and 'social' landlords providing social housing. The main incentive that encourages 'private' landlords to enter into social housing provision is that they are permitted to make profits. 'Social' landlords provided, until 1990, non-profit housing and operated under stricter regulations than private landlords. Since 1990 the regulations concerning non-profit housing have undergone a number of changes and these will be discussed below. Subsidies and loans are available for both rented and owner-occupied social housing. However, the concentration here will be on the social rental sector.

A main feature of the social housing system is that the provisions are temporary in nature. The conditions applicable to social housing apply only until public loans are redeemed. As a result of this, since the mid-1980s large sections of the social housing stock have been lost to the free sector as these loans are paid off. With only limited new social house building to replace these units, the sector is beginning to experience serious shortages.

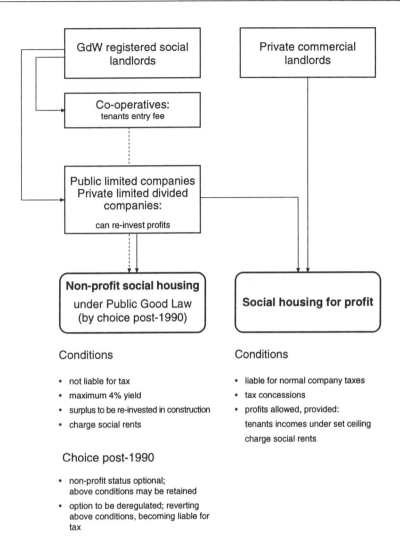

Figure 6.2 Structure of social housing providers: Germany.

6.4.1 Social housing provision and management

The overlaps in the provision of social housing in Germany make classification of different landlord organizations difficult, because each landlord does not necessarily provide one specific type of housing. The basic structures are set out in Figure 6.2. The private landlords who provide social housing are mainly large institutions and private individuals who all make profits on their investments. This form of social housing provision was undertaken in post-war Germany to encourage increased construction in the sector without putting too great a burden on government finances. However, the profits of these landlords will determine future expansion in this part of the social rented sector, and its growth is therefore tied, more so than in other countries, to both the market and the economy. This can lead to a situation where housing managers, aiming to optimize operating conditions, are necessarily less concerned with ideas of social responsibility towards tenants.

In 1993 private landlords controlled just under 1 million dwellings in the social sector. Loans and subsidies are received directly from the government for the construction of dwellings. Private landlords are liable to pay normal company taxes, but the provision of social housing can enable them to take advantage of certain tax concessions. Profits are permitted provided that landlords accept tenants whose incomes are under a specified level, and social rents are charged.

All non-profit housing provided prior to 1990 by social landlords was subject to a Law governing 'Housing for the Public Good' (Wohnungsgemeinützigkeitsgesetz). This law decreed that social landlords were exempt from corporate, trade and capital taxes as a compensation for adhering to the following conditions for supplying social housing (COFACE, 1989c; Norton and Novy, 1991; Power, 1993):

- A maximum of 4% yield on investment.
- The building and managing of housing was to be social landlord's sole objective: all other activities were prohibited.
- A commitment that any surpluses above a 4% return would be re-invested in housing.
- Rents would be set according to a 'social–cost rent principle'.
- Social landlords would be committed to a continuing building programme.
- They would provide for tenants on moderate incomes (within set limits) and in regard to this would limit the size of the dwellings.

Social landlords that adhere to these regulations are Genossenschaften (co-operative associations) or Wohnungsbaugesellschaften (limited liability housing companies). These are registered with the Gesamtverband der Wohnungswirtschaft (GdW) which is the umbrella organization for non-profit landlords. The GdW acts as a lobby and advice centre for the movement, with a regional and federal network.

In 1992 there were 1827 member organizations in the GdW controlling a total stock of over 3.3 million dwellings. However, not all of these were in the social rented sector. Some of the non-profit organizations have a further role as builders and developers of owner-occupied housing and also manage housing for third parties. These landlords may additionally play a role in providing social housing for profit, so that all of their activities are not bound by the 'Public Good' Law.

Co-operative associations make up around two-thirds of the GdW membership (1174 associations in 1992), but control only about 30% of the registered stock, i.e. just over 1 million dwellings. They are private organizations backed by, for example, churches, trade unions and charities, and they have strong local links which influence tenant selection. The co-operative movement is based on collective property, and members are owners and tenants at the same time. Tenants are required to pay a proportion of initial costs of the dwelling and therefore tend to be fairly high income earners.

Housing companies made up a much smaller part of the GdW membership (622 in 1992) yet they manage a much larger proportion of the social rented stock. They are controlled by municipalities, trade unions and national employers, such as the post office, railways and churches. A lot of the companies are very small. However, a small number of them are responsible for large stocks of dwellings. For example, the 50 biggest companies have stocks of approximately 20 000 units each. These companies are usually ones where big city local authorities or Länder governments have a controlling stake.

During the 1980s total dwelling construction in the social sector fell as it appeared that the current housing supply was saturating the market. There were also arguments that social housing was no longer needed and that there were many inefficiencies in its provision. These arguments were reinforced when scandal erupted over Neue Heimat, the largest social housing company in Germany.

Neue Heimat was a housing company owned by the German Trade Union Congress. It managed over 300 000 social dwellings. However, it abused its power by making over ambitious deals and speculating in risky investments. Eventually it emerged that the company had huge financial problems which had left it on the verge of bankruptcy. It was too late for the Trade Union Congress to undo mistakes and finally most of the dwellings were taken over by new housing companies formed by the Länder.

This crisis had a huge effect on German housing organizations and gave the government the impetus to change the social housing sector, even though Neue Heimat was by no means representative of other companies. In 1990 an Act came into effect that repealed the 'Public Good' Law. This meant that social housing companies would be allowed to diversify their activities, they would be liable to the same taxes as private landlords and profit-making companies but would also receive the same tax privileges (Power, 1993).

It is expected that many co-operatives will voluntarily maintain the conditions of the 'Public Good' Law and continue to operate on a non-profit basis. Many organizations have welcomed the changes as they removed many 'excessive restrictions' in social housing (COFACE, 1989c, p. 138). However, there are also fears that the new freedom will lead to increasing rents in the sector, to properties being aimed at higher income earners to increase profits and to declining levels of social housing provision. Indeed the abolition of the 'Public Good' Law has been quoted as being the 'greatest wrong decision since the war' (German Tenant Association, director H. Schlich from *Frankfurter Rundschau*, 21 January 1989, in Norton and Novy, 1991, p. 32).

Municipalities play a vital role in the allocation of housing. Prospective tenants apply to the housing departments (Wohnungsamt) and receive a 'certificate of entitlement' to social housing if they have an income below a set limit. There are three types of certificates that tenants can apply for: an emergency certificate gives access to special reserved stock which has a higher level of subsidy for the landlord; a certificate for households with particularly low incomes gives access to social housing built before 1964 with lower rents; and a normal certificate applies to rest of the stock. Once a certificate of entitlement has been awarded, applicants will be housed according to the priority in each category.

Income is the main criterion for determining whether a household is in need of a social dwelling. Once an individual has a tenancy there are no further reviews of household income. This has led to considerable problems as tenants' incomes rise above the qualifying level and they are still able to stay in the dwelling.

There was much debate in Germany about how to address this problem. With growing need for social housing, it seemed that the sector was not targeted to those in most need and that the rate at which new requirements were being met from the existing stock was very low. In response to this situation the Bundestag introduced a law at the end of 1981 which entitled the Länder to levy an additional tax on certain households. This tax, the 'Fehlbelegungsabgabe', must be paid by tenants if their incomes rise to 20% above the set limit. The setting of the limits and the operation of the system vary between the Länder. The revenue received from this tax is put back into new social housing construction (Hills *et al.*, 1990, p. 155).

Even after some years of operation the additional tax does not seem to have been very effective at providing an incentive for high income tenants to move on. Problems of allocation and access are therefore continuing.

6.4.2 Financing and subsidies for social housing

a. Construction of social rented dwellings

There are three main subsidy paths (Förderungsweg) for the construction of social housing. Their principal aim is to reduce the tenants' rents to below the 'cost rent' and the size of the loan will therefore be different for each development project.

The first subsidy path ('Erster Förderungsweg') is for the construction of publicly assisted social housing reserved for specific sections of the population. This subsidy is awarded on the condition that minimum quality standards are met in building. A dwelling must also be below a maximum quality standard to be allocated to a social tenant. Tenants must have incomes under a set ceiling.

The second subsidy path ('Zweiter Förderungsweg') leads to the construction of dwellings which are slightly above the level of those constructed under the first subsidy path. They are allocated to households whose incomes are up to 40% above the social income limit. They will have a higher rent attached to them and are therefore aimed at tenants who have higher incomes but cannot afford to rent in the free private sector.

Some Länder also offer a third subsidy path ('Dritte Förderungsweg'). This was introduced in 1986 so that Länder can grant further (usually short-term) subsidies for social housing construction with more flexible arrangements concerning rent setting and allocation, which are agreed between the Länder and the 'builder' when the subsidy is awarded (Hallett, 1993, p. 126).

The actual financial instruments used are set out below. There are three forms of aid that are used for the 'Erster' and 'Zweiter Förderungsweg':

1. Capital subsidy in the form of an low interest loan, that will partially finance the construction of a dwelling.
2. Operating costs subsidy, usually paid over a 15 year period with the subsidy decreasing each year. The size of the original subsidy depends on the floor space of the dwelling.
3. Operating cost loans to partially cover capital expenditure. The amount of the loan will depend on floor space. Loans are given for 15 years. Repayments of 2% per year begin from the 16th year. Interest at 6% on the unrepaid part of the loan must also be paid from the 16th year.

Generally, institutions constructing social rented dwellings must finance at least 15% of the building costs themselves. As well as subsidized loans from the Länder, loans can be taken up from the capital market. These are loans on an annuity basis with a term of 30 years (Papa, 1992, p. 61). If an operating cost subsidy has been allocated, subsidies may also be given in the form of sureties for mortgages which are obtained at market rates (Hubert, 1992).

b. Responsibilities for allocating subsidies

The relationships between the government and housing bodies responsible for the construction and improvement of social rented dwellings are shown in Figure 6.3.

The federal government determines the amount of subsidy to be allocated to the social housing programme each year, and also determines the cost rent. The Länder governments are obliged to allocate an amount to social housing equal to that which the central government is allocating to their Land. They are responsible for awarding social housing subsidies and loans resulting

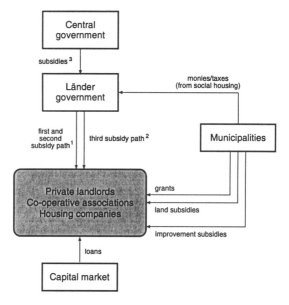

Figure 6.3 Social housing finance system: Germany. [1]Subsidies in the form of Öffentliche Baudarlehen (interest free loans), Aufwendungszuschuss (operating cost subsidy) and Aufwendungsdarlehen (loans to partially cover capital expenditure). [2]The third subsidy path operates only in some Länder and varies between Länder, usually a one-off contribution towards building costs. [3]Not granted 1985–1989.

from the social housing programme together with any they wish to grant from their own budgets (e.g. via the third subsidy path). The Länder decide how funds are allocated between the three Förderungsweg. A large degree of diversity in the channelling of social housing finance and the conditions of loans and subsidies exists between the Länder. The Länder also make decisions concerning the number of dwellings to be built over the year, whether these are to be for rent or sale, and set the criteria for the quality of the dwellings.

The municipalities in turn take responsibility for urban planning matters, issuing construction permits, the allocation of social dwellings and they provide land for the building of social dwellings.

From 1985 the federal government withdrew from the direct financing of social housing as, for reasons discussed earlier, the necessity for social house building was not seen as being so great. This left the responsibility for financing all new social housing developments entirely to the Länder and municipalities, and led to the development of the Dritte Förderungsweg. Even so, the late 1980s saw a dramatic downturn in the construction of new social dwellings. It was only from 1989 that federal government again started to grant direct subsidies for new building. This action was brought on largely by reunification, but was also influenced by the increasing need for housing and the shortfall of '1 million dwellings' discovered following the 1987 census (Eekhoff, 1989).

The federal government has set out a programme for its budget allocations to social housing up to 1997. These have been increased considerably since the late 1980s. In 1988 federal funds for the social housing programme stood at DM 0.45 billion and DM 1.05 billion in 1989. However, between 1990 and 1997 it is estimated that funds will average out at approximately DM 3 billion per annum including subsidies for the new Länder.

c. Improvement subsidies

From 1977 subsidies to encourage the improvement of rented dwellings took two forms: low interest loans and operating subsidies. These were financed jointly by the federal and Länder governments, and were implemented through the municipalities. Schemes were targeted at older urban areas and on energy saving projects (Tomann, 1990).

d. Rents

A scale of social rent levels is set annually by the Länder. These are the rents that tenants in social dwellings actually pay. For individual landlords to arrive at this social rent, they must initially make a calculation of cost rents, which will then be adjusted down to the social rent through negotiation of different subsidies. (The description of the system of social–cost rent calculations relies heavily on Hubert, 1993.)

The cost rent calculation must be made for each individual project and is based on an estimation of construction costs, land costs and (where subsidies are in the form of current allowances) interest on loans throughout the construction period. From all of these items a 'cost rent' is arrived at. The difference between the cost rent and the social rent set by the Länder is made up by a subsidy payment through one of the subsidy paths. The investor gets a return equivalent to the cost rent (social rent plus subsidy). The cost rent is binding until public loans or subsidies are fully repaid and the dwellings revert to the free rental sector.

Increases in rent are dealt with differently, depending on the type of financing and subsidy awarded. The different systems of rent increases caused problems to tenants, as landlords can pass on increased costs. Social rents have been rising at increasing rates. Higher rents have not been accompanied by increases in incomes to the degrees that were anticipated in the methods of rent calculation. Thus, rising rents have been an increasing burden on tenants. A substantial difference has grown between rents of dwellings financed by public loans and those financed by expenditure subsidies.

According to general Tenure Law, 11% of all improvement costs can be passed on in higher rents. This led many landlords to carry out extensive improvements purely so that they could charge an increased rent which means many tenants experienced great hardship in meeting higher rental demands. Changes are being made to the system so that the cost rents are not being set so high.

6.4.3 Evaluation

While a number of recent changes have been made to the system of social housing in Germany, considerable problems still remain in the sector. These include:

1. An increasing pressure on waiting lists from immigrants from eastern Europe and also movement within Germany since reunification.
2. Increased demand on social dwellings due to increasing household formation.
3. Problems of 'under occupation' of social dwellings as households become smaller but remain in the same size dwelling.
4. Access to the social housing stock, difficulties being experienced by 'problem households' as landlords become more and more selective;
5. The question of whether social landlords are really fulfilling their 'social' obligation. This has been brought even more into question as non-profit status is ended for many organizations.

These issues are currently being debated. A number of questions need to be addressed, such as should high income earners be allowed to remain in the social dwelling stock? Should new immigrants who have never paid into the social welfare system be entitled to receive social housing? There are discussions about how the Fehlbelegungsabgabe might be changed, to increase more proportionately with income.

However, a principal concern is still the need to build more social dwellings. Increasing construction in this sector is now a major policy issue, even more so following the changes in the non-profit status of landlords in 1990 and the reduction of the stock as social loans are repaid. It is a topic fraught with political sensitivity in terms of responsibility between the federal and Länder governments.

6.5 HOUSING IN THE NEW BUNDESLÄNDERN

Housing in the former East Germany was said to be a 'social right' that was guaranteed under the constitution. (East Germany will henceforth be referred to as the 'new Bundesländern', as distinct from the 'old Bundesländern' of the former West Germany). To meet this guarantee the government embarked on a huge building programme during the 1970s that has left the country with a crude surplus of housing units. With a total stock of about 6.8 million dwellings, the number of households was about 6.6 million in 1990 (Kornek, 1990).

Because of this 'right to housing', state involvement in housing provision was very high and the government was involved in the subsidization of most types of housing in some form or another. The proportion of income that a household should spend on housing was clearly defined by the government. This was set at a very low level (between 3 and 5% of incomes) to fit in with the concept of housing as a welfare good.

However, while some households devoted exceptionally low proportions of their income on rents (e.g. agricultural workers paid only 0.9%), other household types, particularly low income households, paid significantly more. While households on incomes of less than DM 1200 devoted approximately 4.5% of income to rent, single adults with children and low incomes often paid up to 10%. Even so, the state subsidized these low rents with about DM 20 billion annually (Dienemann, 1993).

Although the state declared equality for all citizens in the GDR, a significant degree of favouritism was targeted to a small number of party officials, both in housing and other service provisions. At the same time many private owners of dwellings were discriminated against by tough rent controls and a lack of state support for maintenance and repairs. Households often queued for up to 10 years on waiting lists to obtain dwellings, and they had no choice whatsoever regarding size and very little with respect to location.

Following the reunification of Germany all housing laws that existed in the former West Germany were to apply to the new German Länder. To quote the federal Ministry; 'From 3 October 1990, and with only a few exceptions for a limited transitional period, the entire body of law on housing, rents and building in the West German Länder will apply in the Länder, Brandenburg, Mecklenburg-Vorpommern, Sachsen, Sachsen-Anhalt and Thüringen, as well as in East Berlin. This basis for a general improvement in housing and town planning has thus been created' (Hallett, 1993, pp. 144–145). The newly unified Germany was faced with considerable problems which the system of provision and subsidization in the former East Germany had created.

The rush to build such large quantities of housing units in the 1970s building programme led to high numbers of industrialized system built blocks. The state preferred high quantities rather than good quality, and took little notice of the need and demand for larger dwellings. Dwellings from the new building programme are becoming more and more unpopular because of their uniformity and lack of ability for 'self-expression' by the tenants. Furthermore, facilities and public amenities for the estates are very poor. Provision of libraries, shops, leisure facilities and other meeting places are clearly insufficient.

The policy of maintaining low rents has also had consequences on the quality of the existing stock, resulting in limited scope for investment in maintenance, repair and improvement work. Although newly built dwellings are of a fairly high standard, the condition of the older rented stock has become so poor as to be uninhabitable in many cases. About 20% of the stock has no inside WC, 860 000 units were without a bath or shower and estimates suggest that 'between 700 000 and 1 million flats are totally unsuitable for living and must be demolished' (Schuler-Wallner and Wullkopf, 1991, p. 14).

Despite the crude surplus of housing units apparent in the new Bundesländern quite extensive problems of both shortages and homelessness have become apparent since reunification. For example, in Leipzig homelessness is estimated at 4% of the city's 500 000 inhabitants. In 1990 it was estimated that in total over 200 000 persons were either homeless or potentially homeless (Schuler-Wallner and Wullkopf, 1991). Thousands of households are continuing to live in dwellings with totally unsuitable conditions. There is a serious need for both new dwellings and modernization of the existing stock.

Many of the best state-owned properties are being sold off at advantageous rates. However, most are sold to former West German citizens, taking advantage of tax deductions and tax subsidies which had essentially been targeted at citizens in the new Bundesländern. These households are often not in a position to buy properties, even with tax advantages, because of limited savings.

Hallett (1994, pp. 139–140) lists five main tasks of housing policy necessary in the 'five new Länder':

1. To mobilize the capital and resources needed for new and improved housing.
2. To devise new, market-orientated forms of tenure and management.
3. To re-establish the legitimacy of private ownership.
4. To do the above without imposing excessive hardship on any group of citizens.
5. To encourage people to stay put rather than move to West Germany.

Some of these goals have been addressed through increasing rents, firstly to cover the necessary maintenance and repair work, but also to act as an incentive for increasing investment by private landlords. In October 1991, rents across all sectors in the new German Länder were raised by DM 1/m². This resulted in an increase in average rents, plus service charges, from DM 83 to 295 per month. This still left rents in the new Bundesländern far behind levels in the west; in 1991 average monthly rents stood respectively, at DM 166 in the east and over DM 400 in the west. In 1993 a second universal rent increase was initiated, which raised rents by DM 3.80/m². One of the main reasons for this was to increase the opportunity for repairs and renovations.

However, rent increases have also led to the problem of rent arrears accumulating as tenants find it difficult to afford rents but, in particular, service charges. In the former East Germany service costs were not levied on the tenants. Non-payment of rents had reached DM 340 million in 1993 (GdW, 1993). Housing allowances (Wohngeld) were introduced in the new housing system, but in 1991 the take up by 1.5 million households out of an estimated 4 million eligible households was particularly slow.

New construction of housing has been very slow due to lack of familiarity with the new systems and availability of credit. Total housing completions in 1991 amounted to 14 000 units (GdW, 1992), almost 100% of which were for rent, while in 1992 new house building had fallen to just 7907 units. New construction is progressing slowly due to large amounts of investment being channelled into modernization and maintenance work. Investment in modernization rose to DM 7.5 billion in 1992, more than double the previous years level. Nearly DM 5 billion of this went to maintenance and restorations, and approximately DM 2.5 billion towards modernizing 260 800 dwellings. The circumstances particular to the social rented sector, in eastern Germany will now be examined (see Chapter 8 for details on the private rented sector).

6.5.1 Social housing in the new Bundesländern

Social housing, or at least housing controlled by the state, makes up nearly half of the new Bundesländern housing stock. In 1992 this amounted to 3.37 million social units out of a stock of nearly 7 million dwellings. This has led to a doubling of the amount of social housing in the united Germany.

Public housing was previously managed by state run and co-operative administrations. The administrations would either own or act as trustees for the dwelling stock. The legal entities responsible for the administration of the state-owned stocks were state run companies such as VEB Kommunale Wohnungsverwaltung (KWV) and VEB Gebäudewirtschaft (GW). The owners of co-operative housing stocks were workers housing co-operatives (AWG) and non-profit housing co-operatives (GWG).

Financing for these types of housing was provided almost completely by the state, due to the provision of housing being seen as a 'social task'. Housing construction was financed by state low interest loans to housing administrations, co-operatives and to a lesser extent to individuals for owner-occupation. The loans usually ran for a period of 41 years with interest set at a rate of 4%. Loans for the construction of owner-occupied dwellings could, in part, be interest free. The repayments were worked out so that the monthly financial commitment never exceeded the equivalent of the monthly rent to be paid by the tenants in state-owned flats.

Rents in state dwellings were set and controlled by government. However, costs of financing and construction were rarely taken into account when determining rent levels. Rents were set according to the circumstances of each household: number of adults and children, age, health and income. The rents on these dwellings bore little resemblance to costs and were set at very low levels.

Reunification has resulted in the ownership of housing being reorganized to fit into the models of the old Bundesländern. For social housing this has meant changing the state housing administrations into non-profit housing associations/co-operatives, joint stock companies or public limited companies. Many of these organizations have taken up membership of the GdW. A breakdown of these organizations is shown in Table 6.2.

Table 6.2 Housing stock in the new Bundesländern with GdW membership, 1992

Type of organization	Number of GdW members	Housing stock ('000s)
State housing companies	472	2250
Co-operatives	762	1120
Total	1234	3370

Source: GdW (1993).

The changeover will be a very gradual process, complicated by the accumulated debts of the GDR housing administrations pre-1989. These debts to state-owned credit institutions amounted to DM 36 billion in 1991. Discussions are continuing about how to deal with the problem. The president of the GdW, Jürgen Steinert, is proposing that these state-owned dwellings should be controlled by non-profit companies along the lines of those previously operating in the former West Germany, and that the federal government should write off the debts so that housing costs in the country would be moderated and more money could be channelled into new investment in subsidized housing.

The claims on land and property from outside of the new Bundesländern have also caused many problems. Vast quantities of land and housing have been thrown into effective 'limbo' while ownerships are being determined. At the end of 1991, about 9% of the total housing stock was caught up in restitution claims from third parties or had doubtful property ownership (GdW, 1992). Of the 3.37 million dwellings in GdW membership, 18% had claims of restitution. Most of these were in the housing companies rather than co-operatives. By the end of 1992, only 83 560 dwellings (14% of all claims) had been returned to their rightful owners. This left 15.5% (522 000 dwellings) of the whole stock with uncertain ownership. This is blocking further investment in these dwellings (GdW, 1993). In the social housing stock there is also a problem of over 90 000 empty dwellings, which need to be made fit to live in. Many of these dwellings can be brought back into use once repairs have been made.

6.6 SOCIAL HOUSING IN THE NETHERLANDS

The Netherlands has the largest social housing sector in Europe with 40% of its total housing stock devoted to social housing. Social housing in the Netherlands is distinctive, particularly compared with the UK, in that it has catered not only for lower income but also for median income households. Dwellings are built to a high standard and until recently a large degree of state intervention existed in the sector to encourage construction and to keep rent levels down. Social dwellings were therefore a much sought after form of tenure and many households remained in social dwellings even when their incomes rose.

Avoiding social segregation and the stigmatization experienced in many other European social sectors is seen as an achievement of Dutch social housing. However, more recently as government intervention and subsidies have been quite dramatically reduced, shortages are being experienced in many parts of the country and questions are being raised about the necessity to target social housing to those in most need. As the sector is expected to take on more autonomy, and at the same time receive fewer subsidies, there are a great deal of changes, particularly for the housing associations.

Most of the policies that are now being implemented were outlined in the 'Policy Document on Housing in the Nineties' which was put together by state secretary Heerma in 1989. Several changes are thus a consequence of the 'Heerma Memorandum'.

6.6.1 Social housing provision and management

The social housing stock in the Netherlands is managed by two groups: housing associations and municipalities. However, it is the housing associations that dominate the sector with about 1100 associations managing 2 million dwellings, which account for around 30% of the total Dutch housing stock. The 330 local authority housing organizations own about 350 000 dwellings.

Housing associations are incorporated as non-profit associations or foundations and are registered with the central government as being exclusively engaged in promoting housing. Originally associations stemmed from social organizations, such as churches or trade unions, and remained small bodies. However, since the late 1960s legislation has required that associations should be the main providers of new social housing and their role has therefore grown considerably.

Housing associations are non-profit organizations. They require certification and authorization from the central government to become an 'authorized institution'. Any surplus or profits made must be re-invested in housing and their objectives are to provide, construct, improve or manage homes to meet general housing need.

As the role of housing associations has increased they have become more professional, with fewer volunteers controlling policy. Associations build dwellings for social renting and social owner-occupation, and have more recently become involved in the selling of social rented dwellings (Chapter 7).

They are monitored primarily by the local authority in which they operate but some supervision also takes place from central government. The housing associations' dwelling stock is relatively young and is generally well maintained.

Until 1965 municipalities were the main providers of social housing in the Netherlands. The dwelling stocks have been managed by municipal housing agencies which are either independently incorporated companies or departments of the local authorities. The dwellings that were provided by the municipalities are somewhat older than association dwellings and have, on average, lower rents (Priemus, 1990). However, following the Housing Act 1965, housing associations were granted 'primacy' giving them the first option to build any new social dwellings. A municipality would only be able to take over the development of a site where all housing associations refused to develop. Now, however, there is virtually no new municipality building in this sector.

As part of the overall changes in the sector these local authority organizations are now required to become housing associations. This was decided partly to confirm the role of the municipalities as local government bodies rather than social housing landlords. However, it was also decided that as the municipality was the primary monitoring body of housing associations, they should not be in a position of having to 'check up' on themselves. Municipalities are therefore 'handing over' their stocks to housing associations and forming new management boards. This has also meant a great deal of deregulation in the sector as more individual responsibility is given to associations. This can be seen particularly in the financing arrangements (Section 6.6.2).

The associations, and remaining local authority housing companies, are grouped into two national federations. The Nationale Woningraad (NWR, National Housing Council) has 720 member organizations, managing a stock of 1 400 000 dwellings. It has traditionally represented the interests of the secular housing associations and municipal landlord companies. The Netherlands Christian Institute (NCIV) has 410 members managing 760 000 dwellings. Members tend to be smaller housing associations with a religious base. The umbrella organizations act as a national lobby for their members' interests and as a source of advice on specialist management issues.

a. Role of government – control and monitoring

Housing associations have had strong links with the government since the 1901 Housing Act obliged them to become registered institutions in order to receive government subsidies. The central government maintains a strong interest in subsidized housing and monitors the financial performance of housing associations. It creates the framework for the execution of public tasks by setting down a national programme of new building and improvement work each year.

Municipalities play a monitoring role in the social housing sector. They are responsible for ensuring that land is available and affordable for social house building. They grant building licences and keep checks on the quality of construction. They effectively have the power to control and steer social housing activity in their area. They receive and allocate funds, have the power to guarantee loans and play a large role in the allocation of housing. The central government has little direct involvement in management although it does set general financial rules, allocate budgets and grants to local authorities, and set rent levels.

An important emphasis is put on a close relationship between the levels of government and housing associations to maintain structured co-operation. While both this working practice and continued subsidies have been largely responsible for the success of social housing, these relationships will be put under pressure as government regulation of the sector changes.

Housing associations are required to make an annual report to the municipalities. In the past this report set out plans for the coming year and needed to be approved by local, and sometimes central, government. However, following the 1993 Social Rental Sector Management Decree, associations will be assessed on their performance in the previous year, rather than planning for the forthcoming year. Their report must state achievements in terms of quality of dwellings, housing provided for low income earners, financial policy and degree of consultation with residents. The annual report goes first to the municipalities who then discuss particular cases with the Housing Ministry if performance is 'below par'. Performance indicators are thus in operation.

Housing associations have been given increased autonomy in achieving goals, but with fewer regulations many are experiencing difficulties. The Dutch umbrella organization, the NWR, reports that some housing associations are not able to cope with the new financial responsibilities. There has been some unorthodox land speculation and investment activities. In response to this the NWR is planning to establish an internal 'code of practice' for its registered housing associations to aid them in their new responsibilities.

b. Access and allocation procedures

Local authorities have the main responsibility for allocating social rented dwellings. Each municipality sets allocation criteria. Although housing associations must follow these regulations they do play a role in negotiating their details. Some housing associations also operate their own waiting lists and allocation procedures. This can lead to a lack of co-ordination as some towns or cities may have several waiting lists functioning concurrently.

Waiting lists have often operated on a point setting system. Where shortages were most acute residents were once required to first obtain a 'residence' permit from the municipality before they could qualify for allocation. However, from July 1993 this regulation lapsed and the new 'Accommodation Act' came into being. This has made a series of changes to the allocation of dwellings. The Act provides a statutory framework for distributing social dwellings, under which municipalities have the power to attach conditions to the allocation of particular parts of the stock. Dwellings below a set rent level may be set aside for households on lower incomes or in greater need. Allocations under the new Act may also be made over a wider area as co-operation at the regional level is encouraged to increase choice and flexibility.

Points systems are becoming less popular now as problems with co-ordination continue. Recently, distribution has become more liberalized with a new 'market system' of allocation operating in some areas. Applicants are encouraged to play a more active role in finding themselves a dwelling. Information is made available to prospective tenants who may then register for any dwelling for which specific criteria are met. The dwelling is then allocated to the most urgent case.

A continuing problem is overall access to the social housing stock and the 'skewed' relationship between high income earners in low rent social dwellings. As the social sector in the Netherlands was never targeted solely at lower income households, but also encompassed many middle income earners, it was not initially seen as a problem when tenants' incomes increased and they did not move. Over time, though, the proportion of households on high incomes in the social sector has grown considerably. With increasing income, many households are choosing to remain in low rent social dwellings rather than move on to other accommodation, even if living space is rather cramped. This is particularly the case if dwellings are located in areas with good amenities. This has become a major issue as household formation continues in the Netherlands at a fast rate.

This distribution problem is currently being tackled by trying to free up cheaper dwellings, through turnover of stock and strategic new construction of more expensive dwellings to draw some households out of the social sector. This new construction is taking place particularly in the owner-occupied sector. In addition, municipalities are urged to target available dwellings to lower income earners as much as possible.

6.6.2 Financing and subsidies for social housing

There have been changes over the last decade in the Netherlands in the emphasis on social housing. The share of new subsidized social housing in new construction has fallen since the early 1980s. An increasing significance is being attached to the owner-occupied sector as the central government cuts back public expenditure and reduces subsidies to social housing.

a. Construction of social rented dwellings

Until 1988 the majority of housing association and local authority housing construction was financed by central government loans aimed at keeping rents down to a controlled, government-set, level and ensuring that high levels of building occurred. However, due to the increasing costs of this subsidy system, government loans for constructing new dwellings were stopped after 1988. As part of the continuing change in government intervention in the housing market, subsidies were cut again in 1995. Money is now targeted more specifically at those in most need and is increasingly channelled through housing benefits rather than new construction subsidies.

Since 1989 the government has also stopped guaranteeing housing association loans or providing new loans for improvements. This has meant that housing associations now rely on the private market for finance. Financing arrangements are illustrated in Figure 6.4.

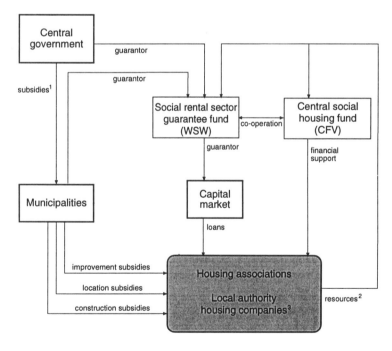

Figure 6.4 Social housing finance system: Netherlands. [1]Pre-1995, operating cost subsidies (one-off payments and supplementary subsidies); post-1995, one-off housing incentive (single budget subsidy). [2]To WSW, payments and lending related to the guarantee loan; to CFV, obligatory annual contributions according to association's means. [3]Local authority housing companies must be transformed into housing associations by 1997 to continue to receive financial support from the central government.

b. Operation of Guarantee Funds

To improve access to the capital market, a Guarantee Fund was set up in 1984 into which housing associations pool a proportion of their resources. This fund, the Social Rental Sector Guarantee Fund (WSW), acts as a private mortgage insurance institution and is backed by the central government, thus giving private financing institutions the confidence to finance 100% of investments. An effect of WSW is lower interest rates because of the additional security. The WSW was set up jointly by the housing associations, the municipalities and the central government.

Since 1990 there has been an extension of the guarantee facilities of the WSW to include all unsubsidized loans taken out by the voluntary housing sector. The WSW will only guarantee a loan once certain criteria regarding an association's financial position are met. While the WSW currently guarantees only 2% of all loans in the social rented sector, this amount is expected to increase dramatically in the future. Associations may also get finance directly from the capital market or may obtain loans with municipal backing. Some existing state guarantees can now be transferred to the WSW.

Working together with the WSW is the Central Social Housing Fund (CFV), also set up by the housing associations. It was established to help out organizations in financial difficulties and it uses its resources to reorganize the funding of financially weak associations. The CFV was set up in 1987 and means that, 'without government aid, the sector itself attends to the covering of risks among weak fellow corporations' (Priemus, 1995, p. 147).

The CFV is financed through annual contributions from the associations according to their size and budget. The fund will measure the financial position of an association and will take on responsibility for reorganizations if certain criteria are met. The CFV will make interest free loans to associations on the condition that cost-effective operations will be possible within 3 years (Priemus, 1995). All registered associations make contributions to the CFV, but the remaining municipal housing companies do not participate. The CFV and WSW work closely together to solve financial difficulties with contributions sometimes coming from both institutions. As such the WSW and the CFV 'embody the independence of the housing corporations in the Netherlands at sector level' (Priemus, 1995, p. 148).

c. Subsidies for construction and improvement

The government has continued to support social housing with subsidies. Under the present system the central government determines the size of the budget for housing subsidies, which it allocates to regional groupings of municipalities. This subsidy is divided between municipalities according to the extent of housing shortage, association reserves, spatial policy and the housing stock distribution ('skewness') in each area. Once this budget has been allocated the municipalities have complete control on how it is spent.

They make decisions, according to need, as to whether the money subsidizes new construction, improvement work or is used, for example, to reduce rents in their area. They will also determine how the money is distributed between renting and owner-occupied occupation.

Subsidies can be allocated in a number of different ways. There have been operating cost subsidies, incentive subsidies and supplementary subsidies.

Operating cost subsidies have been available to housing associations on the conditions that land charges and rents charged fall under a set ceiling, and rent levels are fixed on an annual basis at 6.5% of the investment cost. Major improvements in pre-war rental dwellings have been supported. Rents charged after improvements could not exceed a set ceiling. These subsidies were paid to the municipalities in a series of annual contributions amounting to 10% of the total cost.

One-off incentive payments have been available for more expensive rental and owner-occupied dwellings. These payments were only made in certain urban areas where sufficient cheap rental dwellings already existed. For rental dwellings the payment was around Dfl 10 000 on the condition that the investment cost and rents were below set ceilings.

Supplementary subsidies are available in the form of:

- A location supplement, for differences in costs – particularly land costs.
- A rent reduction supplement, awarded for example for rental dwellings built to replace demolished homes.

These subsidies are targeted particularly to areas of urban renewal. However, it is expected that these will gradually be phased out as urban renewal programmes are reduced (Netherlands Ministry of Housing, 1993).

These subsidies which have been in operation since 1992 are part of a phased plan in social housing subsidization. On 1 January 1995 a new Order on subsidies tied to housing (BWS) took effect. From this date operating subsidies are no longer granted. Subsidies are, instead, in the form of one-off Dfl 5000 incentives to build social dwellings. There is a single housing budget allocated to the municipalities who may then distribute the funds between housing types and sectors as required. This is effectively part of a planned cut in government expenditure to social housing construction and subsidization.

d. Rent policy

From 1975 to 1988 rents in the social sector were set and increased according to the dynamic cost pricing system. Under this method of calculation, rents were laid down by the central government and kept below cost levels for the first years of a development through government subsidies. Increases during this period were set by the government which meant that rents bore little relation to the specific dwellings. A particular problem of this system was that rent levels were anticipated to increase in line with inflation so that costs would be covered and government subsidies could be reduced as time went on. However, during the 1980s particularly low rates of inflation meant that the government was paying very large subsidies to keep costs and rents low.

In 1988 the dynamic cost-price system was abandoned due to the budgetary burden it was creating. Now rent setting has been liberalized so that associations have more freedom in matching rents with costs and quality. Rent increases are also freer and can be set by individual landlords within government limits. However, with less government subsidy, housing associations are also forced to take on more risk and rent levels are expected to increase quite dramatically as associations' costs rise.

Housing associations are facing difficult choices if they are to keep rents low enough for tenants. Concerns within the social housing movement are focused particularly on rent levels in the future as the market plays an increasing role in the financing of social housing.

6.6.3 Evaluation

The social rented sector in the Netherlands is going through a series of major changes, both in its management and financing arrangements. Increasing emphasis is being given to market forces, subsidies have been shifted from the supply side to the demand side, and there is more deregulation and liberalization (some of these issues are discussed in Chapters 4 and 7). The Netherlands seems to going further than other countries by stating that new social housing can be basically self-supporting. In this respect the NWR sees the government at 'an intermediate stage on the road to unsubsidized housing'. There are, however, in relation to the new policy stance, a number of concerns for this sector.

As the government in the Netherlands is withdrawing subsidies and financing for new social housing is coming entirely from the capital market, housing associations are becoming increasingly business-like and operating like entrepreneurs. This change in the role of social landlords is having a series of effects. New construction involves greater risk and housing associations may be more cautious about supplying the quantity of social housing that is needed.

Rents are rising and there are increasing concerns about the future affordability of dwellings in this sector. Pressures on land availability, existing shortages in the sector, especially in the western provinces, as well as increasing numbers of asylum seekers are all further problems.

These problems are exacerbated by the fact that the existing stock is now 'misallocated' to a large degree due to the quantity of high income earners currently occupying social dwellings.

6.7 SOCIAL HOUSING IN THE UK

Social rented housing in the UK is provided principally by local authorities and housing associations, the former being responsible for around 21% of the total housing stock and the latter for about 3%. In Scotland, Scottish Homes is also a major public sector landlord. In Northern Ireland the role of local authorities is performed by the Northern Ireland Housing Executive. Specially created New Town Development Corporations have managed and developed housing in the past. Most of their stocks have now been transferred to local authorities and housing associations. The process will be complete by the end of the century.

6.7.1 Social housing provision and management

Local authorities have until recently had the main responsibility in the UK for constructing and managing social housing. During the 1980s the role of the local authorities was greatly reduced. New construction of 'council' housing fell dramatically from a high point in 1967 of 204 000 homes per annum to a total of only 11 000 completions in 1991. In 1979 35.6% of all dwellings built in the UK were completed by the public sector (local authorities, new towns and government departments). In 1992, only 3.2% of all dwellings were completed by the public sector. This decline has been a direct result of a Conservative government which believed that too much public expenditure was being devoted to public sector housing. Grants from central government to local authorities have fallen considerably and there are severe constraints on new building. Since 1980 over 1.5 million council dwellings have been either sold under the 'Right to Buy' or transferred to housing associations (Section 4.4). Some of the best quality housing has been sold and lower income tenants are left in lower quality stock. The process of 'residualization' (Malpass and Murie, 1990) has left council housing with a strong welfare role to perform without sufficient resources to fulfil its functions adequately.

Local authority housing has become increasingly professionalized. The Chartered Institute of Housing, with members in local authorities and housing associations, has a well developed education and training programme which tries to promote good practice in the housing service. It is important to see this service, in a British context, as more than 'bricks and mortar' provision. There is, in the best authorities, a tradition of concern with the wider well-being of tenants.

The rights of tenants regarding choice and service have been formalized in a Tenants Charter which seeks to improve the tenants' awareness of their rights and the response of local authorities to tenant demands. There is a continuing process of trying to get more tenants involved in the management of their housing by means of tenants' associations.

Since 1988 the government has made it clear that it wishes local authorities not to be housing providers but to be 'strategic enablers'. The enabling role means that authorities oversee and monitor housing provision in their area, working particularly with housing associations, but do not get involved in significant new developments (Bramley, 1993).

Housing associations have been playing an increasingly important role in social housing provision, despite having responsibility for only a small proportion of the stock. In 1992 housing associations managed 3.3% of the total housing stock, having about 788 000 dwellings. Given that there are over 2000 associations, the average size is small by European standards (Section 4.10). In 1992 housing associations built about 25 000 dwellings, which was around 14.5% of total housing construction. Most housing associations are members of the umbrella organization the National Federation of Housing Associations (NFHA) or the Scottish or Welsh equivalent. The federations act as a lobby for the movement and offer advice to members.

Housing associations register with the Housing Corporation or in Scotland, Scottish Homes, and in Wales with Tai Cymru. These bodies, set up by central government, perform both a monitoring and funding role in relation to housing associations. Associations have to prepare regular reports and they have their progress checked against performance indicators.

In England and Wales, which together have 89% of the UK housing stock, local authorities and housing associations control the social rented stock. In Scotland (9% of the UK housing stock) an additional provider is Scottish Homes which manages about 59 000 dwellings (as well as performing its financing role). Scottish Homes is, however, gradually divesting itself of its stock in favour of housing associations. With nearly 35% of the housing stock rented from local authorities, new towns and Scottish Homes and nearly 3% rented by housing associations, the social rented sector is significantly larger in Scotland than in England and Wales (Scottish Homes, 1994).

In Northern Ireland (2% of the UK housing stock) local authority housing was transferred in 1971 to the Northern Ireland Housing Executive. The Executive performs a strategic planning and development role, builds and maintains houses, and assists, by means of grant aid, other organizations, especially housing associations, to provide housing. While over 27% of Northern Ireland's stock is managed by the Executive, less than 2% is managed by housing associations. The Executive is supported by direct government funding. The 46 registered housing associations are financed and regulated by the Department of Environment for Northern Ireland (Williams, 1994).

6.7.2 Financing and subsidization of social housing

A summary of the financial relationships is given in Figure 6.5. Local authorities have borrowed money both from the government and the money market to finance past development. Their ability to borrow to finance future capital expenditure is closely controlled by central government. Every year each local authority produces a Housing Strategy Statement and an associated proposed Housing Investment Programme (HIP). Together these provide an assessment of the housing situation in their area and set priorities for expenditure to tackle problems. Central government responds to HIP bids by giving grants to assist public sector renovation and a Basic Credit Approval (BCA) for each local authority. The BCA is the local authority's permission to borrow money to engage in capital expenditure. As far as council housing is concerned, most of this will now be for repairs and modernization rather than new building. The local authority can borrow up to the BCA limit from a combination of government and money market sources. For agreed additional needs an authority can be granted a Supplementary Credit Approval (SCA).

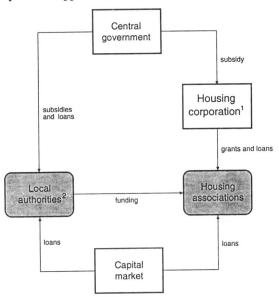

Figure 6.5 Social housing finance system: UK. [1]The housing corporation's financing role is performed in Scotland by Scottish Homes and in Wales by Tai Cymru. Scottish Homes also owns and manages some dwellings. The Department of Environment in Northern Ireland performs a financing and monitoring role for housing associations. [2]In Northern Ireland the role of Local Authorities as housing providers is performed by the Northern Ireland Housing Executive.

In setting credit approvals, government takes account of a council's capital receipts from selling council houses. In England and Wales only 25% of these receipts can be retained for expenditure on housing; the remainder must pay off accumulated debt (Aughton and Malpass, 1994, pp. 38–40). This constraint on use of capital receipts has not applied in Scotland. The increasing stringency of government controls over local authority borrowing has been a major means by which the housing activities of local authorities have been curtailed.

The other highly significant means by which local authorities have been forced to reduce their housing activities is by cuts to the subsidy which central government pays to a council's Housing Revenue Account (HRA). All current costs associated with council housing are met from the HRA. This includes loan charges and maintenance and management expenses. Income from rents and subsidies is paid into the account. Before 1990 subsidy came from central government and by means of discretionary payments by local authorities. The latter were transfers of general income from local taxation. These local transfers are no longer allowed. Some councils made surpluses on their HRAs and transferred money to general expenditure. This, also, is no longer permitted.

The government, in calculating the subsidy to HRAs, makes assumptions about costs and rent increases, and pays an amount intended to meet an assumed deficit. The assumptions that the government makes have a very strong influence on the operation of the HRA. The subsidy mechanism is a very persuasive way of forcing up rents (Aughton and Malpass, 1994, pp. 22–49). In addition to the other items, the costs of rent rebates (housing benefit for council tenants) are, since 1990, met from the HRA and government also pays a subsidy towards these costs. The subsidy to the HRA thus consists of a 'housing element' and a 'rebate element'. While the latter is always positive, the former may be positive or negative depending on the government's view of the financial circumstances of any given HRA. An effect of this is that tenants who do not get rebates can be effectively subsidizing lower income tenants who do receive rebates.

A major financial consequence of council housing has been the rent pooling and cross-subsidization effects which have come about in the absence of cost-price rents (Section 3.2). Local authorities retain their nominal freedom in setting rents but, as indicated above, the subsidy system has a strong influence on rent levels. The government issues guidelines for annual rent increases. The rent increases are related to assumptions about the capital value of dwellings, so the intention is that rents will reflect what the property is worth.

The government's support for housing associations is channelled through the Housing Corporation (in England and its equivalent in Wales and Scotland and the Department of the Environment in Northern Ireland) which has an annual Approved Development Programme (ADP). This is distributed to regions and then to individual housing associations on the basis of bids from the associations. Since 1988 associations have been required to obtain an increasing proportion of their funds from the private capital market. The Housing Corporation pays a one-off capital grant to housing associations which once covered up to 90% of the capital costs of a project. However with the deregulation of housing association funding and rents this Housing Association Grant (HAG) has been reduced and housing associations are expected to raise more funds from the capital market. The average level of

HAG fell from 75% of project costs in 1989/90 to 62% in 1994/95 and is expected to fall even more. It is still possible for housing associations to borrow the remaining funds from the Housing Corporation (or equivalent) or local authorities, but if they are financially strong enough associations are expected to borrow privately (Aughton and Malpass, 1994, pp. 50–62). The aims of the changes were to reduce government expenditure, but at the same time increase investment in social housing through more private sector investment, and to deregulate rents to bring them in line with market levels. Housing associations are therefore having to compete on a more commercial level for private financing. This increases their risks.

Despite the more market-orientated framework, housing associations are still expected to charge affordable rents (Chapter 10) but with grant reductions and little opportunity for quality reductions or efficiency savings the ability of associations to cater for low income tenants in the future is an issue of great concern. The problem is the greater because government is relying on housing associations for new social housing provision.

The net effect of the financial changes in social housing in recent years is a shift towards subject rather than object subsidies and rising rents. In this climate future investment levels and affordability are the major unknowns.

6.8 SOCIAL HOUSING PROVISION IN OTHER EUROPEAN COUNTRIES

Although there are similarities in the provision of social housing in other European countries, the objectives and targeting of the sector are often quite different. For example, in Denmark social housing has been given strong support by the state and is open to a wide range of the population, and was not, originally, allocated according to income level (although this is becoming more of an issue in the 1990s). Social housing in Denmark grew rapidly during the 1970s and this was partly as a response to the lack of new building in the private rented sector (Boelhouwer and Heijden, 1992). Levels of new social construction were kept high up to the late 1980s to meet levels of need. However, as these needs are perceived to be met, building has been reduced and funds redirected to rehabilitation of the existing stock. Denmark also stands out as having a very strong degree of tenant participation in its social housing. Tenants are elected to a management board and take on significant responsibilities for running the non-profit associations.

Several countries, such as Spain, Portugal, Luxembourg and Greece, have a very small social rented sector. However, many of these countries are now beginning to focus housing policies on social provision. In Spain a new 4 year Social Housing Plan between 1992 and 1995 increased public subsidies to social home ownership in new and existing housing, and encouraged the diversification of supply to develop a social rented sector. The Plan aimed to build 460 000 low and medium priced housing units (Landes, 1994).

A 'Plan for Social Housing, 1991' was adopted in Ireland. This has led to greater levels of co-operation and partnership between the local authorities and housing associations. Its objectives were to meet increasing housing needs, increase the choice available to households in need and improve access to low income home ownership. New building in the sector had been declining up to the late 1980s, and following a slump in the housing market in the early 1980s the need for new low cost housing had risen significantly (estimates from local authorities assessments showed an increase in social housing needs of 23% between 1991 and 1993). The housing programme continues to expand in response to need and in 1993 3500 local authority housing starts were approved, compared with only 1000 in 1992 (DOE (Ireland), 1993).

In Greece, where only a minimum of social housing for ownership exists, there are plans to extend the sector slightly. However, the extension is likely to be solely for ownership as pressure for social renting in Greece is not great.

In Portugal, there are enormous problems of unfit housing. Large numbers of people in Lisbon and Oporto are living in squatter settlements. Estimates suggest around 100 000 people in such temporary 'illegal' housing. Over 250 000 people are reckoned to be in unfit housing in Lisbon. More than 40% of the population in central Oporto are estimated to live in dwellings in serious disrepair (Magalhäes, 1995). In relation to the scale of the problems, housing production and social housing provision both existing and planned is small. A net contribution to the Portuguese housing stock of 500 000 dwellings is needed just to replace unfit housing (ENH, 1993). The recently launched plan for re-housing targets the squatter populations of Lisbon and Oporto and will make public land available to private developers to build social housing. These municipally managed programmes will contribute only a little to the reduction in the housing shortage even though the aim of building 40 000 dwellings by the year 2000 is ambitious in the light of previous construction rates.

Many social housing sectors in Europe are clearly facing new and increasing pressures and responsibilities and high levels of need. However, a number of countries are acknowledging the scope of need and have established new policies to provide new social housing dwellings. In spite of the progress of 'privatization' in social housing, it appears that there are cases where governments are still prepared to accept that the level of need justifies policies to promote supply.

Social housing issues 7

A detailed analysis of the systems of social housing in France, Germany, the Netherlands and the UK was provided in Chapter 6. This chapter will attempt to draw out some of the common issues and problems that exist in this sector. While many differences in the systems have been identified there are a number of trends taking place in the sector which are common to all the countries. The strength of the trends, and the countries respective responses to them, is varied. In particular, this chapter will focus on the role that government plays in the social sector. Different approaches to subsidies, distribuitional issues, housing shortages and the future of the social rented sector will be considered.

7.1 CENTRAL AND LOCAL GOVERNMENT AND SOCIAL HOUSING PROVIDERS

The degree of central and local government control, monitoring and influence over social housing bodies varies considerably between different countries. This is shown in the details in the previous chapter. The role of government can be characterized in a number of ways.

In recognizing the role of state it is useful to examine the degree to which the government's role influences the outcomes of housing provision. Does it play an active or monitoring role in management, and how does it influence the financial arrangements for social housing construction?

Governments play a role in setting up different structures which may in turn limit or encourage further investment. Social housing bodies and agencies exist to organize the provision and financing of social housing. The degree to which the state is involved in the running of these bodies will determine how much continued influence it has on their overall policies. For example, bodies could be set up in the form of a governmental agency, or even a government department, that relies wholly upon the state for funding and has limited opportunities for independent initiatives. Alternatively, organizations may be set up that have the backing of government but act as autonomous bodies making independent decisions with respect to providing and financing social housing. In the most 'extreme' case the government may leave all detailed decision making to the market taking no responsibility in any specific arrangements (but may still have some monitoring role or lay down guidelines). The previous chapter illustrated some of these different arrangements in the particular countries.

Although central government is not involved in any significant way in the direct supply of housing in the European Union, local government does own and manage a significant proportion of the stock in the UK and, to a lessor extent, in the Netherlands and Ireland. Both central and local government have important roles in the funding and supervision of social housing throughout Europe. For municipal social housing this can mean the possibility of high levels of control and influence being felt from both local and national housing policies.

In France, central government's representative in the départements, the préfet, has a supervisory role with respect to the HLMs. The municipalities exercise considerable influence over the funding, management and allocation of HLM dwellings. Many other examples could be given of central and local government exercising indirect but significant influence over the provision of social housing without being involved as a landlord. Ultimately, the power of government with respect to the funding of social housing provides considerable control.

The influence of the state is clearly not simply a function of how much housing is 'owned' by the state. Social housing organizations can act as agents of the state or as more independent organizations depending on the details of the financial and supervisory relationships. The variety and complexity of these relationships makes generalizations difficult.

A further aspect of the state's role in social housing is the extent to which housing is politicized in any country and the degree of consensus surrounding housing. For example, in the UK the housing sector has in the past frequently been used as a tool of policy, with short-term goals, rather than there being a specific commitment to the sector in its own right. There is also in the UK less consensus amongst parties concerning the role or priority of housing than exists in some other European countries. This has accounted for a generally more consistent policy towards the sector in France, Germany and the Netherlands.

7.2 THE MARKET APPROACH IN SOCIAL HOUSING

It is tempting to view social housing as a non-market sector and thus see non-profit housing as an alternative to commercially provided private rented housing. Such a clear cut division is, however, misleading. Evidence given in the previous chapter shows that in several countries, including the UK, the Netherlands and Germany, there is an increasing emphasis on making the social rented sector more 'market orientated'. This situation, in many cases, has arisen out of the need for governments to cut public expenditure, but can also be seen as part of the strategic withdrawal of government from detailed housing intervention. A principal strand of this policy is the shift from object to subject subsidies, with government continuing to be involved in 'affordability' through the housing allowance systems but less involved in production and allocation.

Much more emphasis is placed on the supremacy of the market to finance, build and allocate social housing. Key issues for governments are privatization, decentralization and deregulation. Operating with greater freedom and more market-orientated objectives means giving housing associations more private initiative, devolving responsibility to local rather than the central government and removing 'restricting' regulations.

In practice this has a dramatic effect on social housing provision. It means that policies are formulated with the aim of bringing social rent levels nearer to those that would prevail without subsidy. The approach also tends to put an increasing emphasis on raising development finance from the money markets and allowing social housing organizations to make 'surpluses' on their current operations. These factors mean increased risk for social housing providers, higher costs, higher rents and ultimately the possibility of lower levels of construction.

There has been continuing concern in Germany about the operation of the 'social' sector for profit. Krätke (1989) argues that most of the social housing is built, managed and exploited by private investors and large 'social' housing companies, which are run like private enterprises. Following the reversal of the Public Good Law in 1990 (Chapter 6) even more social housing in Germany will be treated as profit-making. Regulations to influence the 'social' rent level are intact but it remains to be seen whether this will amount to sufficient control to maintain the social character of this sector.

As indicated in the previous chapter, this is also a major issue in the Netherlands where the government's declared aim is to make all new social construction self-supporting, with no government subsidy. In the Dutch 'Housing Memorandum for the Nineties' a more market-orientated approach was promoted with central government becoming less involved in the social sector and housing associations being more 'independent'.

This is clearly having a major impact on the roles of social housing providers. While providers were always very clear on their roles of providing subsidized housing at reasonable rents, the changing nature of the sector, its 'marketization', requires changing roles for housing associations. For example, in the UK housing associations have had to become familiar with different management strategies, providing information that funders need in order to provide support from the private finance market. Private funders in the UK are particularly sceptical about providing finance for social housing organizations where they see high risks involved. In a document produced in 1991 on private finance for social housing, it was argued that 'A wider acceptance of social housing as an investment medium' is needed and that 'At the moment risk discourages potential lenders and raises the costs of the relatively little private finance now funding social housing' (Pryke and Whitehead, 1991, p. 39). The housing associations' success in adapting to the private market is therefore dependent on their ability to convince funders of the suitability of social housing as an investment.

Increasing pressure on the role and responsibilities of housing associations is not unique to the UK. In France the objective of the HLMs has always been to accommodate people in need who are not able to find a place in the private rented stock. However, laws introduced in the early 1990s that aimed to give a better balance of dwelling quality and dwelling type in urban areas and to give French citizens the right to a dwelling, have led to conflicting roles for the landlord organizations. These include the pressures of combining the provision of dwellings for people on low incomes, or people with special needs, with their increasing financial role as budget managers. Problems have emerged particularly in the allocation of social dwellings. With a number of different organizations having nomination rights negotiations can be difficult. There is pressure to house those in greatest need but rents are rising and the ability of some landlords to refuse certain tenants if their income is not high enough means that the allocation procedure can involve conflicting principles. Despite a shift to a more market-orientated approach in France it has been claimed that compared to Britain 'there remains a greater recognition that housing is a national responsibility' (Kleinman, 1995, p. 17).

In the Netherlands the removal of a number of regulations controlling the activities of housing associations and the increasing privatization that is taking place has led to a number of 'scandals' within some organizations. These cases of inexperience with dealing with a market framework and exploitation of their new freedom may be corrected as associations become used to their new roles.

The Neue Heimat scandal in Germany at the end of the 1980s also shows how a market-orientated and privately financed system of social housing can be exploited when controls are ineffective (for details, see Chapter 6). The misuse of funds and resulting bankruptcy of the Neue Heimat housing company highlighted the problems in the system of German social housing control. The search for the means to regulate without too much government intervention continues.

As costs are increasing, many countries are beginning to introduce policies to promote the sale of their social rented stock. Initial programmes, outside of the UK, have been tentative and, where they exist, particularly in

France and the Netherlands, no 'Right to Buy' has been established. Cautious measures are being introduced so that some of the problems that have been experienced in the UK can be avoided. In the Netherlands it is the financially weak housing associations that are being forced to sell off part of their stock and in France too the few sales that have taken place are mainly for financial reasons on the part of the landlord.

The debate on how far to pursue a market-orientated approach and the role of markets is still developing. Ultimately, total reliance on a free market approach would mean the end of social housing, for no subsidies would be involved and ability-to-pay would determine allocation. A more market-orientated approach may bring some benefits to the social housing sector. If organizations become more independent in their operations and they are under less pressure from changing government policy, the sector may find itself in a better position to direct assistance where it is most needed. However, if a more market-orientated approach, where profits determine provision, means higher rents and lower levels of construction, tenants will be disadvantaged. The problem of the sector in the future is how organizations can maintain a 'social' perspective in provision if they rely wholly on private finance.

7.3 THE MOVE AWAY FROM OBJECT SUBSIDIES

As demonstrated in Chapter 4, there has been a distinct shift in the type of subsidies being used to support social housing. The use of object subsidies has become less popular with many governments. This has resulted in a switch away from object subsidies towards income related assistance. The reasons for this shift appear to be similar across Europe.

One of the main factors is the widely held belief that the supply of housing is less a problem now than it once was. As we discussed in Chapter 2, there was, instead, greater concern over the quality of the stock and policies for improvements. A second important motive for a reduction in producer subsidies was their burden on governments' budgets. There was a growing desire during the 1970s and 1980s to reduce government spending to control inflation. To achieve this many governments cut back on housing expenditure (Denmark was a notable exception during the 1980s).

The general objective of reducing spending on production also tied in with a further belief of many governments that the distributional effects of an income-related subsidy would be more beneficial than continued support for housing production. It was argued that since the major housing shortages had been alleviated subsidies could be better targeted to those 'in most need'. In this way housing allowances could cushion lower income households from the worst effects (i.e. rent increases) of the reduction in supply-side support.

It was also seen as a more efficient use of government spending as public funds were not 'wasted' on households who did not really need them.

The need for housing allowance schemes was also perpetuated by the move in many countries to a more market-orientated housing policy. Markets were increasingly being seen as beneficent and able to respond both flexibly and effectively to changing consumer demands and tastes (Kemp, 1990). It was thought that subsidies to consumers would therefore interfere less in the market than would producer subsidies. As rents moved more in line with market rents so the need grew for increased subsidies to low income groups.

There has been a movement towards subsidizing consumption rather than production of housing. However, while it was a declared aim to move away from object to subject subsidies to reduce government spending, the subsequent increases in housing allowance budgets (and increasing tax expenditures) have meant that in many countries actual housing expenditures have risen. Table 7.1 shows the increasing percentage of households receiving housing allowances.

Table 7.1 Percentage of households receiving housing allowances: selected European countries, 1980, 1993

	Denmark	Germany	France	Netherlands	Portugal	UK
1980	12.7	6.0	10.5	8.0	3.3	16.0
1993	21.0	6.3[1]	24.3	14.0	16.0[1]	18.0

[1]1990.
Source: European Commission (1993, 1994).

Towards the end of the 1980s and in the early 1990s it was apparent that subsidies should be targeted even more rigorously to cases of specific need. In many countries new programmes were established that focused on groups such as the elderly, the handicapped, asylum seekers and other minority groups. While the amounts of subsidy are not necessarily being increased, a number of governments are trying to put together more coherent policy guidelines with respect to these groups. These policies include, for example, a supplementary subsidy in France which is available for acquiring dwellings to be leased to disadvantaged households – the PLA d'insertion. In 1993 the government in the Netherlands adopted the Act on Facilities for the Handicapped (WVG) which broadens the group which is able to claim additional housing assistance. Germany as well as the Netherlands is being forced to update its provision for immigrants and asylum seekers. Several programmes to investigate experimental housing that could house large numbers quickly have been initiated. In the UK some housing associations have been developed that target particular social or ethnic groups.

7.4 HOUSING SHORTAGES

In the early 1990s shortages and increasing need within the social housing sector were considered to be a problem in many European countries. Governments in Europe are becoming aware that housing needs are not being met. There are greater pressures on waiting lists and allocations procedures, more concern is being voiced over the distribution of the social stock, and there are high levels of recorded homelessness (Chapter 5).

The reasons for increasing need are complex. However, a key contributory factor to the growing housing need is the rate of household formation. This was discussed in Chapter 5. Demographic projections are the starting point for estimates of future housing needs.

In the UK there have been numerous estimates of need and housing shortage. Estimates range between a requirement for an annual social house building programme of 74 000 and 122 000 units compared to a rate of 28 781 dwellings per annum between 1986 and 1991 (Wilcox, 1990; Bramley, 1991; Audit Commission, 1992).

In the Netherlands, housing ministry estimates suggested a future housing requirement of 1 million dwellings (all sectors) between 1988 and 2015 or approximately 400 000 between 1990 and 2000 (de Gans and Oskamp, 1992).

Statistics on housing shortages in Germany (East and West) compiled by DIW estimate that in 1987 between 800 000 and 950 000 persons were either living in substandard conditions or were homeless (Schuler-Wullner and Wullkopf, 1991). Following the massive influx of immigrants to Germany an annual rate of construction of 500 000 homes (all sectors) for 10 years is considered necessary, by the DIW, to meet need from the early 1990s (Observatory on European Social Housing, 1994).

Estimates in France by INSEE suggest a requirement for an average of an extra 330 000 dwellings per annum (all sectors) compared with the recent construction rate of around 220 000 units per annum (Geindre, 1993b).

While shortages are increasing, housing ministries are facing pressures to cut capital expenditure on housing construction. This has meant that new alternatives have been sought to finance and provide social housing. The response to this problem varies between countries, and is related to the perceived urgency of the situation and to the priority given to housing. In some countries, where housing in considered a high priority, governments have tried to continue to subsidize new construction. For example, in France, for a short period, funds available for PLA loans were increased. In the Netherlands guarantee funds were set up to help housing associations get finance from the capital market and to provide support for housing associations in financial difficulty. Some specific problems and the responses in different countries will now be examined.

In Germany a number of factors working together have created serious shortages. A shortage of social housing was 'discovered' when the 1987 census found a shortfall of 1 million dwellings (Eekhoff, 1989). Problems in the supply of housing were caused partly by many households living in dwellings too large or too small for their household size. At the same time, rent levels were pushed up while incomes did not grow, resulting in high rent burdens for many households. In 1988 it was estimated that the lowest income decile paid over 40% of income on rent (Schuler-Wanllner and Wullkopf, 1991).

These conditions were exacerbated by weak mobility rates among low income earners, the loss of social rental dwellings through condominium conversions (to the owner-occupied market) and the transference of social rented dwellings to the private sector as 'social' loans were repaid.

The fall of the Berlin Wall in 1989 and the huge wave of immigrants from both eastern Germany and the former iron curtain countries put even more pressure on the housing market. It has been estimated that 3.5 million immigrants have come into Germany creating a need for 2.5 million new units, including 1 million in the former GDR. Between 25 and 30% of the homeless in Germany are estimated to come from the former GDR (Schuler-Wallner and Wullkopf, 1991).

The need for higher levels of construction has been acknowledged by the German government. After a period during the mid-1980s when federal housing subsidies were suspended, the new crisis of housing shortages prompted a re-introduction of support for the social sector (Chapter 6). The level of spending is not, however, expected to continue once immediate requirements have been met. There is an on-going debate concerning the future provision of social housing including suggestions for alternative finance and monitoring arrangements.

The housing shortage in France has hit the social rented sector particularly hard. The HLM umbrella organization UNFOHLM has estimated that the need for HLM dwellings stands at more than 1 million and is expected to keep rising (Geindre, 1993b, p. 23). The sector is under pressure from the increasing number of homeless persons but also because alternatives are limited. There is a rapidly declining private rented sector. Foyers, which are hostels for young people where training and education facilities are provided, have become over-subscribed. The availability of dwellings in the intermediate rented sector is also limited. In addition, increasing rent costs, as in Germany, have reduced tenant mobility and access to the stock.

The Netherlands has been facing a mounting housing shortage since the late 1980s. In 1988 the Fourth Report on Physical Planning produced by the Dutch housing ministry stated that in the period 1985–2015 the total housing stock should increase by 1.5 million dwellings, and that 1 million of these should be built in the Randstad area (de Gans and Oskamp, 1992). The Randstad area contains the main urban areas of the Netherlands, including

Amsterdam, Rotterdam, The Hague and Utrecht. It is in these cities that the need is greatest, but at the same time these areas are also suffering from a lack of building land for new housing. Ways of addressing this issue are therefore linked to the increasing shortage of land.

The housing ministry had aimed to reduce the housing shortage from 3.5% of the stock in 1995 to 2% by the year 2000 (Nationale Woningraad, 1994). However, by 1993 it was clear that this would not be achieved. Part of the reason for this is that the government has gradually been withdrawing subsidies for social housing. This has resulted in less subsidized housing being built, and a reliance on new construction from the unsubsidized, mainly owner-occupied sector. Construction in this sector is heavily susceptible to interest rate changes which during the early 1990s were not very favourable.

Finally, in the UK a number of facts illustrate the need for more dwellings, particularly rented dwellings. Throughout the 1980s the number of homeless persons has risen dramatically, especially the number of homeless young persons. Waiting lists for local authority and housing association dwellings have increased. During the 1980s many councils were using bed and breakfast accommodation to provide temporary housing for families. At the same time the rate of construction in the social rented sector was falling.

7.5 MANAGEMENT PROBLEMS

While much of the social housing in Europe is of a high standard there are many problems in the management of social rented housing which manifest themselves in the form of arrears, high vacancy rates and disrepair. These problems vary greatly in their intensity between and within countries. In the Netherlands while the overall quality of social housing is high, a variety of physical defects, locational disadvantages and adverse rent/quality relationships have been identified as contributing to high vacancy rates on some estates (Priemus, 1988).

Problems of rent arrears, empty properties, allocation and maintenance associated with the polarization of social housing have been identified in similar ways for both Britain and France (Willmot and Murie, 1988). In France the problems are seen to be concentrated in the large HLM estates, the grandes ensembles, where they are compounded by issues of physical defects and vandalism.

The residualization of social housing has become a particular problem in the UK and France. Many estates have become run down and are isolated from transport networks. In the UK the success of the 'Right to Buy' policy has resulted in the best properties being sold off, leaving a remaining stock which is in many cases in poor condition and houses a large proportion of low income and benefit-dependent households.

Other countries in Europe, especially the Netherlands, are introducing new policies to prevent this residualization, and the threat of 'ghettos' being formed. Policies are encouraging mixed tenure developments including owner-occupied units alongside rental units, and aiming to maintain mixed income neighbourhoods.

Some countries, particularly Germany and the Netherlands are also facing pressures from the increasing number of immigrants entering their borders and the potential problem of new immigrant ghettos forming.

Such problems in the management of social housing are clearly major issues. It is important to note that the problems are not unique to specific countries and can exist, albeit in differing degrees, under a variety of funding, management and allocation regimes.

7.6 DISTRIBUTIONAL ISSUES

Inequality in the distribution of social housing is an increasing problem in many European countries, particularly the extent to which relatively high income earners are occupying low-cost housing, with low income earners being forced into poorer quality expensive private rental accommodation. This trend in much of Europe has been synonymous with a more market led social housing sector. Deregulation and the reduction in government supply subsidies has resulted in both increased costs and higher rents.

With higher costs and greater operating risks, social landlords are becoming more and more selective in the tenants they are allocating to their housing. Many landlords are now more wary about allocating housing to low income earners because of the possible financial risks.

In Germany the social rented stock has become available to a broader set of income groups, as income ceilings have risen with costs. It was expected that with rising incomes tenants would move out of social housing. However, this has not been the case, and over time this has produced a situation in Germany where about a third of the social housing stock is let to tenants whose incomes are over the set limits (Hills *et al.*, 1990). To counteract this, many Länder introduced the 'Fehlbelegungsabgabe' (Chapter 6) which is a fee to be paid by any tenants in social housing whose incomes are above a set limit. This works as a sort of negative housing allowance.

The government in the Netherlands is facing similar problems, but has rejected the German 'fee' solution. A proposal for fixed-term tenancies to tackle the problem has met with protest from housing organizations and is now effectively off the agenda.

The criteria for tenant selection are being re-examined in several countries to make allocation methods more efficient and to improve the relationship between rents and incomes. In Germany it has been stated that 'there is an urgent need for reformed and extended "social" restrictions' (Krätke, 1989,

p. 288), together with a reassessment of allocation procedures so that access to social housing for low income groups can be improved.

7.7 THE DETERMINATION OF RENT LEVELS

Deregulation of rents within the social housing sector is a feature of policy in many European countries. This has thrown up questions regarding the future role of governments in both setting and regulating rents in the social sector.

While the liberalization of policy is seen as vital in the move to liberalized market operations, initial rent levels and increases are still to be set in many cases, by central, regional or local governments. At the same time non-profit landlords have been given the responsibility of maintaining their rents at levels which will ensure that all costs are covered. This has resulted in rent increases that have simply contributed to a bigger housing allowance bill.

The function of rent is called into question by the changes that are occurring. There are questions about whether rent does in practice, and should in principle, perform a market allocation function instead of 'need' being a principal determinant as to who gets what. If rents are to make more significant contributions to costs, they are likely to absorb an increasing proportion of incomes unless housing allowances pick up more of the bill. We return to problems of affordability in Chapter 10.

7.8 THE FUTURE OF A LIBERALIZED SOCIAL HOUSING SECTOR

Examining systems of social provision in other European countries has revealed many important differences. The use of the private sector to provide social housing has developed most strongly in Germany, and the advantages and drawbacks of the German system are particularly relevant to the developments elsewhere in Europe. The alleged exploitation of the social sector by private investors has caused problems, especially concerning the affordability of dwellings. The idea that social housing provides an incentive for investment rather than is firstly a form of 'welfare provision' can create conflicts.

Part of the differences between the countries is explained by the different roles that are played by governments. For example, the direct role of local government in the UK has been considerable when compared to the other three countries. No other country gave its local authorities the degree of power as did the UK, and while the government still plays a role in provision in France, Germany and the Netherlands, it could be argued that because of this local government control, housing became far more politicized in the UK.

One of the challenges for a more market-orientated social housing system is how to retain a degree of social control over housing suppliers while getting the assumed benefits of more decentralized decision making. Control in the past has often been by means of financing mechanisms. As finance is decontrolled, leverage over housing organizations can become less effective unless there are clear rules about the limits to the degree of freedom granted to 'social' landlords. One of the benefits of less direct public ownership of social housing in several countries is that more housing expenditure is outside of the public sector. As enthusiasm grows in the UK for local authority housing companies (Joseph Rowntree Foundation, 1993a) to whom local authority housing would be transferred to get the financing benefits of some German, French and Dutch housing organizations, the issues of social and political control will have to be addressed.

The experience of these countries shows that some market liberalization with social control is possible but requires detailed regulation to be effective.

Private rented housing provision

This chapter examines the size of the private rental sector in European countries and considers its contribution to production. Financing, subsidies and rent regulation are considered. The more detailed material again relates to the Netherlands, France, Germany and the UK.

As we discussed previously tenure-orientated approaches cause problems of definition. It is less easy to distinguish, clearly, a separate private rented sector outside of the UK. The division between 'private renting' and 'social renting' as explained in Chapters 4 and 6 will be especially blurred in some countries.

In Germany, given the ownership of similarly subsidized and controlled properties by housing associations and private landlords, a watertight distinction between private and public rented housing is impossible. There are estimates of privately owned rented housing but some of this housing is more like social housing given the conditions under which it has been supplied. Some sources relating to West Germany define the 'private rented sector' as:

1. Rented stock built before 1948.
2. Non-social housing built since 1948.

Included in (1), however, is much government controlled non-profit housing and (2) specifically excludes non-profit housing. Category (1) is included in the total because official statistics do not identify the 'public' and 'private' components of this stock.

In France, it is possible to identify four types of rented housing:

1. Rent controlled sector: mainly pre-1948 dwellings owned by individuals.
2. Regulated sector: mainly Habitations à Loyer Modéré (HLM) ('non-profit housing').

3. Private subsidized sector.
4. Free sector: post-war rented housing not subject to controls.

It is possible to consider all rented housing not owned by HLMs to be 'the private rented sector'. One study (Duclaud-Williams, 1978) which is less clear on the private/public sector division, produced figures for a 'semi-public subsidized sector'. This is basically the same as category (3) above. The difficulty arises because of the existence of a large volume of accommodation which is subsidized and, in many cases, also financed directly by government loans. This is subject to rent controls and in some cases to government tenant selection criteria but owned by private individuals and companies.

Discussion and statistics on rented housing in the Netherlands tend to distinguish a subsidized from a non-subsidized rental sector. The subsidized sector, however, comprises non-profit housing association dwellings and 'premium dwellings' which are privately owned but built with state subsidies. There are estimates of the proportion of the rental stock owned by private individuals and commercial companies in the Netherlands.

On the basis of combining several estimates, the size of the private rented sector in all of the European Union countries is shown in Table 5.10. The figures however, must be interpreted in the light of the comments above and those in the country sections which follow.

8.1 THE PRIVATE RENTED SECTOR IN FRANCE

8.1.1 The size and nature of the sector

The private rented sector in France today stands at about 20% of the total housing stock and contains just over 4 million dwellings. Table 8.1 illustrates the change in the housing stock between the tenures over time. The private rented sector has experienced a continued decline over the last few decades. In 1963 the sector accounted for 66% of the rented stock, but by the early 1990s this proportion had fallen to 54%. The contraction in the sector has been particularly marked since 1980. The sector lost 700 000 dwellings in the 1980s. The reasons for this trend will be looked at more closely later. However, the main contributory factors are the sale of private rented dwellings for owner-occupation, the demolition of poor quality housing and the lack of incentives for new construction.

The private rented stock is made up of dwellings built under the '1948 law', in the controlled private rented sector, and those in the 'free' private rented sector. The 1948 Act laid down distinct structures and controls for the provision of private rented dwellings in the post-war period. Dwellings built under the 1948 Act were subject to strict controls on rents and tenants were given specific rights regarding security of tenure. Such private rented

Table 8.1 Housing tenure: France, 1955–1988

	1955	*1963*	*1973*	*1984*	*1988*
Owner-occupier households (%)	35.0	42.2	44.5	51.2	54.3
Renting households (%)	48.8	45.2	44.3	40.1	38.0
Households in 'Free' housing (%)	14.2	12.6	10.2	8.1	7.2
Others (%)	2.0	–	1.0	0.6	0.5
Social rental:					
size of stock (%)		7.4	13	16.2	17.1
number of dwellings		(1089)	(2230)	(3263)	(3538)
Private rental					
size of stock (%)		32.1	27.6	22.2	19.7
number of dwellings		(4762)	(4732)	(4460)	(4088)
1948 Law dwellings		(1433)	(1187)	(705)	(502)

Source: French Housing Ministry (1994b).

dwellings play a social role. The rents are lower than social rents and those in the 'free' private sector. Originally income ceilings limited access to 1948 dwellings. The households living in these dwellings tend to be elderly, have low incomes, and be entitled to state benefits. This act only applied to a limited number of dwellings and this number has been gradually declining over time. At the start of the 1950s around 3 million dwellings in the private rented stock were subject to the conditions of the law of 1948. However, since then this part of the sector has been declining at a rate of 50 000 dwellings per year. This has been due to a large number of sales of these dwellings and the end of contracts. This means that the dwellings revert to the 'free' private rented status, not bound by the 1948 law. By 1993 less than 400 000 dwelling units, or 10% of the stock, remained in this part of the private rented sector. It is estimated that the 1948 dwellings will be almost gone by the end of the century (CDC, 1993a).

The introduction of many different rent regulations and controls, particularly in the 'free' rented sector has led to wide range of rents being charged. This partly explains the substantial differences in the amenities provided and the general conditions within the private rented stock.

8.1.2 Type of investors in private renting

Investors in private rented housing include both institutions and private individuals. Of the total private rented stock, 87% is owned by 'les baillers personnes physiques' (individual investors) and only 13% by 'les baillers personnes morales' (institutional investors). Nevertheless, it is institutional investors that have ownership of the newest accommodation. Nearly a third of the stock owned by individual investors was built before 1948 (CDC, 1993a). The role of institutional investors has been declining especially since the 1970s. Their share of the private rented sector in the provinces fell from 44% in 1972 to 26% in 1989 (CDC, 1993a).

Property investment societies (sociétés immobiliéres d'investissement) exist who specialize in the investment and ownership of private rented accommodation. The other significant institutional investors are insurance companies. They are heavily influenced by the rate of return they are likely to receive on the rented property.

The organizations investing in the private sector do not reach the scale of those, such as HLMs and OPACs, in the social sector. Two of the most important organizations are the UAP, owning 35 000 dwellings and the Axa Midi with 20 000 units. The Crédit Foncier France and the Caisse des Dépôts et Consignations who provide finance for social housing also own housing and provide funding in the private rented sector.

Private individuals own over 3.6 million rented dwellings, compared to only 500 000 owned by institutional investors. Privately owned dwellings are smaller on average and have lower values. Private individuals who have invested in private renting tend to be wealthy; 54% of investors are in the top income decile and 14% are in the next decile; but investors also tend to be elderly and nearly half are retired or 'inactive' (CDC, 1993a). Dwellings from the sector will be lost when property is passed on to children as this tends to prompt the liquidation of assets. New generations favour assets that have a higher rate of return and are easier to manage.

8.1.3 Investment and construction rate

As investment in the private rented sector has, over time, come to be seen as less and less profitable, so the quantity of new building has declined. During 1974, 54 000 new private rented dwellings were constructed, yet by 1984 the annual construction total had fallen to 5000. Private sector investment in the rented market seems to have been hit particularly hard by the general decline in the construction industry in the mid-1980s.

It was just as the supply of new housing began to fall that demand for rented housing in particular began to increase, especially in the cities. Measures to help stimulate housing construction were introduced in the mid-1980s, with specific targeting to the private rented sector. In 1984 tax reductions on new investments were introduced for both individuals and institutions, and broadened from 1986 in the Quilès-Méhaignerie Law. Initially, these included enabling investors buying property for rent to write off between 5 and 10% of the capital invested, and freeing private rented sector rents from rent controls in certain situations (Boelhouwer and Heijden, 1992, p. 224). Incentives were, however, extended further in later years.

The 1986 measures have had some positive effect on new construction. From the low of 5000 dwellings built for private renting in 1985, there was an increase to approximately 20 000 new houses destined for the sector in 1990 (Louvot, 1992, p. 26).

8.1.4 Financing and subsidies

The private rented sector in France has always had access to some form of financing or fiscal subsidy, and yet the sector has still tended to decline over time. There are increasing efforts by the government to try and boost investment in this sector, as programmes for housing generally are being given higher priority in France.

Central government subsidizes some private rented housing through loans and grants from state funded financial institutions. Some loans which are granted to the HLMs for social housing are also available for private investors, providing they adhere to certain conditions. The Crédit Foncier France will grant Prêts Locatifs Aidés (PLA) loans for the building of private rented housing. The loans can be obtained by private individuals and institutions to finance the purchase of land and construction of dwellings, and purchase of dwellings for renovation. These dwellings will then be let at sub-market rents. They can be classified in the 'intermediate' rented sector (Chapter 6 for details). The dwellings are only available to lessors below a certain income level and some control on rent ceilings must be followed. The loan may cover a maximum of 65% of the construction costs and it could have either a fixed interest rate for 25 years or a variable rate for 30 years (French Housing Ministry, 1992).

Private landlords can also receive subsidies for the improvement or renovation of dwellings from the Agence Nationale pour l'Amelioration de l'Habitat (ANAH), the National Agency for Habitat Improvement. Subsidy is usually restricted to two areas of improvement. Firstly, improvement work on dwellings built before 1948 which are lacking either an inside toilet, a bathroom or central heating, and secondly, work to improve the energy-efficiency of dwellings built before 1975. Subsidies are allocated normally at a rate of 25% of costs. However this may rise to 35% for dwellings that have a contract with the state to enable tenants to receive APL. There is then an income ceiling for eligible tenants and a limit on the rent to be charged. The subsidy may also increase to between 40 and 70% of costs when the dwellings are allocated to a particularly disadvantaged household. Subsidies are allocated on condition that a lease is granted for a minimum of 10 years after completion of the work. The ANAH subsidy was successful in reducing the number of pre-1949 dwellings lacking one of the three basic facilities listed above from 37% in 1978 to 19% in 1988 (French Housing Ministry, 1992).

A number of fiscal incentives are available to investors in the private rented sector. Tax reductions for investing in private renting were introduced in 1984. Up to 1989 tax relief on the first FF 40 000 of an investment was granted if a landlord bought or constructed a new dwelling and rented it for more than 6 years. In 1990 this was reviewed and new conditions were laid down for all new dwellings. Tax reductions on investments are available to private individuals and institutional investors for the purchase of a new property, the construction of a new property or the renovation of a derelict property for the use of private renting. Again, the dwellings must remain in the private rented sector for at least 6 years.

For investment in new construction, tax concessions can be equal to 10% of the original investment, for individual investors, or 7.5% for institutional investors, with limits of FF 300 000 per dwelling for individuals and FF 600 000 for married couples. (From 1997 tax reductions will increase to 15% with a married couple maximum of FF 900 000, Geindre, 1993a.)

Demands from within the private sector led to the introduction of new measures during 1993 as part of a package to try to stimulate investment in housing. This included raising the annual capital allowance which individual investors can charge against property income from 8 (the 1986 level) to 10%, and allowing landlords to deduct property deficits from total income, subject to an annual limit of FF 50 000 (Oxley and Smith, 1994). The rate was, however, still lower than for other investments.

As well as investing in the supply side of private rented housing, the government grants housing allowances to tenants. If a landlord qualifies for a PLA loan the occupant is entitled to receive the APL (Aide Personnalisée au Logement) housing allowance provided household income is below a set level. In 1988 approximately 24% of private rented households were in receipt of APL, down slightly on the percentage for 1984. Private rented households may also qualify for AL (Allocation Logement). AL was introduced as a way of encouraging improvement and modernization in the private sector. It is a lower payment than APL and can only be received if a certain quality standard in the dwelling is reached.

8.1.5 Rent regulation

There is a history of tight rent control and security of tenure in France. Rents are determined by a complicated system which involves calculating a 'corrected surface area', taking into account quality and maintenance, and then multiplying this by an annually reviewed value per square metre. The rent available influences investment 'landlords make very precise calculations as to what is more profitable: no maintenance or just minimum jobs on a building which yields low rents, or to invest in maintenance and charge higher rents' (Boucher, 1988, p. 321).

In the 1970s housing policy began to change in favour of an enhanced role for the market. This was influenced by a series of government commissioned reports (Nora and Eveno, 1975; Barre, 1975). The 1977 Housing Act provided for a greater reliance on market forces, increasing rents and mortgage interest rates and reducing government expenditure. A revised system of housing finance was introduced which involved giving private rented sector investors access to the PLAs which were discussed previously.

The principles of the policy changed little during the 1980s. However, in 1982 a Rent Act was introduced which aimed to protect tenants of pre-1948 housing – to ensure that rent increases were fair and took account of real incomes. Six year tenancies were also established with a choice of 3 years for individual as opposed to company landlords.

During the 1980s landlord organizations continued to argue that investment in the private rented sector was not worthwhile and that controls were too tight. From 1986 greater deregulation was introduced and rent controls were relaxed. It was thought that deregulation would help to improve the profitability of housing and reverse the trend of investors leaving the sector. The provisions of the 1982 act were suspended and more limited security of tenure was introduced. In some areas, particularly Paris, rents rose dramatically. This led, in 1989, to an amendment to the 1986 Act which decentralized rent regulation allowing limited control within certain regions. There is a gradual movement towards market rents following the 1986 Act, which will not have taken full effect until the mid-1990s.

8.1.6 Evaluation

After having a period of relative stability from 1963 to the mid-1970s the private rented sector has declined rapidly. Although four times as big as the social rented sector in 1963 it was about the same size 30 years later (Geindre, 1993a).

A statement issued in May 1993 by the ANAH illustrates the problems of the increasing pressure in the private rented sector: 'The fiscal burden on private rental landlords and investors has continued since 1975, the accumulation of legislative texts and regulations have, without doubt, put the position of the sector in question. This has produced a devastating effect: in 15 years, the private rented stock has lost nearly a million dwellings. The number of young one-person households, the increase in divorce, the increase in the student population, the low level of real wages in the tertiary sector and the high level of professional mobility, all generate a need for rented housing which can not be met solely by the HLM stock' (translated from CES, 1993, p. 150).

There are a combination of circumstances working against the sector at a time when demand is particularly high. One of the main reasons has been the general consensus among investors that housing investment is no longer profitable. This is the conclusion of a report to the Prime Minister for the preparation of the Eleventh Plan, '*Housing: A Priority for the 11th Plan*', by Geindre (1993a). The report claims that the lack of fiscal incentives as compared with those for other investments means that housing is still suffering from under investment.

Table 8.2 Pre-tax performance of different investments (% return on capital): France

	1960–1970	1971–1980	1981–1989	Over 30 years
Housing	2.4	3.1	2.8	2.8
Bonds	3.3	1.5	7.6	4.0
Shares	0.1	0.7	17.3	5.2
Liquid savings	0.6	3.2	1.3	0.9

Source: Geindre (1993a).

Table 8.2 (from Geindre, 1993a, p. 52) suggests that while the returns on investment in housing, at approximately 2.5–3% per annum after tax, have been comparable with other investments over a long period of time, in the short and medium term other investments can be more profitable and therefore more attractive.

Between 1981 and 1989 housing investment gave a yield of 2.8%, bonds 7.6% and shares 17.3%. Estimates from other sources confirm this situation. 'Les cahiers de habitat' suggest an average return of less than 0.8% after tax; Daniel Lebègue, former director of the Treasury, calculated that in 1990 the return on housing was 3% while on other assets it was 14% (translated from CES, 1993, pp. 150 and 168).

The condition of much of the stock has caused many problems. A housing enquiry carried out by INSEE found 218 000 dwellings to be disused or dilapidated and yet only 33 000 were condemned to be destroyed (Louvot, 1992) leaving large quantities of poor quality dwellings in the stock. Landlords are not prepared to invest in repairs and renovations as they do not see returns to compensate them. Many of the good quality dwellings are being sold for owner-occupation. Since 1985, 33% of previously rented property has been sold to its occupants. In total over the period 1984 to 1988 the private rented stock lost 441 000 dwellings while during the same period only 72 000 were constructed. More recently a tight home ownership market, especially for low income earners, has increased the demand for renting: both private and social. However, with a shrinking private rented supply landlords are becoming more and more selective in their choice of tenants (Lefebvre, 1992). Landlords will only take on tenants if they believe that their income will continue to support the rent and not lead to an accumulation of arrears.

A further disincentive to investment was legislation protecting pre-1948 tenants, that was in force between 1982 and 1986 (Section 8.1.5), an increase in the risks attached to the private rented sector left landlords with few options for eviction or ending a contract, even when rents were not being paid.

Although the fiscal effects of the 1986 Méhaigherie Law (Section 8.1.3) and the improved tax concessions in 1993 (Section 8.1.4) are slowly increasing the annual construction of new dwellings (from 5000 to 20 000 per annum between 1984 and 1990) there are calls for still more incentives for the sector, so that more of the 70 000 dwellings per year leaving the sector can be replaced. While the 1986 Law has encouraged the building of smaller dwellings, there is an increasing demand for larger rental units. The 1986 Law also makes no contribution to preventing the erosion of the existing stock. The measure has been described as a 'tool for sustaining new construction rather than an element of a coherent policy to maintain the private rented sector' (Geindre, 1993b, p. 145).

Various proposals have been put forward to meet the aims put forward for the Eleventh Plan (Geindre, 1993a). The proposals concentrate on the system of taxation for housing in France arguing that the poor fiscal position in relation to other investments has exacerbated other barriers to investment. Housing investment should be made a more viable option in the long term by introducing 'stabilizing qualities' into the system to make short-term fluctuations in inflation or interest rates of negligible importance. For those properties remaining in the 'controlled' rented sector it is suggested that all rental income should be tax free, as for HLM housing, and there should be a greater difference in the tax conditions imposed on qualification for ANAH subsidies between the controlled and uncontrolled private rented sectors. A more generous treatment of depreciation as in Germany is proposed (Geindre, 1993a). Generally it is suggested that the system in Germany might offer some solutions to problems in France. We now turn to an examination of the German private rental market.

8.2 THE PRIVATE RENTED SECTOR IN GERMANY

8.2.1 The size and nature of the sector

Germany has the largest private rented sector in the European Union accounting for 43% of the total housing stock and containing over 11 million dwellings. The sector continues to play a much more important role in Germany than in most other European countries. The main investors are large commercial lessors and high income private individuals. Although there have been significant constraints on the operation of the sector since rent regulations in the early 1970s, investors have continued to go into the private rented market because of generous fiscal incentives related to both capital and income. These incentives have, over time, ensured the supply of private rented dwellings and the sector has stayed at a fairly constant level during recent decades.

About half of the private rented stock was built before the Second World War and was constructed mostly in large cities. Despite the success of the sector, there has recently been a fall in new building, especially in the cities where serious shortages have developed.

Tenants in Germany have traditionally had strong legal rights which have been seen by some landlords as a negative influence on investment. Some concessions have been made to landlords in an attempt to maintain interest in the sector. The condition of the private rented stock has become a major issue. While tenants are made responsible, in most cases by a written clause in contracts, for minor repairs and periodic renovation work landlords are still responsible for structural maintenance. However, it is argued that in practice maintenance has often been neglected and this has resulted in some buildings being demolished, because of their poor condition (Leutner and Jensen, 1988).

Table 8.3 Additions and reductions in the supply of rented dwellings ('000s of dwellings): Germany, 1980–1989

	1980	1981	1982	1983	1984	1985	1986	1987	1988	1989[1]
Total completions	130	140	140	150	180	130	90	60	60	70
Total reductions[2]	60	70	80	90	80	80	80	80	80	80
Net additions[3]	70	60	60	60	90	50	0	–20	–20	–10
Total extra indirect increase in supply[4]	190	160	140	130	150	120	110	110	110	120
Net additions and release of stock	260	230	210	190	240	170	120	90	80	110

Items do not add to totals because of rounding in the original source.

[1]Estimate, [2]due to demolitions, amalgamations, conversions and sales, [3]accounting for all reductions, [4]release of stock as tenants move to owner-occupied sector.

Source: DIW (1989, p. 273).

8.2.2 Investment and construction rate

Additions and reductions to the stock of rented dwellings in Table 8.3 are shown for all rented housing. As data is not available to separate private from social renting in Germany, we will consider trends in the rented sector overall, making special reference to the private sector where possible.

In 1989, an estimated 70 000 new rental units were constructed. The Deutsches Institut für Wirtschaftsforschung (DIW), estimates approximately 40 000 of these dwellings to be in the social sector and 30 000 in the private sector. The data shows how the construction levels of rented housing has declined over the past 10 years. This trend began when the provision of private rented accommodation was seen as less profitable. Many investors became disillusioned with strict contractual agreements, limiting rent increases which were introduced in the early 1970s (DIW, 1989).

At the same time new temporary leases were introduced which could be set for a maximum of 5 years. These limited contracts encouraged landlords to rent the dwelling for only a short time after which they might either occupy it themselves or sell it. In addition an increasing number of private rented dwellings were being sold to owner-occupiers. This had a double effect on stock levels: whilst some stock was being lost to owner-occupation, incentives for new building were too low to encourage investors to replace or make up for losses.

In response to this situation, and so the size of the sector and level of provision could be maintained, new measures, in particular tax incentives, were introduced in 1989 in an attempt to revive the provision of private rented housing. Lower building prices and a general increase in rent levels noticeably improved opportunities for investment in the sector (DIW, 1989). Consequently, the number of rented housing completions have been making some recovery since 1989.

8.2.3 Financing and subsidies

Government support for the private rented sector has been maintained in the post-war period. While other countries, particularly the UK, supported mainly social housing, in Germany the promotion and support of private renting was also seen as a key element in policy to promote housing production and private enterprise. Up to the late 1970s a number of loans and subsidies contributing to operating costs and rehabilitation were available, together with certain tax exemptions. Some Länder also made lump sum contributions to private renting through the 'Third Subsidy Path' which enables the provision of short-term subsidies to promote housebuilding without the need to impose strict regulations concerning rent levels. The Länder are now responsible for providing grants, while the federal government supports renting indirectly through tax reliefs.

Private rented housing in Germany has always been treated in the same way as any other investment for tax purposes. This means that any costs including interest payments, maintenance and management and depreciation can be deducted from revenue before tax is levied. Any losses from housing investments can be set against other sources of income, though this has become significantly restricted over time. Up to 1990 all investors in any tenure were exempt from land tax for the first 10 years after construction. This was a considerable incentive, particularly in private renting, but from 1990 the privilege was withdrawn. Rented dwellings are liable to both capital assets tax (0.5% of the value of the dwelling less the debts relating to it) and

Table 8.4 Depreciation allowances on new investment in rented housing: Germany

Before 1989			After 1989		
Years after construction	*Annual rate (%)*	*Accumulated depreciation (%)*	*Years after construction*	*Annual rate (%)*	*Accumulated depreciation (%)*
1 – 8	5	40	1–4	7	28
			5–10	5	58
9–14	2.5	55	1–16	2	70
15–50	1.25	100	17–40	1.25	100

Source: Hubert (1993, p. 24).

municipal land tax (levied on the owner and charged on the value of land and buildings erected on it). Rented property is exempt from capital gains tax if the property is held for more than 2 years (Boelhouwer and Heijden, 1992). Although a generous system for deducting depreciation costs from income already existed, in 1989 the government improved depreciation allowances to revive construction in this sector. The changes are set out in Table 8.4.

The period during which depreciation can be included as a deduction was reduced from 50 to 40 years, but the rate of depreciation was increased. The new system gives a higher rate of depreciation in the first few years. Depreciation can be deducted at a rate of 28% over the first 4 years and 58% over 10 years (the rate had previously only reached 45% in the first 10 years). This will benefit investors in the early years of an investment when it had previously been more difficult to make a profit (Boelhouwer and Heijden, 1992, p. 132). This policy change has lead to a dramatic increase in expected tax losses for the government. In 1989/90 losses stood at DM 362 million but were expected to reach DM 566 million in 1991, and DM 960 million by 1992, as the supply of rented dwellings increased (DIW, 1990). In addition to these depreciation rates, if owners rent their dwellings for a minimum period of 5 years to a low income household and do not exceed a rent level fixed by the Länder for social dwellings, the depreciation allowance increases further so that during the first 10 years a depreciation rate of 85% can be reached. In 1989 a further fiscal incentive was introduced to encourage renovation and repair work. Expenditures contributing to the creation of rental dwellings through extensions or renovations to existing dwellings could be deducted from income for tax purposes for 5 years (at a rate of 20% per year). This measure applied only to those dwellings started after October 1989, and completed before January 1994. There was a cost ceiling of DM

60 000 for the construction of these dwellings. Many of these new measures were a direct result of the increasing housing need that was apparent in Germany after reunification.

Tenants in private rented accommodation are eligible for housing allowances. The housing allowances system is outlined in Chapter 6 and is the same across all the sectors. Approximately 95% of all claimants are tenants and about 63% of these are renting privately. With an increase in the number of claimants of Wohngeld, especially since reunification, the cost of housing allowances have gone up considerably. However, despite the Wohngeld system many tenants are still confronted with financial problems. Tenants that do qualify for Wohngeld often find that payments do not reduce housing expenditure to an acceptable level as rents have increased more quickly than payments are revised under the Wohngeld system (Chapter 10). In addition the Wohngeld system does not effectively alleviate problems caused by the gap that exists between old and new rental contracts. We will now discuss this further below.

8.2.4 Rent regulations

Rents were rigidly controlled in the immediate post-war period and up to the 1960s. Gradual increases in controlled rents were allowed during this time. From the 1960s rents were deregulated and controls were relaxed. However, by 1970 there was increasing pressure on the government to re-introduce controls to combat rapidly increasing rents. In 1971 the government introduced the Rent Regulation Act which limited rent increases for existing tenancies in unsubsidized privately rented housing, and introduced new security of tenure measures. These gave tenants an infinite contract term and protection against eviction. Since the 1971 Act the legal framework for residential leases has been based on three elements:

1. Unilateral security of tenure for the tenant.
2. A limitation on rent increases for sitting tenants, to the level reached by comparable accommodation ('Vergleichsmiete').
3. Free negotiation of initial rents on a new lease (Hubert, 1993).

Tenants can only be asked to leave if the landlord or a member of the landlord's close family take up occupancy or if the tenant does not adhere to the conditions of the tenancy. Eviction with the objective of receiving a higher rent from a new tenant is forbidden (Leutner and Jensen, 1988). As a concession to landlord organizations, temporary leases of up to 5 years have been available since 1983. These relax the conditions for evictions or the ending of contracts. However, many landlord organizations have still criticized the protection given to tenants claiming it is a disincentive to investment.

The value and calculation of the 'Vergleichsmiete' was not completely clear on its introduction. It was only in 1982 that the issue was clarified. 'The

Vergleichsmiete is determined by the rent of contracts which have been agreed upon during the last 3 years' (Hubert, 1993, p. 14). The main aim of this system was that 'new' rents would not move ahead of 'old' rents. However, in the high inflation of the 1970s a substantial rent-gap had already emerged between existing tenancies and new contracts. Also, because initial rents are not restricted, rent controls have only a limited impact. Rent increases can only be enforced with respect to specific criteria. These are:

1. Increases in operating costs or interest charges.
2. Increased expenditure due to improvement work.
3. Evidence of comparable local units fetching higher rents.

In meeting these criteria an increase can only go through if it has been a year or more since the last rent increase and if the rent does not increase by more than 30% in 3 years. Tenants can dispute a rent increase in court. Landlords may increase rents in relation to improvement expenditures made on the dwelling. Eleven per cent of the total cost of improvements can be passed on to the tenant, provided that the tenant has agreed to this improvement work prior to it being carried out.

Rent levels have increased steadily and the difference between old and new rental contracts is becoming increasingly pronounced. Official data on monthly rents show how rents in older dwellings are considerably lower than many new contracts. In dwellings built pre-1949 average rent levels stood at DM 5.94/m², while for those built between 1979 and 1987 average monthly rents reached DM 8.76/m², and as high as DM 11.95/m² for some small units (Hubert, 1993).

There are a number of factors that are influencing rent increases. Rents have increased partly because the size and the quality of the dwellings that households are consuming have also increased (this is discussed more fully in Chapter 10). A second pressure on rents is the growing shortage of housing especially since 1989. Although this has been felt across the whole housing market, the private rented sector has been hit especially hard (Bundesmisterium, 1992a).

A further contributory factor concerns the emphasis, in Germany, on subsidizing modernization and renovations in this sector. 'The tendency of private landlords to provide *deluxe* accommodation, at corresponding rents, has been to some extent a response to demand, but it may also have been encouraged by an excessive emphasis in public policy on renovation as against new building but the outcome was nearly always higher rents. It can, indeed, be argued that housing became "too good", as dowdy but cheap housing was modernized' (Hallett, 1994, p. 5).

The legal restrictions concerning old and new rents are also likely to have had an effect. The gap appears to have widened since changes were introduced in the 1980s. 'This trend indicates, that the restrictions on rent reviews protect the sitting tenant too much, probably at the cost of those who have to move' (Hubert, 1993, p. 33).

There are special tenancy arrangements for occupants of private rented dwellings which are to be converted into condominiums. These are usually single units in a multi-dwelling building which have been sold for owner-occupation. The change in tenure status increases the vulnerability of tenants and the conversion of properties has become a major issue in Germany. There is a high probability that landlords will choose to live in their dwellings once converted, or at least try to evict the tenant so that the property can be sold. To protect tenants in this position, 'freeze' periods have been introduced during which time the new owner may not terminate a contract. This period was extended in 1993 from 3–5 to 5–10 years, depending on the local authority (Hubert, 1993).

8.2.5 Evaluation

The data presented in Table 8.3 on levels of construction suggests that investors became disillusioned with the private rented sector; 'rising building costs and land prices, in combination with the income structure of the population ... had a negative effect on the cost-effectiveness of investments in housing' (Leutner and Jensen, 1988, p. 173). This trend went hand in hand with transfers of stock to ownership and co-ownerships, and of landlords maintaining vacancies for speculative reasons, especially in inner-cities.

Working together, these effects meant that new construction levels have not been high enough to replace demolished and sold stock. Between 1987 and 1989 the net change in stock levels, estimated by calculating the number of completions in the rented sector less reductions in stock (due to demolition and sales), was actually negative by between 10 000 and 20 000 dwellings. The number of units supplied annually was a positive total due to rented dwellings becoming vacant in the stock as tenants moved into, for example, owner-occupied housing (see Table 8.3).

Low construction levels have had a striking effect on the ability of the stock to cater for the increasing demand for rented accommodation. A large proportion of 'new' households choose to live in rented accommodation. Between 1980 and 1984 an estimated 90% of new households who desired rented housing were able to find accommodation. However, between 1985 and 1987 the situation had worsened considerably due to a lack of new building, and the release of rented stock for owner-occupation (DIW, 1989).

The limited number of dwellings that were available were also affected by steep rent increases due to the high inflation and excess demand. In the cities this had not just become a problem for low income households, but was beginning to affect wider sections of the population, as private rented housing became less and less affordable (DIW, 1991). The difference in rent levels has in particular reduced the mobility of tenants. In many cases, moving means entering a new contract at a higher rent, so many tenants become trapped in unsuitable accommodation.

The affordability problems in the private rented sector have contributed to a greater call for increasing state social housing programmes. This it is argued may encourage investors back into the private market as expected yields increase (DIW, 1990). In fact the high level of demand and housing shortage as a result of reunification led the federal government to make considerably more funds available to housing, and to modify the financing arrangements. Large increases in tax expenditures increased levels of supply considerably, from 26 700 completions in 1988 to an estimated 66 800 in 1991 (DIW, 1992).

Many increased subsidies were also directed to the new Bundesländern. These measures largely mirror the system in the former West Germany but are generally set at higher levels. These are examined in the next section.

A further expansion of the private rented sector is taking place as stock transfers from the social rented sector at the end of the contractual financing periods. Due to the nature of the financing of social housing in Germany support is only given for the length of time it takes to repay initial construction loans (see Chapter 6 for details). Once these have been repaid social dwellings receive no further government support and revert effectively to the private rented sector. This process is highly significant. Estimates suggest that of the 4 million social rented dwellings in 1984 half will have been transferred to the private rented sector by 1995 (Boelhouwer and Heijden, 1992).

8.3 PRIVATE RENTING IN THE NEW BUNDESLÄNDERN

While much of the land and housing in the former GDR was nationalized after 1960, private construction of dwellings was still encouraged. Substantial help in the form of low interest loans was provided by the state, although most of these were granted for construction of owner-occupied units. The state encouraged private owners and landlords to continue to take responsibility for their own repair and maintenance, to provide some relief to the burden of state resources allocated to housing investment.

Strict rules were established to control the operation of private landlords. Tight controls were in place on rents, evictions, sales and even occupancy of private rented dwellings. While the expansion of owner-occupation was permitted, building of new private rental units was forbidden, as was the rental of privately owned units in multiple-unit structures. This was, 'to prevent either unearned profits or distribution based on income or wealth, in violation of the preference accorded to workers and farmers' (Marcuse and Schumann, 1993, p. 88).

Pre-war rent controls in Germany were not changed substantially in the GDR. Allocation was undertaken directly by the local authorities and sales required their approval. Landlords had little control over occupancy and tenants had a high degree of security. Low-state-regulated rents were the main factor preventing the growth of the private rented sector. The letting of private dwellings was often more of a financial burden than a source of income. Many of the dwellings were in poor condition with rents not covering the costs of repairs.

Landlords were, in some cases, able to 'relinquish ownership' of their private rented property to the state who would then be responsible for letting the dwellings. This was often done with units in multi-dwelling buildings, where maintenance and repair costs were highest. However, the sale of private rented units was not always popular with local authorities who would then become liable for repair costs, and face demands from tenants to carry out work. Therefore, in many cases, landlords simply abandoned their dwellings. It has been estimated that almost 10% of the total stock in the former East Germany, having been formally private rented, was either abandoned or taken over by the state.

Even so, state subsidies to private rented dwellings were still relatively large. Figures from 1989 reveal that 2353 million marks (old Ostmarks) were planned to be devoted to the operating costs of private renting. Landlords themselves contributed 2265 million marks to operating costs (purely from rent payments) which means 51% of all operating costs in the sector were covered by state subsidies.

GDR policy has been summarized in this way: 'A strong preference for non-private forms of housing ownership, whether state or co-operative, the prohibition of new private rental housing construction, the devaluation of existing private rental housing, and the encouragement of private home ownership only as supplemental to other forms of housing provision' (Marcuse and Schumann 1993, p. 131).

The structure of ownership of the housing stock illustrates the emphasis on state control. In 1950, 91% of the total stock was in private ownership. However, by 1990 the state owned or controlled over half of the stock with only about 40% in private ownership (Hallett, 1993).

Increasing the levels of owner-occupation in the new Bundesländern is now a main aim of housing policy. Many rented dwellings are being sold to the tenants. While owner-occupation stood at around 20% in 1990 the government hopes that levels of 40–45% can be reached, in line with the size of the sector in western Germany.

The quantity of private rented stock in poor condition is particularly high. Much of the stock needs modernization and repairs. It is hoped that the phased increase in rents, also applying to private landlords, will act as an incentive to private landlords. The government has set up generous subsidies for landlords to encourage investment in modernization and renovation work, although these activities are likely to be confined initially to landlords with higher incomes.

The structure of subsidies is broadly the same as for the former West Germany. For private landlords this includes depreciation allowances, tax treatment in line with that for other types of investment, and subsidies for modernization and renovations. Loans with low rates of interest are also available to build new dwellings, but as many households have few savings, it will be difficult initially to fund the costs they must cover themselves. Most loans and subsidies are paid through the newly established Kreditanstalt für Wiederaufbau (Loan Bank for Reconstruction). Subsidies in the new Bundesländern are set at significantly higher rates than those in the old Bundesländern, reflecting the extent of support needed. One of the main aims of policy is to improve the dwelling stock so that the population of the new Bundesländern are encouraged to live and work here, rather than moving to the west of Germany.

8.4 THE PRIVATE RENTED SECTOR IN THE NETHERLANDS

8.4.1 Size and nature of the sector

During the 1950s the private rented stock in the Netherlands accounted for about half of the total dwelling stock. However, since that time the sector has seen a continual decline, similar to that experienced by France and the UK.

Table 8.5 Housing tenure (% of total stock): Netherlands, 1950–1992

	Owner-occupied	Social rented	Private rented	Other rented
1950	28	24	47	1
1960	30	23	47	
1975	39	34	37	
1980	42	38	18	2
1992	45	42	13	

Source: own calculations, based on Ghékiere and Quilliot (1991), Van Vliet (1990) and Van Weesep and Van Kempen (1992b).

Estimates in 1993 put private rented dwellings at only 15% of the total stock (Netherlands Ministry of Housing, 1993).

Table 8.5 shows the development of the stock over time. Until the 1960s the private rented sector was the dominant tenure in the Netherlands, containing 47% of the total stock. It housed many low income groups who were unable to afford the higher rents in the better quality social housing being constructed. However, the rapid expansion of the social rented sector and its aim of providing accommodation for both middle- and low-income groups meant that it gradually took on more and more tenants from the private sector. New construction for private renting declined as the demand and provision of good quality social housing increased.

The sector's decline was dramatically exacerbated by a rent setting system that was introduced in 1975. The dynamic cost-price rental (DCPR) system was applied across the whole rental sector and, throughout the period in which it was in operation (1975–1989), caused problems in both sectors. In the private rented sector, the DCPR system (Section 8.4.4), acted as a disincentive to investors who both withdrew dwellings from the stock and ceased new building in this sector. This helps to explain the more rapid decline during the 1980s, from a level of 37% of total stock in 1975 to only 13% in 1992.

It is important to note that the national figures illustrated in Table 8.7 are not evenly distributed throughout the country. Indeed, the housing stock in the four largest cities (Amsterdam, Rotterdam, The Hague and Utrecht) differs considerably from the rest of the Dutch housing stock, with generally much less owner-occupation and higher rental levels in these cities (Van Weesep and Van Kempen, 1992b).

Pre-war private rental dwellings and properties bought by municipalities, although constituting only 17% of total stock, represent almost 60% of all dwellings of very bad quality (Netherlands Ministry of Housing, 1993). The pre-war housing does generally tend to be smaller and cheaper, and is often in medium rise blocks in city centres. Tenants are usually the young or very old and a high mobility rate exists in this housing. Much of this housing is now being sold to housing associations or local authority organizations. In contrast the majority of post-war private rented dwellings, mainly built by institutional investors, comprise fairly large, good quality accommodation. This tends to be more expensive and attracts high income earners to areas where housing is in high demand.

8.4.2 Nature of investors

The private rented sector accounting for 13% of the stock includes private individual landlords (7% of the stock) and institutional investors (6%), owning together approximately 750 000 dwellings. The pre-war private rental stock is dominated by the individual landlords and the post-war stock by institutional investors, particularly pension funds and insurance companies.

The proportion of the stock owned by individual investors has been declining at a faster rate than that owned by institutional investors. Falling

Table 8.6 Housing completions in the private rented sector: Netherlands, 1970–1992

	With subsidy	One-off grant	Without subsidy	Total
1970	26052	-	2890	28942
1975	23454	-	777	24231
1980	9820	-	1267	11087
1985	16201	—— 4009 ——		20210
1988	8794	1507	1018	11319
1990	5950	1393	1606	8949
1992				6500

Source: Ghekiere and Quillot (1991), Netherlands Ministry of Housing (1993) and own calculations.

returns and greater risk during the 1970s and 1980s increased the number of individual landlords who sold their dwellings to local authorities, to housing associations or for owner-occupation and conversions to condominiums.

8.4.3 Investment and construction rate

Table 8.6 shows the reduction in construction of private rental dwellings. In 1970 24% of completions were for this sector but by 1992 this had fallen to 7.6%.

Many investors began to leave the private rental market when the DCPR came into effect in 1975. At the same time there was an increase in new construction for the owner-occupied market. The stock of owner-occupied dwellings increased through the sale of tens of thousands of private rented dwellings per year to owner-occupiers (Priemus, 1988). Table 8.6 shows a continual decline: in 1992 only 6500 new private rental dwellings were constructed.

8.4.4 Financing and subsidies

Landlords operating in the private rented sector are able to receive subsidies from central government, and a distinction is made between these dwellings and other, unsubsidized private rented housing. Those landlords owning unsubsidized dwellings are free to set initial rent levels. However, rents for subsidized dwellings must adhere to rises set by national rent policy.

The financing and subsidization of new construction in the private rented sector has changed considerably over the last two decades. Until 1975 a system of annual payments to subsidize operating costs was used to encourage private rented housebuilding. The owners of the rented housing were then required to charge rents at government set levels.

However, this was seen as an expensive and ineffective system and was therefore changed under the 1974 Rent and Subsidy Policy. This introduced the DCPR system for the whole rental sector. Long-term subsidies were still available, but they were determined in a different way. Under the DCPR system, cost rents were calculated over a 50 year period to take into account future increases in rents. The system anticipated higher returns in the future due to inflation and rent increases. So while an annual subsidy was still paid for the whole 50 year period, the difference between the contract and cost rent was expected to decrease over time as the subsidy was gradually reduced. The theory behind this system was that because the subsidy was calculated over a longer 50 year period, subsidies would be more efficient (Conijn, 1993), resulting in lower costs to the government.

However, in practice landlords investing in new housing, mainly pension funds and insurance companies, received lower returns on their investments as subsidies were decreased. This was mainly because low inflation rates meant rents did not increase at the expected rate and were not high enough to cover costs. This in turn led to a reduction in investment in new private rented housing.

The DCPR system was also applied in the social rented sector, and it was mainly the problems of financing and subsidization in the private sector that led to its downfall. The government was having to provide for unexpected increases in finance and subsidies because:

1. Low inflation and subsequently low rent increases were not meeting the anticipated rent levels.
2. An uncertain capital market meant that low start loans for construction were not widely available.
3. The costs of subsidy payments rose while rents were low (this is covered in more detail in Chapter 6).

Therefore, from 1989, the DCPR system was abandoned. Rent increases were subsequently set annually and came under new regulations. The government reverted to a grant system. Subsidies can still be provided as incentives to investment, on the condition that the investor charges the controlled rent for the property.

Sector 'C' grants have been available to private rented investors since 1984. These are one-off grants of Dfl 5000 for the development of houses whose construction costs are below certain limits. These subsidies are targeted at lower income households whose income falls between a set minimum and maximum. Sector 'C' grants are also available in the owner-occupied sector. In 1990 Dfl 990 million was paid out in sector 'C' grants of which Dfl 123 million was allocated to the rented sector (BIPE, 1991). Grants are available for improvement and major maintenance work. These are also tied to rules concerning rent increases. Loans for the construction of private rented housing come solely from the open market; no government subsidized loans are available.

Subsidies are available to lower income households in the form of housing allowances. The same housing allowance system applies to both social and private tenants. The system is described in Chapter 6.

8.4.5 Rent regulation

Rent controls have continued to be a strong feature of the private rented sector in the Netherlands. While the DCPR system was in operation, the actual contract rent charged was determined by a points system: the government would set a standard increase which could then be adjusted, by agreement between tenants and landlords, on the basis of particular features of the dwelling. Points were awarded for certain facilities which could result in either an increase or decrease in the rents. The system was expanded in 1986 to take into account more features of the dwelling and its environment.

This system of rent control had been abandoned by the late 1980s. At the top end of the market rents are freely determined but below certain valuation thresholds rents may only be set and increased according to a scale set by the government. Over time rents have increased considerably. In 1979 average rent levels in the private sector stood at Dfl 244 per month, had almost doubled by 1989 and reached Dfl 539 per month in 1994 (Nederlandse Woonbund, 1995).

Rents differ considerably between institutional investors and private individual landlords. Individual landlords charged average monthly rents of Dfl 498 in 1994, but institutional landlords charged Dfl 860 (Nederlandse Woonbund, 1995).

8.4.6 Evaluation

The changes in rent and subsidy policy over the last 20 years have had a dramatic effect on the role of the private rented sector and the proportion of housing being built in the sector. The number of private individuals able to afford to supply private rented housing has fallen. Dwellings owned by private individuals are of poorer quality. The strict rent policy, inflation and increases in management and maintenance costs had a detrimental effect on private landlords.

While the reduction of new building in the private rented sector has been a cause of some concern in both France and Germany, and policies were initiated to re-introduce incentives to the market, there has in the Netherlands been a very limited response to the situation. With a considerable stock of good quality social rented dwellings neither the demand for private renting nor concern over the future of the sector are so apparent. There is little discussion on maintaining a balance between sectors. The Dutch Housing

Union, which represents Dutch tenants, does however object to policies in the private rental sector, especially excessive rent increases, poor security of tenure for tenants and poor quality of private rental dwellings (Nederlandse Woonbund, 1995).

Although there is a serious housing shortage which is forcing up rent levels in the private rented sector, especially in the main cities, the demand for new housing is being focused on the social sector, due to high quality standards, and the owner-occupied sector for higher income earners.

8.5 PRIVATE RENTED HOUSING IN THE UK

8.5.1 Size and nature of the stock

As in the other European countries that we have considered, the private rented sector in the UK has been declining rapidly. However, the extent of the sector's decline and its prospects for the future are particularly bleak in the UK. The UK has the smallest private rented sector in the European Union. Table 8.7 illustrates the extent of the decline in the UK from over 50% of the total stock in the 1950s to only 9% in the early 1990s.

The sector has changed from housing the majority of the population to a marginal housing sector containing more unfit dwellings than any other sector. Its comparatively old stock has had little investment and is often used by households as a last resort.

There is some evidence which suggests a small increase in the size of the stock since 1991. Data for 1993 put the sector at nearly 10% of the stock (Table 8.7). A scheme initiated in 1988, the residential Business Expansion Scheme, outlined later, has had some impact on new construction. However, a large part of the increase has been a consequence of the slump in the owner-occupation market which has increased the number of dwellings let

Table 8.7 Private rented dwellings: UK, 1950–1993

Year	No. of dwellings ('000s)	Total stock (%)	Region
1950	7.36	53.0	GB
1960	4.60	32.0	England and Wales
1970	3.67	19.6	GB
1975	3.12	15.7	GB
1981	2.28	10.9	GB
1989	2.08	9.0	UK
1993	2.29	9.6	UK

Source: Forrest and Murie (1988), Kemp (1988), DOE (1982, 1994) and Down *et al.* (1994).

temporarily while they cannot be sold. The number of households needing to rent dwellings has increased following repossessions. Many of these dwellings will revert to owner-occupation when the housing market picks up.

The introduction of rent controls in 1915 certainly had some effect in triggering the decline in the sector. However, other factors have also been important. The level of slum clearance in this sector has been particularly significant. Estimates suggest that 80% cf all dwellings demolished through slum clearance between 1914 and 1975 were in the private rented sector. Other major losses occurred due to the sale of dwellings to owner-occupation and sales to Local Authorities.

In 1989 the General Household Survey revealed that 56% of private rented dwellings were built before 1919. Much of the best private rented stock has been sold to owner-occupiers and local authorities, which has left conditions in the remaining private rented dwellings particularly poor. There has been a distinct lack of investment in the repair and maintenance of private rental dwellings, largely due to the reluctance of landlords to incur losses. The English House Condition Survey, carried out in 1991, found that since 1986 the private rented sector had experienced the worst decline in conditions of all the sectors. The level of general disrepair in the private rented sector was 85% higher than in the owner-occupied sector. The sector had the highest rate of unfitness, at 20% of its stock.

At the other extreme there is some better quality private rented housing. This includes dwellings whose lettings are related to employment. Many dwellings have benefited from programmes of urban regeneration and gentrification in inner cities, seen for example in Docklands and enterprise zones.

Within the sector two sub-sectors can be identified. The unfurnished subsector tends to contain the older housing stock with fewer amenities and have longer term tenancies. The furnished sub-sector, on the other hand, is made up of relatively newer, slightly better quality, but smaller, dwellings and houses younger people often sharing and on short-term tenancies. There are a number of different tenancy types and rent regulations applying to these subsectors.

The types of household living in private rented accommodation are diverse, reflecting the role it plays in the housing market (DOE, 1993b). A wide range of socio-economic groups rent privately. Older households are most likely to live in old, poor quality private rental dwellings and the lowest income groups are also quite strongly represented. However, there is additionally a proportion of high income private tenants in newer, more expensive units. Many households move into private renting when they are unable to find alternative rented accommodation, or cannot afford to buy their own house. The diversity of demand and need suggests that the private rented sector still has a potentially significant role to play.

8.5.2 Type of investors in private renting

Private landlordism in Britain has always tended to be mainly on a small scale. Private individuals owning a small number of properties predominate. Tenancies were traditionally set up by non-resident landlords, with only a small proportion of resident landlords. In addition, some housing in this sector is provided by companies and institutions for employees. While this used to make up a fairly significant part of private rental supply, it is estimated that these large landlords accounted for only 10% of the stock in 1990, and have continued to decline since then (Best *et al.*, 1992).

Most individual landlords manage the properties they let themselves in their 'spare time'. However, some are also handed over to housing management agencies who will select tenants, collect rents and deal with arrears and organize repairs on behalf of the owners.

Motives for renting privately are varied. The small number of companies still owning private rental stock were motivated initially by rates of return, but also by future capital gain. When rental income declined many landlords tried to get vacant possession of rental dwellings, to sell them and liquidate their investment. As it became apparent that rental dwellings were more valuable without tenants than with tenants, a 'valuation gap' developed, which led to a considerable difference in the market value of properties depending on whether they had sitting tenants or they were empty. In the past, some speculative investors bought dwellings with sitting tenants, and kept them for as long as the tenancies ran. With vacant possession the properties could be sold with considerable capital gain.

8.5.3 Investment and construction rate

In the 1930s up to 66 000 dwellings per year were completed for private renting. However, since 1945, investment in new construction has been almost non-existent (see Kemp, 1988). The government has tried to reverse the decline in private renting. Assured tenancies and Shorthold tenancies were introduced in the 1980 Housing Act. These allowed registered landlords to charge market rents and permitted tenancies, in certain circumstances, to run only for 12 months. Changes in 1988 made assured tenancies with market rents possible for any landlord and allowed shortholds to be for as little as 6 months. The higher rents and reduced security of tenure for tenants were expected to encourage an expansion of the sector. The measures have had only a limited success. The residential Business Expansion Scheme (BES) from 1989 encouraged the setting up of companies which have invested in new private rental construction and the purchase of existing housing for private letting (Section 8.5.4).

Under the 1986 Building Societies Act, the government has tried to encourage building societies to finance, develop, build and manage private rented dwellings, by giving them new powers. However, while these arrangements were well received by the Building Societies Association, the actual response in new development has been sluggish (Garnett *et al.*, 1991). One example has been the creation of a company called 'Quality Street' with backing from the Nationwide Anglia Building Society. At its launch the building society invested £600 million in the company, and aimed to own and manage 40 000 homes by 1992. However, by early 1994 Quality Street, by then a 75% subsidiary of the building society, owned only around 2100 dwellings and managed 1100 dwellings for a third party.

The small increase in the sector over the past 5 years has led to debate over whether a change in attitudes has taken place in favour of private renting. However, it has become apparent that the small shift from owning to renting is largely a consequence of uncertainty in the housing market, and is only a temporary phenomenon. Following the ending of the residential BES in 1993, there is a widespread acknowledgement that further incentives are necessary if the sector is not to slip again into gradual decline.

8.5.4 Financing and subsidies

There are no on-going government incentives to invest in the private rented sector, in the way that there are in Germany and France. This has been the major contributory factor to the absence of new construction in the sector. After legislation on rent controls, the growth of home ownership and fairly limited levels of demand in the sector, many landlords were no longer able to make a worthwhile return on their investment. While investors in the private rented sector in Germany are treated in principle in the same way as all other investors, in the UK private landlords are treated unfavourably compared to other investors. No tax breaks on sinking funds or depreciation are allowed (Crook, 1988). The only capital subsidy given by the government to private landlords come in the form of improvement grants.

Improvement grants are awarded by local authorities to cover a proportion of improvement and renovation costs. A number of different types of grant are available. One of the main changes initiated under the 1988 Act affected landlords by making most grants discretionary rather than mandatory. At the same time the act also reduced the minimum standard of improvement to be attained. Local authorities have the power to serve a notice on landlords which stipulate by law that repair or renovation work must be done. These notices are served in cases where dwellings are in very poor condition, lacking basic amenities or below set standards. A mandatory grant is usually awarded in these circumstances. Landlords can apply for discretionary grants to carry out repairs, which a local authority might award depending on resources and need. To determine the amount of subsidy a means test is applied to the income of the applicant (either tenant or landlord). Depending on income level (or rental income in the case of landlords) a proportion of costs will be determined that will qualify for subsidy. Grants are allocated on the condition that landlords continue to rent out the property for at least 5 years. If they were to sell the property before this time period was up they could be asked to repay part or all of the grant.

The recent changes that have put more emphasis on discretionary grants will reduce assistance and have serious consequences for the private rented stock, particularly since so many dwellings are already in very poor condition.

The first fiscal encouragement given to landlords for a considerable time was the extension of the BES to cover investments in housing. The Finance Act of 1988 provided incentives for private individuals to invest in rented housing. The BES was originally set up to encourage the supply of capital into small firms that were investing in risk bearing activities. Extending this to investment in private rented dwellings, meant private individuals could invest a minimum of £500 and a maximum of £40 000 by becoming a shareholder of a BES housing company. This investment could then yield a dividend with tax relief at the investor's marginal tax rate and full capital gains tax relief if the shares were disposed of after 5 years. The housing must be let on a purely commercial basis, which excludes housing associations from the scheme. Dwellings must be held for 5 years to get tax relief on capital gains.

Table 8.8 Government housing benefit expenditure to the private rented sector: Great Britain, 1986–1996

Year	Government expenditure on rent allowances[1] (£ million)
1986/87	996
1987/88	1030
1988/89	1055
1989/90	1336
1990/91	1597
1991/92	2322
1992/93	3257
1993/94 (estimate)	3817
1994/95 (plans)	4320
1995/96 (plans)	4900
1996/97 (plans)	5500

[1]Includes payments to housing association and private tenants.

Source: Ford and Wilcox (1994).

On the demand side, the private rented sector is assisted by government expenditure in the form of housing benefit payments to tenants. Although there is a high level of housing benefit eligibility for private rental tenants, the sector has the lowest level of take-up. While 95% of eligible council tenants are estimated to actually receive benefits, the figure is only 88% for private tenants.

Table 8.8 shows how rent allowances have increased from just over £1 billion in 1987/88 to £3.8 billion in 1993/94, and are expected to rise to £5.5 billion in 1996/97. Under the current system, the Department of Social Security (DSS) estimates that rent allowance costs will continue to grow at a rate of 7.1% per annum (Ford and Wilcox, 1994). The data on rent allowances includes payments to both private tenants and housing association tenants. Data from the DSS, for Great Britain, reveals that together these two sectors had 1 290 000 claimants receiving rent allowances in 1992. Of these 949 000 were private rented tenants (for further details, see Ford and Wilcox, 1994).

8.5.5 Rent regulations

Regulations covering rents are complex in the UK and vary according to the different tenancy agreements and types of accommodation. Regulations have changed considerably over the years. Rent controls have existed in the UK in different forms since the First World War. A substantial measure of decontrol was introduced in the 1957 Rent Act. This deregulated rents in the belief that higher rents would mean greater profit and lead to an increase in the supply of private rented dwellings.

The measures did not unfortunately have the desired effect and the sector continued to decline. However, the 1957 Act had further negative consequences that were not anticipated. The legislation allowed for rents in the unfurnished sector to be increased at each new letting, which was encouraging some landlords to intimidate, harass and illegally evict sitting tenants so that rents could be increased. This led in some cases to an increase in homelessness with an already existing housing shortage in the country. This situation was taken advantage of by notorious landlords like one named Rachman, who built up a portfolio of poor quality 'slum' properties in London during the 1950s and 1960s, and because of the housing shortage was able to charge very high rents. This unacceptable face of private renting became known as 'Rachmanism' and influenced the environment in which the Labour government introduced the 1965 Rent Act (Kemp, 1992). This introduced a system of regulated tenancies and 'fair rents' that could be assessed by independent rent officers. Rents were set according to the characteristics of the property, and at the same time security was returned to tenants in unfurnished accommodation. Further changes in rent regulation were introduced in 1974.

The new assured and shorthold tenancies introduced in 1980 and modified in 1988 have decontrolled rents for new tenancies and, in the case of short-

Table 8.9 Rented dwellings, tenancy types and rent levels: England, 1988–1993

	Assured			Regulated						
	Shorthold	Other post-1988	All	With registered rent	Without registered rent	Resident landlord	Not accessible to public	No security	Protected shorthold and pre-1989 assured	All
Thousands of tenancies										
1989	–	–	–	472	599	109	508	62	65	1814
1990	143	357	500	322	268	89	482	87	38	1787
1993	826	377	1203	244	162	158	376	22	–	2166
Percentage of all private tenancies										
1988	–	–	–	26	33	6	28	3	4	100
1990	8	20	28	18	15	5	27	5	2	100
1993	38	17	56	11	7	7	17	1	–	100
Rent (£ per week)										
1988	–	–	–	21	36	24	31	38	41	30
1990	66	61	62	27	36	35	31	30	46	43
1993	80	60	74	31	32	41	43	50	–	60

[1]Numbers and percentages include tenancies which are rent free, but these are excluded from the average rent figures.
Source: DOE (1994).

holds, allowed limited-term contracts. Of all lettings, in a survey carried out by the Association of Residential Letting Agencies (ARLA) in 1992, 70% were assured shorthold tenancies (Joseph Rowntree Foundation, 1993b). However, the increase in the number of assured shorthold tenancies has also led to an increase in average rent levels. Table 8.9 shows the increases in rent levels by type of tenancy, since 1988. The data shows how the number of assured tenancies (rather than regulated tenancies) has increased between 1990 and 1993, from 28 to 56% of all tenancies. Regulated rent tenancies have been declining rapidly as contracts are terminated, and will continue to do so in the future.

8.5.6 Evaluation

There has been a growing convergence of opinion in the UK on the need for reform in the private rented sector. There is arguably a need for more rented housing (see Chapters 5 and 6 on levels of need and shortages). It is unrealistic to expect the social housing sector to meet all of the need: 'for the foreseeable future, the social landlords are unlikely to cater for the more mobile, for the full range of single people, or for those with moderate – not low – incomes. A major contribution to meeting these needs could and should be made by the private landlord sector: a healthy private rented sector can supply extra flexibility, diversity and choice' (Best *et al.*, 1992, pp. 3–4).

However, if the decline in the sector is to be significantly reversed, improvements in financing, subsidization and operation of the sector are necessary to encourage investment and restore a positive reputation. Some of the suggestions for changes in policy and some comparisons with the relative incentives and profitability of the sector in France, Germany and the Netherlands are discussed in Chapter 9.

8.6 ASPECTS OF PRIVATE RENTED HOUSING IN OTHER EUROPEAN COUNTRIES

Table 5.10 shows that the size of the private rented sector across the member states of the European Union varies considerably, reaching highs of 30, 35 and 43% in Luxembourg, Portugal and Germany, respectively, down to lows of 8 and 7% in Ireland and the UK.

In most of the European Union countries there is a declining private rented sector. Provision of private rented housing is divided between two main groups: private individuals and institutional investors. Over time, the balance between the shares of these two groups has been changing. While the number of individual landlords is declining, particularly in Italy, and to a certain extent Portugal, institutional investment in private rental housing is increasing in relative terms. Between 1981 and 1988 in Italy, private individual investors reduced their holdings from 77 to 71% of the total rented stock, while institutional investors increased their share from 5.9 to 8.1% (Ghékiere and Quillot, 1991). Although this is a relatively small change, it does reflect the more European wide experience that a general lack of returns is rendering investment in rented housing unprofitable, particularly for individual investors. Withdrawal from the private rented sector, as dwellings are sold or put to alternative use, is true in Portugal, Spain, Denmark and Luxembourg.

However, the reasons for this become more complex when each country is taken individually. For example, in Denmark high land prices and high building costs throughout the 1980s have, together with a subsidy system that does not encourage investment, contributed to the decline.

In Luxembourg, new investment in the private rented sector was falling during the 1970s and 1980s. There were tight rent controls which fixed initial rent levels and subsequent increases. To try to re-introduce investment into the sector some of these controls were relaxed in 1987 for newly constructed dwellings.

A further notable trend affecting the decline in the private rented sector has been the concurrent increase in the owner-occupied sector. This is particularly apparent in both Spain and Portugal. In Portugal, for example, 50% of new construction was destined for the rented sector in 1970, yet by 1983 this had fallen to 4.8%, as the proportion of new construction for home ownership increased (COFACE, 1990). A similar building boom in the owner-occupied market has been experienced in Spain where increases in speculation and house prices have led to a loss of interest in the private rented sector.

Government intervention in the private rented sector has been high in Europe, usually taking the form of rent controls and tenant protection. Legislation typically provides for regulations on initial rent levels, rent increases and some form of tenant protection. Controls have been particularly strict in Portugal, Luxembourg, Denmark and Ireland. However, as new investments began to fall there was a general relaxing of controls in an attempt to stimulate the market. In many cases this has had only a limited effect on new construction and has left tenants in a weak position.

For example, in Belgium a temporary Rent Act established in 1983 gave all tenants a degree of protection from eviction, yet this was amended in 1985 effectively leaving landlords to decide whether to have a contract stipulating tenants' rights. There is no legislation governing minimum or maximum rent levels and although only annual revisions are permitted, little tenant protection exists. With no national housing benefit system there is a lack of guidelines relating the level of rent to the tenants' ability to pay and no direct housing support for low income households.

New incentives within the private rented sector in a number of countries seem to have been having only a limited effect on new construction levels. At the same time there is increasing concern about evidence which shows poor conditions and low quality levels concentrated in older private rented housing. There is still a significant role that private renting might play. Housing shortages have become more apparent. The lack of investment that many countries are experiencing in this sector is likely to contribute to increasing problems in the future. The prospects for the future and possibilities of new policy measures will be examined in Chapter 9.

9 | The changing position of private rented housing in Europe

In Chapter 8 we examined the operation of private rented housing, particularly in France, Germany, the Netherlands and the UK, and we followed the trends of the sector over recent decades. Some similarities in terms of decline and policy issues have been identified. However, differences between the countries, particularly between the UK and other European countries, are very significant. The private rented sector in the UK stands out as (1) experiencing the greatest decline and (2) currently being the smallest in the European Union.

This chapter examines some of the differences and similarities. It then explains some of the reasons for private renting being more significant in certain countries than in others and, in particular, examines the reasons for the decline in the sector in the UK.

Furthermore, it will advance some explanations for the lack of success in reviving the private rented sector in the UK. This will involve an examination of political attitudes to the sector, the types of households in need and the shortage of private rented housing. It will consider some government responses to need and look at why policy initiatives have been ineffective in stimulating a lasting recovery in the sector.

Finally, it will examine the prospects for private renting in Europe, particularly in the UK, and consider whether there are experiences of private renting in other countries that might suggest ways of reviving private rented housing in UK.

9.1 THE DECLINE OF THE PRIVATE RENTED SECTOR IN EUROPE

There has been a decline in the private rented sector in most European countries. Data in tables from the previous chapter show the extent of the decline. In France 32% of all dwellings were in the private rented sector in 1963; latest estimates show the current level to be around 20%. In the Netherlands the size of the sector fell from 47% in 1950 to 15% in 1990. The sharpest decline has however been in the UK where private renting fell from 53% of all dwellings in 1950 to just 8% in 1990. The data shows that the trends in decline have been somewhat different between the countries. In the UK the greatest decline was between 1950 and 1970; in France the decline was less dramatic and much more gradual over the past four decades; the Netherlands also followed a more gradual pattern, but experienced a sharp drop between 1975 and 1980. These trends coincide with political and economic events and policy changes towards the sector in the respective countries and are discussed in the previous chapter.

It is interesting to note, however, that private renting sector in Germany has not experienced a similar decline. While levels of new development in the sector fell towards the end of the 1980s, legislation introduced in 1989 provided incentives for investors to remain in and to enter the market to meet the growing demand from householders.

One of the major arguments put forward to explain a reduction in, or a low level of private rented housing, particularly in the UK, has been the existence of rent controls. This is emphasized in much of the literature. For example, Minford *et al.* (1987) maintain rent control played 'a major role' in the decline of the sector in the UK even though it was not necessarily 'the major cause' of decline. Ricketts (1987), too, suggests that rent controls are one of the major factors but also puts forward additional major contributory factors, such as increasing investment in owner-occupation. Other works have attributed a lesser role to rent controls. These include Kemp (1988) and Harloe (1985).

Some studies claim that controls have had a direct effect in lowering the rate of construction of private rented dwellings in other countries (Gyourko, 1990). For example, in France in the early 1980s, the imposition of strict controls led to a decline in production in the sector. The size of the sector dropped from 26% of the stock in 1978 to 22% in 1984. This represented a fall in the number of private rented dwellings of 369 000. At the same time many landlords were removing dwellings from the stock because of low returns. Gyourko also makes a direct connection between British policy which has favoured rent controls and the small size of the private renting sector. He goes on to argue that rent controls, for this and other reasons, are ineffective and suggest that they should be eliminated as a form of government intervention (Gyourko, 1990, pp. 781–791).

However, while rent controls do seem to have had some effect on the sector, they can only be part of the cause of decline in the UK. Maclennan puts the role of rent controls into perspective: 'Landlords invest in an asset such as housing because of the net rate of return and the risks associated with that class of investment relative to other forms of investment, including other forms of housing investment. Similarly households choose between renting and owning not solely as a function of the price of rental units but because of the relative price of owned housing, the range of quality offered and the other costs and benefits associated with particular tenures, including costs of movement' (Maclennan, 1988, pp. 163–164).

Rent controls therefore also work together with many other factors to reduce both landlords' incentives to invest and householders' propensity to demand rented dwellings. This accords with the theoretical exposition on rent controls in Chapter 3 (Section 3.7). Evidence in Chapter 8 shows how other regulations relating to landlord and tenant contractual arrangements have affected rent levels and behaviour in the sector across Europe. Where strict regulations are written into contracts, including length of tenancy, powers for eviction *and* rent controls, evidence suggests that landlords become less inclined to continue to let their properties and prospective private landlords are discouraged from investing in new construction.

For example, strict contractual regulations in France such as specific conditions for termination of tenancies and rent increases may have contributed to the decline of the sector. Deregulation since the late 1980s has reduced some of these barriers to investing in private rented dwellings but nevertheless led to dramatic rent increases causing hardship for tenants.

The pattern of deregulation and rising rents is similar in many countries. Whilst in the past tenants may have benefited from greater security in their tenancy agreements, deregulation policies do appear to be favouring investors and landlords. A further influence on investment in this sector is the rate of return on private rented dwellings. Some of the data given in Chapter 8 shows how rented dwellings have fared in comparison to other investment types. For example, Table 8.2 shows how in France the short-term yields on housing are significantly lower than yields on shares and bonds. In the UK too there is considerable evidence that poor relative returns are a major disincentive to investment.

In the Netherlands it is thought that the need for private renting is not great, and there are few incentives for investors. Households in the Netherlands benefit from a large and good quality social rental sector capable of providing housing for both low and middle income tenants. This has taken some pressure off the demand for private renting.

In Germany the high rate of return has continued to attract new investment. Tax incentives have historically been very generous, and have even been increased (1989) in response to housing market conditions and rising demand.

A further feature of the decline in private renting has been the changes in the control of the private rented stock between private individual landlords and institutional investors. Over time there have been common trends in the changing ownership of private rented dwellings. The two main groups who have historically invested in private rented dwellings are private individuals and institutions (particularly insurance companies and pension funds).

Insufficient returns on property and an increase in other problems associated with renting privately (management costs, problem tenants, etc.) has contributed to a change in the nature of investors in private renting. For the larger institutional investors the prime motive for entering into the market has been financial. A degree of inertia and less sensitivity to financial returns has kept some smaller investors in the sector.

9.2 WHY IS PRIVATE RENTING LESS SIGNIFICANT IN THE UK?

Despite problems of definition, it is clear that the private rented housing sector is significantly larger in all the other European Union countries (except Ireland) than in the UK and the sector has declined less in other countries than in the UK.

The reasons for the larger private rented sectors are the results of market conditions and government activity over a long period of time, and simple uni-causal explanations based on observations of current circumstances are of limited value. We can, however, argue that for the countries examined, there are sets of factors which have made both demand lower and supply higher than in the UK. The demand factors are related, from the household's viewpoint, to the cost and availability of substitute accommodation, and the supply factors are related, from the landlord's viewpoint, to the returns on investment in rented housing, taking account of the risks and the returns associated with alternative investments.

Demand has been higher in some countries because of the very small stock of public rented housing. This is especially the case in Germany where households who could not afford or did not wish to enter the owner-occupied sector have, in large numbers, had to turn to the private sector.

Demand for private renting has, in certain cases, been enhanced by the cost of owner-occupation. Average house prices in large West German towns in 1987 were estimated to be between seven and eight times the annual gross income of industrial workers (Leutner, 1987), and calculations based on 1984 figures suggest that the average UK manual worker needed to work 9165 hours to buy the average UK house compared with 20 453 hours in West Germany (Eurostat, 1986).

The periodic cost of home ownership is influenced by (1) the type of housing finance system, which in turn affects the cost of credit, and (2) government subsidies. These factors have worked to keep down periodic costs in the UK compared with Germany. In the 1950s and 1960s the lack of long-term credit for house purchase was also a serious impediment to the growth of home ownership in France.

There are certain groups for whom the propensity to rent appears to be higher in many countries, e.g. young persons, single person households and mobile households (Howenstine, 1981). The demand for private renting by young households has been reduced, relatively, in the UK by the high levels of owner-occupation in younger age groups. Even countries with higher overall levels of home ownership do not have the very large proportions of young owner-occupiers that have existed in Britain. This must have a significant relative effect on the demand for private rented housing.

Housing allowance systems have supported the demand for private housing in other countries. While a national system of rent allowances has existed since 1972 in the UK, allowances may have had a more significant effect in reducing the proportion of household income devoted to housing than in raising the demand for renting. Since the 1970s housing allowance systems have, with increasing significance in each of the countries, given lower income households income supplements which have been a positive function of income. This has been true of the German Wohngeld, the French Aide Personnalisée au Logement and the Dutch Individuele Huursubsidie. Without this assistance, demand for private renting would almost certainly have been significantly lower in each country.

On the supply side, a variety of factors have combined to make private rented housing a better investment in other countries than in the UK. These factors have related both to the revenue from, and the costs of, the investment.

Despite various forms of rent controls in the 1950s and 1960s, a range of direct subsidies helped promote new construction and the continuing supply of rented housing. In each country except the UK some form of direct cash assistance, cheap loans or tax concession was available. While the 1970s and 1980s saw rather less direct assistance, cheap finance, for at least a proportion of the stock, and tax concessions, for all the private rented stock, have been available in other countries. In the UK tax incentives in the residential BES only had a limited impact due to their very short-term nature.

Returns to renting have been enhanced by the gradual lifting of controls in France and Germany. The stronger continuing rent controls in the Netherlands have been compensated by on-going subsidies, where, it is argued, rent controls have necessitated subsidies and there is a 'virtual absence of non-subsidized construction of rental housing' (Oosterhaven and Klunder, 1988).

A variety of measures have been used in other countries to provide low cost finance for the construction, improvement or purchase of housing for rental. In some cases the state supplied cheap finance as, for example, under the 1950 and 1956 Federal Housing Acts in West Germany and with the Crédit Foncier loans from 1950 in France. In other cases, lump sum subsidies were related to loan costs as, for example, under measures introduced in 1950 in the Netherlands.

It can be argued that direct subsidies to private housing have declined, but that very significant indirect subsidies in the form of tax concessions have made private renting a more attractive investment (particularly in France and Germany) than in the UK. The much less favourable taxation treatment in the UK helps in a large measure to explain the difference in the net profitability of private renting between the UK and the other countries. This has been illustrated by the data given in Chapter 8.

There has been widespread concern for many years that the private rented sector has not been supported or utilized to the extent that was needed in the UK, especially when comparisons with other countries were made. As early as 1965, a section of the Milner Holland Report contrasting private renting in Paris, Copenhagen, Amsterdam and Hamburg, stated 'it is clear that in most of the cities examined, governments have assumed more comprehensive responsibilities than our own has adopted for regulating and revising rents, for securing the rights of tenants to remain in their accommodation and for controlling the distribution of rented housing' but in addition 'it is clear that governments in most of the other countries we studied have given more encouragement for the building of private rented housing', while in Britain, 'private landlords and their tenants have not been subsidized, either directly or indirectly, to the extent that they have in other countries' (Committee of Enquiry into Housing in Greater London, 1965, pp. 215–216 and 223).

More recently there have been arguments for a more comprehensive policy toward the sector, with the provision of incentives, clear regulations and more certainty for both tenants and landlords (for further discussion, see e.g. Harloe, 1985; Kemp, 1988; Best et al., 1992; Crook et al., 1995). Much of this recent literature has responded to policy changes implemented in an attempt to revive private renting.

Political attitudes have influenced the fortunes of private renting. The British political system lacks continuity and consensus in its approach to housing policy as a whole. This has had a substantial impact on the private rented sector, in particular, because of the need to gain the long-term confidence of investors. Private investors will anticipate future policy changes as new governments come to power and consequently continuous levels of investment will not be maintained. In the UK support for private renting has been attached to a particular political party, historically the Conservative party. However as the sector has declined, despite lip service given by politicians on the right to the case for revival, the political significance of the sector has inevitably fallen. Private sector landlords do not command many votes and do not have an effective political lobby.

This is an area where the UK, again, differs from other European countries. There exists, particularly in Germany, France and the Netherlands, a greater degree of political consensus on many housing policy issues. In practice this means that consecutive governments have often reached agreements on policies that make major changes to the housing system and there is little evidence of one political party specifically promoting or discouraging any one tenure type.

9.3 WHAT DOES THE EXPERIENCE OF OTHER COUNTRIES SUGGEST ABOUT WAYS OF REVIVING PRIVATE RENTED HOUSING IN THE UK?

Examining the situation in other countries should make one realize that the odds are stacked firmly against the private rented sector in Britain. It should also alert us to the wide range of alternative means of promoting private renting that exist elsewhere. There is indeed much to be learnt from this sort of comparative analysis. As the House of Commons Environment Committee (HMSO, 1982, pp. xlv–xlvi) noted '...if further attempts are made to generate significant investment in private rented housing, certain aspects of the foreign experience would repay close examination' and new forms of support may be necessary: 'other possible mechanisms by which assistance could be provided include some wider ranging American and European subsidy systems aimed at both landlords and tenants'.

A number of factors have been put forward that characterize the situation of the private rented sector in the UK, in comparison to other European countries.

In contrast to the UK (Housing Research Foundation, 1989; Best *et al.*, 1992):

- Private landlords often provide general needs housing.
- Renting from a landlord is seen as perfectly normal.
- Landlords do not in general have the poor image that they have in Britain.
- Although in many countries the private rented sector is smaller in size than it once was, it still usually accounts for a significant share of the housing stock.
- New construction for private rental still occurs on a not insignificant scale.
- Tax incentives for private landlords are of long standing and pervasive in many industrial nations.
- Support for the publicly rented sector in the past and for the owner-occupied sector more recently, has not been as strong as in Britain.

In its efforts to revive the private rented sector the government has deregulated rents, introduced new terms for tenancy agreements and from 1988 to 1993 encouraged investment in the residential BES.

While the number of privately rented dwellings increased from 1.8 to 2.05 million between 1988 and 1993 (Down et al., 1994), this is likely to be less an indication of a long-term response to deregulation and more a short-term response to tax incentives and the slump in the housing market.

The government's attempt at encouraging the supply side through the residential BES has been described as being a short-term, if expensive, success. The following points can be noted in connection with the scheme: 'It has generated the first significant wave of new investment in the private rented sector for half a century. The dwellings supplied by BES landlords have been of a higher standard than exists in much of the existing private rented sector. It has brought new property companies into private letting (whereas only 10% of all lettings are currently owned by companies). It has brought the venture capital industry back into touch with private housing to let. It has shown that it is politically viable to provide subsidies to private landlords in Britain' (Best et al., 1992, p. 15).

However, there are drawbacks with the system. While is was an aim of the government to 'kick start' the private rented sector through this initiative, and evidence clearly shows that there is both demand for private rented dwellings and a willingness to supply them when returns are worthwhile, the residential BES has been only a temporary measure. Private individuals will sell their shareholdings in order to get tax relief on capital gains, and it is unlikely that the housing companies that have been formed will continue to operate with no further incentives in the future. The scheme has also been costly and the government is unlikely to extend subsidization at the level involved in the BES.

Many studies have debated the costs and benefits of various frameworks and incentives (Maclennan et al., 1991; Best et al., 1992; Crook et al., 1995). Here it will be useful to summarize some of these findings.

What is emerging as a crucial factor in Britain is the need for the introduction of a framework, which includes financial incentives, that will revitalize both the demand and supply sides of private renting. The reforms should be seen as long-term and command political consensus. There is a growing consensus, outside parliament, on the need for a more viable private rented sector. But in political circles this level of agreement has not yet been reached.

It has been suggested that for a revival in the private renting sector to be a success four main issues need to be addressed (Crook, 1992, p. 58):

1. *The role of the private rented sector.* This would require a recognition of the range of households in need or demanding private renting dwellings, including transitional households who are not housed in the social rented

sector. This might include newly formed households in the housing market, young single persons, students, owner-occupiers wishing to rent temporarily, households moving with employment and new one-person households recently separated or divorced. For these household types the private rented sector could provide cheap, flexible ready access short-term accommodation or alternatively better quality housing for those who prefer to rent.

2. *Rate of return required by investors.* To encourage sustained investment in a variable private rented sector landlords must be able to achieve a competitive rate of return. To ensure that this can be established a number of factors must be considered. These include the level of rental income and opportunity for capital gains on property, the level of risk attached to owning private rented dwellings, and their relative liquidity (compared to other investments), the stability of the legal framework in the sector and the reputation attached to private renting.

3. *The level of demand and the need for subsidies.* Demand may be promoted by a rising number of households who find the risks of owner-occupation on a low income too high and, were it a viable option, would prefer to rent. At the same time if changes in the status of private renting are to be achieved, changes which involve all tenures are necessary. Private renting is more successful elsewhere because of factors influencing owner-occupation and public rented housing, not just the private rented sector. One sector cannot be considered in isolation. If public sector housing continues to wane, there is more of an opportunity for both the supply and demand for private renting to increase, if the necessary conditions prevail. At the same time, however, to ensure that this demand can be met the capability of the private sector to meet this demand must be increased by cutting costs of supply. Two significant sources of cost reductions stand out from the examination of other countries. These are the availability of low cost, long-term finance and generous deductions for taxation purposes. Depreciation allowances for private rented investment exist elsewhere, but not in the UK. The taxation position of both builders and landlords in the UK needs to be re-examined. Significant depreciation allowances and capital gains tax exemptions are important features of the German system, in particular, which should be seriously considered. Any changes in the financing costs and taxation position of suppliers of private rented housing need to be underwritten in some sort of form, so that any additional assistance is certain for several years ahead. It has been noted that support in other countries is on a long-term basis. In the process of arguing for support, careful attention needs to be given to the definition and interpretation of 'subsidy'. It can be argued that private rented housing thrives in Germany without subsidies. However, important proportions of the stock have been supplied in the past with the aid of direct subsidies, even if they are not getting them to

the same degree now and, most importantly, indirect subsidies in the form of tax concessions are significant. It is important to note, again, that in Germany these 'subsidies' have had, according to analyses within the country, two effects – increased supply and lower rents.
4. *The need for regulations.* The degree of control and regulation in any proposals for the private rented sector will have a vital effect on its success. These controls would relate to the level of freedom in rent setting, variations in rents across the stock, the range of tenancies and terms available, the possible registration of tenancies, and the approval of landlords who are to receive subsidies.

Some form of regulation in private renting may be necessary to provide the sector with the stability of cross-party support and to improve its reputation (Crook, 1992). Rent controls, however, continue to be a contentious issue with disagreements over whether fewer controls might be more likely to encourage investment or, alternatively, whether tight controls could lead to further problems of monitoring and increase risks.

A number of recommendations for the private rented sector have been made following the analysis of a national survey of private landlords undertaken in December 1993 and January 1994 by the Joseph Rowntree Foundation (Crook *et al.*, 1995).

Policy options that are suggested include:

1. Levelling the playing field by reducing owner-occupier's tax reliefs; reducing or eliminating tax paid by landlords; granting landlords the right to set depreciation against taxable income.
2. Allowing the establishment of Authorized Housing Investment Trusts (AHITs). While this option costs nothing in public or tax expenditure, AHITs must first be convinced of the competitiveness of returns and be encouraged to have confidence in investments.
3. Providing financial assistance to close the 'yield gap' and encourage and retain investment in the private rented sector. The form that these financial incentives might take include capital allowances, remitting tax incentives on rental income and realized capital gains or grants. What specific form these payments should take and what level of return an investment might yield are documented elsewhere (Kemp, 1988; Best *et al.*, 1992; Crook *et al.*, 1995).

The evidence from other countries does not point to a thriving 'free market' private rented sector. Rather it points in most cases to one of decline in the face of growing home ownership. However, it also shows, in the case of Germany, the possibility of contractual relationships between the state and private landlords which can provide fiscal incentives that increase returns while at the same time limiting landlords' freedom of contract with tenants.

The most significant lesson to be learnt from examining the 'private rented sector' in other countries is that it does not exist anywhere in the sense of a textbook 'free market' where demand and supply interact unimpeded. Where the sector is large the state supports both demand and supply.

Affordability | 10

In this chapter we will consider the principles associated with affordability and look at the relationships between incomes, expenditure and payments for housing in France, Germany, the Netherlands and the UK. The implications of affordability problems for housing policy will be set out. We will examine the meaning of the affordability problem and look at the different approaches that are taken to tackle the problem.

10.1 DEFINING AFFORDABILITY

We found in Chapter 2 that a major aim of housing policy in the countries of the European Union has been to secure decent housing for all households at a price within their means. When the price is not 'within their means' it can be argued that there is an 'affordability' problem. In Chapters 3 and 4 we identified some of the policy instruments that can be used to close the gap between the cost of providing rented housing of an acceptable standard and what households are able to pay. The basic elements of affordability have thus already been outlined. The affordability problem has, however, become such a focus of attention in the UK and other countries, that we now examine the concept of affordability in more depth.

An oft quoted definition of affordability states that 'affordability is concerned with securing some given standard of housing (or different standards) at a price or rent which does not impose in the eye of some third party (usually government) an unreasonable burden on household incomes' (Maclennan and Williams, 1990, p. 9).

There must, to operationlize this definition, be some judgement about what households *should* pay for housing. Much of the data recorded on the relationship between incomes and rents is inevitably about what households *do* pay. Some discussion is about what households *might* have to pay if some event occurred such as housing association grant levels being cut.

There are thus three affordability measures:

1. 'Should' affordability measures are normative and only definable with respect to the appropriate value judgements,
2. 'Do' affordability measures are positive and can be determined empirically.
3. 'Might' affordability measures involve some sort of forecasting.

Affordability is usually discussed in terms of a relationship between household income and payments for housing. Sometimes it is described in terms of the proportions of total household expenditure which are devoted to housing. The corollary of this is that there is some proportion of income left for expenditure on other goods and services and what this figure 'should be', 'is' or 'would be if...' can equally be the subject of debate and/or measurement.

A lack of precise detail in the definition is often associated with sloppy thinking and can lead to misleading comparisons. The exact definitions of *payments for housing*, *household income* and *household expenditure* need to be apparent for any useful comparisons, policy discussions and debates on the logistics of implementing changes in practice. To give some examples to illustrate the point:

1. *Payments for housing* might include only rent for 'space' or it might include heating and water charges or other service charges. In the owner-occupied sector, mortgage payments might be considered or some measure of imputed rent used. The payments could be gross or net of rent rebates, tax reliefs or other assistance.
2. *Household income* could be gross or net. It could be only from income from work or it could include housing allowances and/or additional state benefits. It could include or exclude tax, national insurance and other deductions. It might be that only 'disposable income' is considered which takes account of deductions for various items.
3. *Household expenditure* could be gross or net, with the latter being adjusted for taxes and subsidies.

With the definitions clarified and agreed, for any consideration of what households 'should', 'do' or 'might' pay, we need to be clear about *which* households are to be considered.

Some affordability measures are average proportions for large populations. The macro housing expenditure ratios are averages for the whole populations of countries. Some figures are estimates for all households in a given tenure; others relate to households in different income groups; some to differences between the tenures; some relate to age.

The affordability measure is typically presented at a point in time. The consideration is *current* housing payments, incomes and/or expenditure in a static framework. A consideration of variations in the items over the life cycle of households would produce another set of measures.

To be used in any definitive comparative sense, whether internationally or within a country, an affordability measure must ideally examine *what* is the quantity and quality of the housing which is, or might be, consumed.

10.2 AFFORDABILITY AND POLICY

Affordability cannot be separated from the concept of housing quality. Governments may be concerned that households acquire housing of a minimum standard. Thus we might identify:

$H*$ = the volume of housing of an acceptable standard which a household should consume each month

The question then arises as to how this minimum standard relates to household income and how much expenditure is required to achieve $H*$.

Let:

$$Y* = \text{monthly household income}$$
$$E_h = \text{expenditure required to purchase } H*$$
$$E_h = P_h \times N_h$$
$$P_h = \text{price per unit of acceptable housing}$$
$$N_h = \text{number of units of acceptable housing deemed appropriate for a given household each month}$$

There might be concern that if $H*$ is purchased there will be insufficient income $(Y* - E_h)$ left to buy other goods and services.

Let:

$O*$ = a bundle of non-housing goods and services of an acceptable size and composition to be consumed each month
$$E_o = \text{expenditure required to purchase } O*$$

Then:

$$E_o = P_o \times N_o$$
$$P_o = \text{price per unit of other goods and services}$$
$$N_o = \text{number of units of such goods and services deemed to be appropriate for a given household each month}$$

$H*$ and $O*$ have to be pre-determined. They will vary with the composition of the household. We may take the composition of the household to be given although governments might wish to pass judgement on the existence of certain household types and decide that there should be no normative $H*$ and $O*$ measures for them!

From a government's point of view, a satisfactory position might be defined as:

$$Y^* \geq E_h + E_o$$

Thus household income is sufficient to buy both decent housing and enough other goods and services according to standards set by governments.

Assuming there are no supply constraints on H^* or O^*, three formulations of the 'unsatisfactory' position are:

$$Y^* < E_h + E_o \qquad (10.1)$$
$$E_o > Y^* - E_h \qquad (10.2)$$
$$E_h > Y^* - E_o \qquad (10.3)$$

All three formulations do, of course, amount to the same thing but the perception of the problem and the appropriate responses is different in each case. In equation (10.1) the problem is that household income is too low and in equation (10.2) that the required expenditure on housing is too high. In equation (10.3) the problem is formulated as the expenditure required to purchase a satisfactory bundle of other goods and services being greater than that which can be met from residual income (for another formulation of an economic approach to affordability, see Hancock, 1993).

The appropriate policy responses might be to tackle any of the influences on E_h, Y^* and E_o. Thus, there might be policies to influence prices generally or the price of housing in particular. There might be policies to raise income generally or to raise incomes selectively in the light of the values for E_h and E_o. There might be policies to reduce expenditure on housing, without unduly affecting the volume of consumption, by adopting tactics which reduce the consumption price of housing either generally or selectively in the light of the values of E_o and Y^*.

There is logically no way of determining whether or not the 'satisfactory position' is achieved by arranging that E_h/Y^* conforms to some sort of magic rent-to-income ratio. The notion of defining affordability in terms of such ratios or giving a universally applicable percentage of income or expenditure which *should* represent the maximum devoted to housing does not help to solve the problem.

It does not, furthermore, necessarily follow that the problem lies with the price of housing. If governments do decide to influence the price of housing consumption they need to (1) understand how prices are currently determined and (2) take a view on what they want house prices and rents to represent.

It is clear that one cannot separate the issue of the price of housing, or expenditure on housing, from a set of inter-related issues. Housing affordability cannot be isolated from broader questions about the level and distribution of income. Nor can it be isolated from policy on a wide range of factors, including social security payments, which influence the ability of households to consume a satisfactory level of non-housing goods and services.

10.3 THE MACRO HOUSING CONSUMPTION EXPENDITURE RATIO

The macro housing expenditure ratio has been calculated for 12 European Union countries for the period 1970–1990 and is illustrated in Figures 10.1 and 10.2. The methodology adopted by Menkveld (1993) was employed.

To calculate the ratio the following equation was used:

Macro housing expenditure ratio = gross rent, fuel and power expenditure/final consumption expenditure of resident households

(Two sets of data have been used in calculations over the 20 year period – the detailed tables of the OECD National Accounts years 1970–1982 (1983) and 1978–1990 (1991). While data is in the same format in both editions of the National Accounts, it should be noted that some degree of continuity was lost between 1977 and 1978. The latest available data has been used where possible. Calculations of housing consumption ratios were made using 'current prices' of consumption volumes.) There are several limitations ('which can lead to distortions in cross-country comparisons'), in basing a comparison on this formula (for a full discussion, see Menkveld 1993).

Firstly, the method of defining 'consumption' in statistics on private household consumption and government consumption in the different countries could produce misleading variations. Quantities of private versus government consumption can differ depending on the route of housing subsidies. For example, subsidies weighted to households will tend to increase levels of household consumption; while those weighted to buildings will reduce housing consumption of private households.

Secondly, comparisons of the housing consumption data must also take account of the different items included in national housing statistics. For example, the inclusion of items such as maintenance, repair work, services or whether second homes are included, but especially differences in definition of the value of imputed rent.

Thirdly, using percentages as an indicator also has disadvantages as this is only a relative measure and can mask real volume changes in housing consumption. While, 'an international comparison of relative housing consumption ... is hindered by the relatively poor data that international organizations like the OECD provide' this measure was 'the best available' (Menkveld, 1993, p. 48) and the ratio can serve as an indicator of housing consumption trends.

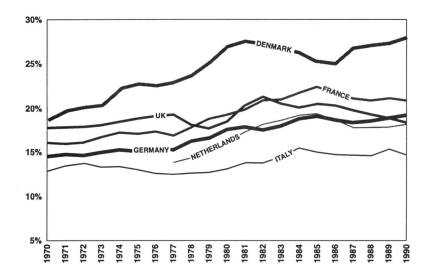

Figure 10.1 Macro housing consumption expenditure ratio I: selected European countries, 1970–1990. Source: OECD (1983, 1991).

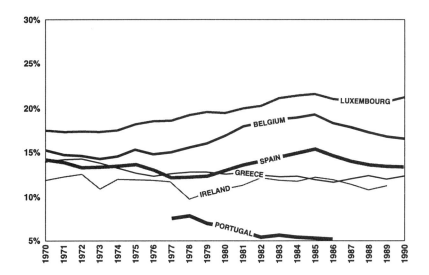

Figure 10.2 Macro housing consumption expenditure ratio II: selected European countries, 1970–1990. Source: OECD (1983, 1991).

From Figures 10.1 and 10.2 it is clear that over time most of the countries have experienced some increase in the ratio. However, Greece, Ireland, Portugal and Spain actually saw a decrease in the ratio during the period. The graphs for a number of countries have followed similar patterns, experiencing a steady increase in the ratio up to about the mid-1980s and then levelling off, or even declining, after that time. The fall in some countries (e.g. the UK) brought the ratio almost down to the 1970 level.

Denmark clearly saw the greatest increase in its housing consumption ratio over the period, with a rise of 9.5 percentage points. France, Germany, Luxembourg and the Netherlands all increased by around 4 percentage points, while Italy, the UK and Belgium only rose slightly overall.

For some countries it is possible to examine the gross rent in isolation from household fuel and power payments as a measure of housing expenditure. This narrower definition of housing payments, which includes rents and imputed rents for owner-occupiers as well as water charges, has been used for the calculations in Table 10.1.

Table 10.1 Gross rents as a percentage of household consumption expenditure: European Union, 1978, 1990

	1978	1990	Change	Relative volume change	Relative price change
Denmark	18.31	22.99	3.68	0.97	2.71
France	11.87	15.58	3.71	1.85	1.86
Germany	13.35	16.70	3.35	2.53	0.82
Greece	10.26	9.25	−1.01	1.46	−2.47
Ireland	4.73	5.90	1.17	1.20	−0.03
Italy	9.87	11.24	1.37	−2.10	3.37
Luxembourg	13.24	14.88	1.64	−0.34	1.98
Netherlands	10.09	14.32	4.23	2.19	2.04
UK	13.41	14.88	1.47	−1.08	2.50

Insufficient data for Belgium, Portugal and Spain. Calculations are percentage of household expenditure devoted to housing at current prices.

Source: OECD (1991) and own calculations.

As with the macro housing consumption expenditure ratio shown in Figures 10.1 and 10.2, for most countries the proportion of expenditure devoted to rent is rising over time; Greece is the only exception in Table 10.1. By using the OECD data on expenditures in constant prices as well as in current prices it has been possible to divide the changes in gross rents from 1978 to 1990 into a volume and price component. Thus, for example, in the case of Denmark of the 3.68 percentage points increase in the average proportion of household expenditure devoted to gross rents, 0.97 percentage points were due to an additional volume of housing consumption and 2.71 percentage points to an increase in relative prices. In the case of the UK (and Italy and Luxembourg), the volume change was negative. Thus, using constant prices the volume of expenditure devoted to housing fell (15.37% in 1978 to 14.29% in 1990 in the UK) so in the UK relatively less housing compared to other goods and services was being consumed. The method used here is a variation on the method used to calculate 'volume mutations' and 'price mutations' used by Menkveld (1993, pp. 43–48).

For most countries the increase in housing expenditure is partly associated with a rise in the relative price of housing (Ireland and Greece are exceptions in Table 10.1). This rise in relative prices is likely to be, in part, a function of falling production subsidies.

In Table 10.2 a number of housing cost measures have been calculated in real terms for 1992 comparing the position with 1980. The UK stands out as the country with the greatest increases in real housing costs over this period with rents in the social housing sector rising by 92% in real terms.

Table 10.2 Indicators of changes in housing costs [index numbers in real terms 1992 (1980 = 100)]: European Union, 1992

	'Housing costs'	*Social rents*	*Private rents*
Belgium	92.3		
Denmark	118.3	111.8	111.8
Germany	104.3	122.2	105.0
Greece	92.4		91.5
Spain	95.6	95.6	95.6
France	116.0		116.5
Ireland[1]	83.8		
Italy[1]	108.3		
Luxembourg[1]	92.2		91.3
Netherlands	115.6	142.2	134.8
Portugal[1]	116.1		32.2
UK	143.5	191.7	168.6

[1]1991.

Housing costs = gross rent fuel and power in private consumption.

Source: European Commission (1993) and own calculations.

10.4 COUNTRY BY COUNTRY RELATIONSHIPS BETWEEN RENTS AND INCOMES

A consideration of relationships between household rents and incomes at a more micro level reveals similar trends across Europe. Namely, that households are spending an increasing amount of their income on housing. This is examined below in more detail for specific countries.

10.4.1 France

In France an increasing proportion of incomes are being devoted to rent and housing costs. Between 1984 and 1988 the average rent to income ratios of French households increased from 12.5% to nearly 15% (Bessy, 1992).

The fact that tenants are generally devoting a larger proportion of their income to rents is not surprising when it is noted that rents have been increasing at a higher rate than incomes. During the period 1984–1988 incomes rose by 15% while expenditure on housing increased by 37% (over the same time inflation was 14%). As in most countries the proportion of income devoted to housing is highest for those on the lowest incomes and lowest for those on the highest incomes. Table 10.3 shows how the rent to income ratio changes between the different tenures.

Table 10.3 Rent to income ratios: France, 1988

	Gross rent to income ratio		Net rent to income ratio	
	Paris region	Provinces	Paris region	Provinces
Households receiving subsidy				
AL	18.5	18.7	10.7	9.9
APL	24.4	27.6	14.4	16.7
Non-beneficiary	15.1	14.5	15.1	14.5
All households	15.7	16.5	14.9	14.3
Owner-occupiers				
APL	32.1	32.0	23.6	22.2
non-beneficiary	20.5	21.4	20.5	21.4
HLM regulated				
APL	19.9	20.0	8.8	7.3
non-beneficiary	11.3	11.7	11.3	11.7
HLM unregulated				
AL	13.0	13.6	6.0	5.3
non-beneficiary	10.2	10.0	10.2	10.0
Free rented sector				
AL	24.1	21.2	15.6	11.3
non-beneficiary	17.4	14.6	17.4	14.6

Source: Bessy (1992).

In 1988 it was the owner-occupiers who spent the highest proportion of their incomes on housing with a ratio of just over 20% for those not receiving benefit but up to 32% for those receiving APL (Allocation Personalisée Logement). In the rented sector, households in the unregulated HLMs devote the lowest proportion of their income to rent – regardless of whether the household receives benefit. This sector also has the lowest ratio once subsidy has been subtracted with households paying only 5.3% of income on rent in the provinces.

In contrast, those tenants having the highest rent to income ratio are in the private rented sector, reaching a level of 24.1% in the Paris region, for those receiving AL (Allocation Logement) and 17.4% for non-beneficiaries. In the rented sector households receiving housing allowances have comparable incomes yet, as Table 10.3 shows, the net rent to income ratio in the private rented sector is double that of the HLM sector. The private rented sector also has the greatest difference between the Paris region and the provinces.

The two sectors with the highest net rent to income ratios in 1988, private renting and owner-occupation, have experienced the largest increases since 1984. This increase has been due in the main to increases in rents or in loan charges which have not been compensated by a subsequent increase in subsidies. A major cause of this increase in the private rented sector was the Méhaignerie Law of 1986 which deregulated rents for new tenants in this sector. While rental increases were previously controlled at renewal or revision of contracts, the 1986 Law enabled new contract rents to be set at free market prices, therefore a change in occupancy could also lead to a rental increase. 'In total the contribution to the increases in the rent index of new leases is four or five times higher than that of simple revision or renewal of contracts' (Curci and Taffin, 1991).

In the private rented sector between 1984 and 1988 the average rent per square metre increased by 37%. Of this increase 26.2% was due to rent inflation, which means the effects of any improvements in the quality of the dwelling has been at the rate of about 2.2% per annum over this period (Curci and Taffin, 1991). Rents in this sector have increased further since 1988, as deregulation has continued.

The government is trying to address this problem by increasing incentives to the owner-occupied sector and by introducing a policy to encourage households to move on as income increases – a policy of temporary leases for some social housing is currently under discussion. However, in the meantime many low income households continue to have problems meeting rent costs.

The housing allowance system has important consequences for affordability of housing, especially for low income groups. One in six households (one in three tenants) receive a housing allowance (Curci and Taffin, 1991). Table 10.3 shows the effects of the system on the gross and net rent to income ratio. Considering the gross ratio which includes the housing subsidy it is clear that those in receipt of housing allowances (APL or AL) pay higher proportions of their gross income (including benefits) than do non-recipients.

The data shows that subsidy reduces the rent to income ratio by between 7 and 13 percentage points and, with the exception of owner-occupiers, the housing allowance system leaves households on benefit devoting smaller proportions of their net income to rents than non-beneficiaries. There has been a large increase in expenditures on housing allowances. In the HLM sector, where low income groups are concentrated, the increase in subsidies to households, at 30% (1984–1988), was higher than the increase in household expenditure on rents which was 25%.

10.4.2 Germany

In Germany, the affordability rate has been affected by policy decisions about the supply of housing, especially social housing. The increasing number of properties reverting to private rented status as loans were paid off and the reduction in government subsidies to social housing up to the late 1980s both had adverse effects on the rent burden. Rent increases are also partly a consequence of general rent inflation and an increase in the consumption of rented housing with higher quality housing being consumed. With cuts in object subsidies, more households came to rely on housing allowances. By the end of the 1980s, more than one in 10 households were recipients. However, as in most countries, housing allowances are not paid automatically: an application has to be made. Many eligible households do not apply. This is the problem of 'take-up'. It has been estimated that only half of those entitled actually claim the Wohngeld in Germany. Only about 20% of those who receive Wohngeld are in employment. The remainder are unemployed or are pensioners who are entitled to other benefits, and thus there is a problem of a complex relationship between housing benefits and the social security system generally. The ideal in Germany, as in other countries, might be a fully integrated benefits system covering housing and other benefits.

Affordability issues in Germany are linked to the problem of the 'rent-gap' between the rents of older and newer dwellings as described in Section 8.2.4. Although various policy measures have addressed this long-standing gap it remains as a significant policy issue. The Wohngeld is not sufficiently generous to those in newer housing to close the gap. This is an example of an affordability issue which links in with efficiency and mobility problems and which is largely a consequence of rent setting policy.

Owner-occupiers tend to have a lower rent burden than tenants partly because they tend to have higher incomes. As owner-occupiers' incomes have risen more sharply than those of tenants the former have achieved a more favourable affordability rate (Ulbrich, 1992).

Table 10.4 illustrates the development of the rent to income ratio since 1981 and the effects of the Wohngeld housing allowance. Without the rent allowance, housing costs for households receiving benefit, in 1990, were about 28% of gross income. The reduction after allowances gave a rate of 18%. In 1986 the housing cost ratio was lower and the subsidy effect of Wohngeld was even higher than in 1990.

Table 10.4 Rent burden of tenants in receipt of Wohngeld [average share of housing costs in gross monthly income (%)]: Germany, 1981–1990

	1981	1985	1986	1990
Before Wohngeld	23.5	28.5	26.8	27.9
After Wohngeld	14.8	19.1	16.6	18.0

Source: Ulbrich (1992).

The level of the housing allowance is adjusted every few years in line with inflation. Towards the end of the period housing costs become particularly high in relation to incomes and affordability becomes more of a problem immediately before readjustment occurs. In Table 10.4, for example, the sharp fall in housing costs as a proportion of 'income after Wohngeld' from 1985 to 1986 is largely a consequence of the readjustment that occurred at the end of 1985.

10.4.3 Netherlands

Data on the relationship between rents and incomes in the Netherlands also reveals an increasing rent burden over time. This is illustrated in Table 10.5. Over the period 1982–1993 rents as a proportion of income have increased from 12.6 to 17.1%. Over the period rents increased by 88% compared with only 24% for incomes.

Table 10.5 Housing expenditure ratios by tenure: Netherlands, 1982–1993

	1982	1985	1986	1989	1991	1993
Rental sector						
Net monthly income (Dfl)	2205	2207	2253	2307	2566	2722
gross rent (Dfl)	299	389	401	427	465	518
net rent (Dfl)	279	358	369	390	423	466
rent/income ratio (%)12.6	16.2	16.4	16.9	16.5	17.1	
Home ownership						
net monthly income (Dfl)	2702	2789	2879			
net charges (Dfl)	393	439	423			
charges/income ratio (%)	14.5	15.7	14.7			

Gross rents include individual subsidy for rent; both gross and net rent exclude energy costs and taxes.

Source: COFACE (1989a) and Nationale Woningraad (1993).

For the owner-occupied sector, while only limited data is available, a quite different situation exists. In 1982 costs were more compared to incomes for owner-occupiers than tenants. However, by 1985 rents had increased at higher rate than costs to owner-occupiers and the latter actually fell back again in 1986.

Inequality in the distribution of housing is currently a major problem in the Netherlands. This is due to the 'mismatch' between the incomes of households and the costs of their housing, identified in previous chapters. In the social sector there is 'the widespread use by higher income groups forced into inexpensive subsidized dwellings' (Van Weesep and Van Kempen 1992b, p. 982). This is creating 'affordability' problems for lower income groups forced into high rent dwellings and also putting increasing demands on the housing allowance system to help to pay for this accommodation.

It has been claimed that 'some 50% of households with above median income live in either pre-war or post-war inexpensive rental housing' (Van Weesep and Van Kempen, 1992b, p. 984).

Subsidized social housing has in the past made up a large percentage of new construction, particularly in the cities, so that even though higher income households might wish to move into more expensive rental or owner-occupied housing there is little suitable local supply.

The problems low income households are experiencing are inextricably tied up with the housing allowance system and recent changes made to it. Changes to reduce government expenditure have directly affected low income households. A maximum monthly payment level has been introduced for newly allocated housing (with some exceptions). This has meant that low income households are virtually barred from the newest and best quality housing in the social rented sector. This leaves low income households with even more problems of finding 'affordable' housing. It is claimed that 'minimum income households still pay almost twice as much for housing (in relative terms) as households earning two or three times the modal income' (Van Weesep and Van Kempen 1992a, p. 8).

10.4.4 UK

Approaches to affordability in the UK have been 'tenure orientated' and indeed there are considerable differences between tenures due to financing and rent regulations. However, as in other European countries, there has been a general increase in rents and mortgage repayments since 1970. Table 10.6 shows the increase in expenditure on housing as a percentage of disposable income in the UK between 1970 and 1991.

This shows a 38% increase in the proportion over the time period. The increase from 1980 to 1985 was clearly the greatest, with an increase of 11.4% over the 5 year period. Increases during this period were due largely to policy changes introduced by the Conservative government that came to power in 1979. Central government subsidies to local authorities for housing were cut dramatically and this led to a doubling of local authority rents in the early 1980s. Together with the 'Right to Buy' policy this encouraged more households to move out of council housing into owner-occupied accommodation.

Table 10.6 Household income and expenditure on housing: UK, 1970–1991

	1970	1975	1980	1985	1989	1990	1991
Weekly disposable household income (£)	29.54	58.15	121.50	175.30	247.73	278.17	299.63
Weekly expenditure on housing (£)	3.59	7.14	16.59	26.65	38.35	44.42	50.24
Rent to income ratio (%)	12.15	12.28	13.65	15.20	15.48	15.97	16.77

Disposable income = gross weekly cash (plus imputed income) less income tax, national insurance, etc. Housing expenditure = expenditure on rent, rates, community charge, water, etc. (less housing benefit). Discontinuity occurs, in 1976 and 1983, due to changes in the methods of calculating income and expenditure (see source for details).

Source: CSO (1991) and own calculations.

Further major changes in 1988/89 introduced more deregulation to all rented sector housing (including local authority, housing association and private rented provision) which had considerable 'affordability' consequences for tenants. It has mainly been because of these changes that affordability has become such an important issue in UK housing.

Local authority rented housing is one of the least expensive forms of housing. At the top end of the scale it is households in private rented and owner-occupied (outright owned) accommodation that have the greatest expenditure on housing, with households devoting 25.9 and 23.2% of their total expenditure to housing in 1991 (CSO, 1991). The deregulated private rented sector has experienced the greatest decreases, while at the same time the quality of this accommodation is often much lower (Maclennan and Williams, 1990). Problems of affordability in the owner-occupied sector increased, particularly for those with low incomes, in the early 1990s after mortgage interest rates rose.

For the housing association sector a different measure of affordability has been defined by the National Federation of Housing Associations: 'The current official NFHA guideline on affordability levels is that in taking up assured tenancies, tenants should pay no more than 22% of their net incomes as rent (including service charge)' (NFHA, 1993, p. 34). The calculation of affordability before 1991 expressed the affordability rate as a proportion of median net weekly income for those households with at least one person in work, excluding the household's housing benefit entitlement. The current position is that 'affordability is calculated by dividing the gross rent figure which includes service charges eligible for housing benefit by the household's net income. The net income includes the household's estimated housing benefit entitlement' (NFHA, 1993, p. 35).

However, on average households had an affordability rate of 25% and this rate was as high as 30% for some household types, with 'single elder', 'single adult' and 'lone-parent families' having the highest rates.

The housing benefit system in the UK has been blamed for failing to solve affordability problems for low income groups. This is due to the way in which housing benefit is reduced as income increases. Changes introduced in the early 1980s mean that where an individual's income is just above the level for receiving benefit, significant problems are experienced as the benefit is withdrawn (Whitehead, 1991).

10.5 EUROPEAN AFFORDABILTY COMPARISONS

In France and the UK it is in the private rented and owner-occupied sectors that households experience the highest affordability rates, while in Germany and the Netherlands owner-occupiers appear to be better off. Rents in the social rented sector in all countries are adjusted to below market rents once housing allowances are taken into account. However, low income households, and particularly some household types (such as the unemployed, lone parents, one-person and elderly households), within social housing accommodation still face affordability rates of up to twice those of households with higher incomes.

The housing allowance systems in each country are essential to enable low income households to afford their housing. For the lowest income groups housing allowances reduce their rent to income ratio by up to a half in France and the UK, and by more than a third in Germany. Some housing allowance systems actually set down a 'desirable' amount that households should devote to housing costs and calculate benefits around this. This was, for example, the case in the Netherlands.

In Germany, 'The basic idea behind the German housing allowance scheme is that the payment for adequate accommodation should not exceed 15–25% of the total spending of the household' (Hills *et al.*, 1990, p. 160), payments can, however, reach 30% for individuals. The allowance is calculated according to family income, family size and certain criteria of 'adequacy' which vary across the regions.

Some governments have taken the initiative in specifying percentages which might be reasonable for households to pay and the value of such judgements will be discussed later. However, in contrast, the UK government does not include any explicit definition of an affordability rate, despite professing that housing should be 'affordable' to all households.

10.6 AFFORDABILITY ISSUES

Distinctions were made, at the beginning of this chapter, between affordability in terms of what households 'should', 'do' and 'might' pay for housing.

Policy discussion is largely centred on the 'should' view of affordability as coloured by information on 'do' measures and estimates of 'might' measures.

The implied value judgement of governments seems sometimes to be that for some households higher ratios are better than lower ratios and some households *should* devote more of their income or expenditure to housing. Why? Because the current proportion is too low given the quality consumed. Too low compared to what? This is an area simply of normative judgement. Whether it is better to spend, say, 20% rather than 30% of income on housing is not a question which can be answered with an unambiguous 'yes' or 'no'.

The arguments over affordability have become more significant as governments have reduced expenditure on the direct provision of housing and have expected some households to devote more of their income to housing.

To search in the abstract for some proper or acceptable affordability rate is to search for something worthless. To have some proportion of income or expenditure which *should* be paid for housing is no more valid than a figure for expenditure on say food or clothing or transport. This is not to say that the proportions of income which households *do* allocate to housing are unimportant. They are and changes in these proportions matter. Such changes might be associated with significant changes in welfare.

Affordability is a notion that has come to prominence in the UK in relation to housing association rent levels (Kearns, 1992). This has arisen largely since the 1988 Housing Act introduced changes in the way new developments are funded. This has meant higher rent levels and has caused associations to take more account of the relationships between rents and incomes.

Producing 'should' statements on the basis of international comparisons is dangerous in that one may not be comparing like with like. The problems of definitions, comparability of data and quality in this area are particularly difficult. In 1990 the National Federation of Housing Associations (NFHA) argued that, partly on the basis of evidence that 'rent payments represent between 14 and 19% of income in European countries', a 'maximum of something between 15 and 20% seems reasonable' and 'on the basis of all these indicators, it seems sensible to conclude that, in broad terms, rents are not 'affordable' (at least for any length of time and for the average household) if they absorb more than 20% of the income of the tenant' (NFHA, 1990, p. 19). As noted previously, the NFHA has a more recent *should* statement, 'that tenants should not pay more than 22% of their income as rent' (NFHA, 1993, p. 35).

Through its CORE data the NFHA monitors in some detail what different categories of tenants *do* pay on average and expresses these as affordability levels. Their data for 1991/92 shows an overall affordability rate by households with at least one person in work of 25%. For new assured tenancies it was 29%.

If the affordability rate is 'too high' what responses are possible? Housing associations might respond by trying to cut costs but this might mean a reduction in quality. More generally, there is a relationship between rents and subsidy levels and there have been arguments to the effect that as subsidy levels fall rents will rise and become increasingly unaffordable. One response to this situation is that less will get built. Thus higher affordability levels might mean less investment. If governments are not prepared to accept quality reductions in new housing provision and they are sure that housing suppliers cannot make more efficiency gains, they may wish to increase assistance to consumers (higher housing benefit levels). In fact affordability rates have been rising in many European countries as production subsidies have been cut and output has fallen.

In the owner-occupied sector affordability questions have been linked (in the UK) to claims that house prices are too high for first time buyers or rising mortgage costs make current housing 'unaffordable' and lead to mortgage default. This is something which can be compounded, as experience in the UK shows, by problems of 'negative equity' in a period of falling house prices.

10.7 POLICY APPROACHES

The questions of affordability cannot logically be separated from questions of quality and quantity. Governments do not appear to argue that housing as a commodity is on average too expensive (or too cheap) within a country. The more usual concern is that housing is too expensive for some households to acquire dwellings of an acceptable standard. If the standard is absolute then policy must attack factors which influence housing costs. An alternative approach would, of course, be that standards are allowed to fall.

The concern becomes, as one moves away from averages, one of distribution. Specifically the relationships between the distribution of incomes and the distribution of housing costs. We then get to the nub of the major housing problem for all countries which is that some housing costs are 'too high' compared to the incomes of some households.

The Dutch government has argued that housing subsidies 'are for a very considerable part used by households who, ... in the light of international comparisons, can easily pay for higher housing costs' (Netherlands Ministry of Finance quoted in Menkveld, 1991). In its Housing Memorandum for the 1990s the Dutch government argued that, 'If those living in accommodation which is too cheap move to more expensive housing, more affordable dwellings become available for those who are living in accommodation which is too expensive and the government will not be required to provide as much funding' (Netherlands Ministry of Housing, Physical Planning and the Environment, 1989, p. 9). Here is a government making explicit its desire to see some affordability rates raised so that government expenditure can be reduced.

In a broad sense, governments across western Europe have reacted to high housing costs by trying to reduce them through conditional object subsidies which assist suppliers and conditional subject subsidies in the form of housing allowances for consumers. As production subsidies have fallen in recent years housing allowances have not risen sufficiently to compensate, on average, and so average affordability rates have risen.

If society does not like the housing outcomes of a current housing system then either some structural changes in the system or some changes in the payments which occur within the system are called for. One of the dangers with the affordability debate is that the issue may become one of how to make housing cheaper. This might be by concentrating on a special class of housing – 'affordable housing' – which is for those with low incomes. This identification of particular people with particular types of housing raises a wide range of additional issues – not least of which is stigmatization.

The idea that there is a special class of housing which is 'affordable' has manifested itself in Britain in policies designed specifically to supply this housing. The major confusion in this approach is that the government does not define 'affordable housing'. However, *Planning Policy Guidance Note 3* (DOE, 1992) states, 'A community's need for affordable housing is a material planning consideration ... Where there is a demonstrable lack of affordable housing to meet local needs, authorities may indicate an overall target for the provision of affordable housing throughout the plan area'. Local authorities may use 'planning agreements' to increase the supply of affordable housing by effectively getting some sort of cross-subsidy from some other development (Chapter 4). The contribution of such schemes is likely, however, to be small (Barlow and Chambers, 1992). A variety of strategies have been used by local authorities to obtain land and negotiate deals with the private sector for the provision of 'affordable housing' (Dunmore, 1992).

There are problems with an approach which concentrates on special ways of providing housing which is affordable. Thus the issues become how to make more land cheaply available for this special type of housing or how to do special financial deals to develop this special type of housing.

Such approaches separate 'affordable housing' in a way which avoids the major distributional issues. Across Europe the major questions are about the distributions of housing quality, household incomes and housing costs and the role of government in influencing those distributions. A consideration of the consequences of this action for housing investment must be part of any long-term housing policy.

10.8 SUMMARY

Comparing the proportions of household income or expenditure devoted to housing is difficult because of problems of definition and consistency of data. However, on the basis of OECD data, within the European Union the proportions of expenditure devoted to housing varied in 1990 from under 6% in Ireland to over 21% in Denmark. The proportion in the UK at 14.88% was a little lower than the figures for France and Germany (15.58 and 16.70%) but higher than for the Netherlands (14.32%). Other data presented from additional sources does not seem to show the average burden of housing expenditures in the UK to be significantly different from that in France, Germany and the Netherlands.

Across the European Union countries (with the exception of Greece) a common trend is clear: the proportion of income spent on housing is rising. One of the causes is an increase in the relative price of housing consumption. The relative price rises have been particularly marked in the UK and especially in the rented sector. Evidence from several countries points to low income groups experiencing the largest rent increases and a consequent rise in rent to income ratios.

Some housing allowance schemes in other countries do implicitly or explicitly assume that not more than a given proportion of income should be devoted to housing. It would be wrong to argue that no more than 'x' per cent of income should be devoted to housing in the UK because this is a norm for other countries. Problems of definition, data and quality comparisons make such judgements impossible.

The more useful comparisons relate to the policy approaches used to tackle affordability issues. Most countries have used a combination of supply subsidies and housing allowances to make housing cheaper for some households. As supply-side subsidies have been reduced, housing allowances have not generally been generous enough to prevent rent burdens rising.

In the UK the affordability debate has focused particularly on the problems of making housing association rent levels 'affordable' as grant rates are lowered and on the question of how to use planning measures to produce more 'affordable housing'. There is a danger that concentrating on the supply of a particular type of housing and trying to distinguish a special class of housing – 'affordable housing' – from the rest clouds the real issues which are those of the distribution of incomes compared with the distribution of housing costs.

11 | Conclusions

11.1 POLICY AND PERCEPTIONS

The way that a problem is perceived influences the definition of the problem and the measures that are taken to deal with the problem. Drawing boundaries around 'housing problems' and separating them from sets of personal, social, national and even international problems creates analytically unsustainable divisions. In one sense housing is about everything and everything is about housing. However, policy action which comes out of a box labelled 'housing' cannot be expected to alleviate a multitude of evils. Attacking poverty, unemployment and social deprivation would, on the other hand, do much to improve housing circumstances. The systematic integration of housing initiatives with wider policies is something which governments have yet to properly address.

The value in narrowing the policy focus to 'housing' is that it can allow us to examine the issue of the quality of accommodation which households occupy or their failure to have any accommodation at all. If there was no concern about the quality of the environment in which people live there would be no reason to have housing policies. The concept of an acceptable standard of housing is central to housing policy analysis. We have shown that housing policy is in key respects 'national' and not 'European' in nature. In this very important respect, the determination of an acceptable standard of housing, it is the national rather than the European perspective which prevails. If a similar standard of adequacy was applied across Europe the severity of housing problems would be seen to vary enormously from country to country. Policies are based, implicitly, on minimum standards but these minimum standards can vary geographically and temporally.

Assuming a minimum standard is applied within a country at a given point in time, we have made a distinction between what people 'need' according to a societally determined value judgement and what they can 'demand' given their financial circumstances. We have shown that governments in Europe have tried to close the gap between (1) what is demanded and supplied by housing markets, and (2) what housing is needed, by using a wide range of measures which influence housing demand and housing supply.

Perceptions about the extent of the shortage of housing of an acceptable quality change. A general tendency to believe that the shortage is less than it once was has, as we have observed, led to a reduction in the emphasis on eliminating physical housing shortages. This is consistent with viewing housing less as a production problem and more as a distribution problem. As a distribution problem, the issue of 'affordability' of housing by particular sections in society is stressed over and above issues of a general shortage. The associated shift from production to consumption subsidies that we have discussed does, however, present many problems including adverse effects on investment, increased risks for suppliers and uncertainty over the effective incidence of the subsidy.

We have challenged aspects of welfare economics which lend support to the idea that subsidies to individuals are best in welfare terms because they maximize individual choice and satisfaction. If choice is impeded and the consequences of higher demand are dissipated by the supply side of the housing market, putting more resources at the disposal of individuals addresses only part of the problem. Housing problems can still be correctly perceived throughout Europe to be problems of both demand and supply.

The assumed benefits of more individual choice and more atomistic decision making have combined with claims in favour of less public expenditure to put more emphasis on market processes. We have emphasized, however, that governments continue to play a very significant role in affecting these processes.

The degree of involvement by governments in housing markets cannot be assessed simply in terms of expenditure on housing. We have shown that measuring the extent to which housing is subsidized in any country is extremely complex. In fact the analytical and empirical investigation of housing subsidies in Chapters 3 and 4 suggests that much greater caution, and much more clarity than is common, is required in the very use of the term 'housing subsidy'. The range of government involvement goes far beyond direct expenditures and in to such areas as tax concessions, effects on land supply and the provision of financial guarantees. All of these make an assessment of the degree to which policy influences provision fraught with difficulties.

Neither the degree of public expenditure on housing nor the classification of housing ownership shows the extent to which governments influence the production and allocation of housing. Rented housing provision is significantly affected by the degree of freedom that governments allow housing suppliers in setting rents, selecting tenants and making surpluses. With respect to all of these we have shown that there is much diversity both between and within 'social rented' and 'private rented' housing.

Although there has been a shift in favour of market processes, rents continue to be strongly influenced by governments. A free market rent is less the norm than rent which is moderated by political decisions and regulated by administrative procedures. What rent is supposed to represent is often unclear. In a 'free market' rent is intended to clear the market. Administratively ordered rent setting procedures variously try to relate rents to the 'quality' of accommodation, the cost of provision or 'what can be afforded'. Given that rents in several countries remain strongly tied to the age of dwellings and that, typically, several rent setting systems operate within a country, the problems of 'consistent pricing' continue, as they have for many years, to adversely affect the efficiency and equity of allocation.

The gap between what tenants pay and what landlords receive is getting larger in many countries. Housing allowances bridge the gap. With this growing subsidy, it is somewhat ironic that these same countries are said to be simultaneously in the process of creating a more market oriented housing system.

In such situations future investment levels will be strongly influenced by government. The volume of investment in housing and the distribution of that investment continues, despite a shift away from object subsidies, to be strongly influenced by government decisions. Although wider forces in society both influence investment and influence policy, the decisions made by governments in Europe have major consequences not just for investment but also for the rents which households pay and the processes by which housing is allocated.

11.2 CONVERGENCE VERSUS DIVERSITY

It is sometimes claimed that housing systems in Europe are becoming more like one another, that there are many similar things happening in different countries, and thus there is a process of 'convergence' in housing systems and in housing policies. This process is often described as if it is an inevitable function of broad trends in society. Whilst we have referred to many similar developments in different countries and, at a very general level, similar policy objectives, the operation of housing systems and the mixture of policy approaches points to great and continuing diversity throughout the European Union.

Although falling housing production levels have been a feature of Europe for over 20 years, the extent of the fall varies considerably and, in some countries, production has increased in the 1990s. Wide variations in annual dwelling production rates exist. The physical attributes, and the tenure mix, of this output vary widely as detailed in Chapter 5. The generalization that social renting is under threat holds true for several countries, but construction for social renting was of growing significance relative to total production in the early 1990s, e.g. in France, Denmark and Germany.

The quality and tenure composition of the stock vary widely. Despite the problems of definition and measurement, it is safe to contrast the relatively high quality of the housing stock in Scandinavia, Austria, the UK and the Netherlands with the lower quality in southern Europe.

Whilst over 50% of the housing stock is rented in Germany, the Netherlands and Sweden, only around 20% is rented in Ireland, Spain and Greece. The ownership, control, pricing and access to this stock varies widely. The great diversity in the institutional arrangements, financing mechanisms and categories of landlords is apparent in Chapters 6 and 8. It would certainly be wrong to enunciate a standard 'European model' of either social or private renting.

Despite a general trend in favour of object subsidies, the relative strength of the trend and the balance between supply- and demand-side subsidies varies a great deal as was demonstrated in Chapter 4.

There are wide divergences not only in the processes by which housing is priced but in the proportions of income devoted to housing and the rates of increase in housing costs. The data in Chapter 10 contrasts the less than 10% of household consumption expenditure devoted to housing in Ireland and Greece with over 20% in Denmark.

In considering housing systems, policies and outcomes across Europe the notion of diversity is much easier to defend than that of convergence.

11.3 IS THE UK DIFFERENT?

In several respects the UK is different. Policy is much more tenure oriented in the UK than in the other countries we have examined. Policy has been geared to tenure change. Subsidies have been explicitly targeted at a reduction in council housing. Increases in the numbers of home owners has been a criterion by which politicians have urged that policy be judged. The issue of housing investment, in the sense of the volume of resources going to create new and improved housing, has not been as significant as tenure-orientated managerial reforms.

The UK has had one of the lowest levels of housing investment in the European Union for many years. Between 1970 and 1992, the average proportion of Gross Domestic Product devoted to housing investment was 3.5% in the UK; it was between 5 and 6% in France, Germany and the Netherlands. These countries built an annual average of six to eight dwellings per 1000 inhabitants; the UK built less than five per 1000. The differences, as we stated in Chapter 5, cannot be explained away simply by such factors as varying rates of demographic and economic change or contrasting sizes of housing stock. Policy approaches will have played an important part in producing the variations. We have shown that there are many ways of providing supply-side support in other countries which do not involve explicit public expenditure. This is sometimes because the expenditure of 'social' housing providers does not count as public expenditure, as they are formally outside of the 'public sector' but also because of the range of fiscal concessions and land market interventions used. The range of measures have been detailed in Chapters 5, 6 and 8. We have also shown, particularly in Chapter 6, that a large degree of public control over housing providers is possible without these providers being 'owned' by the government. This has important implications for discussions about the future of the governance of housing in the UK.

The supply-side support for a range of rented housing providers in Germany and France contrasts with the narrow support for once council housing and then housing associations in the UK. The very small private rented sector in the UK is partly a function of this narrow approach. The lack of support for private sector landlords is a distinguishing feature of British policy. We set out the arguments on this in Chapter 9.

Given the tenure bias, the building of new houses to rent in the UK is crucially dependent on public expenditure decisions. Building for renting is less significant in the UK than in other countries. The 17% of all housebuilding intended for renting in the UK in the early 1990s contrasts with the 25–37% levels in France, Germany and the Netherlands. The degree of change in this respect has been extremely marked in the UK; over 45% of all construction was intended for renting in 1980.

The narrowing of the quality range and the residualization of the social rented stock is not unique to the UK but the extent of the residualization and the residualization of renting as a whole does make the UK stand out. The much larger rented sectors in Germany and the Netherlands have a wider quality range and cater for relatively more above-average income earners. The status of rented housing and the policy approaches are different.

The consequences of policy change since 1980 have been more dramatic in the UK than elsewhere in Europe. The effects on the pattern of production have already been indicated. The consequences for housing costs were shown by the data in Chapter 10. Social rents increased much more in real terms in the UK than the other countries between 1980 and 1992. Coupled with this is the high degree of dependency on housing allowances in the UK. This dependency creates much uncertainty.

A major distinguishing feature of the UK is the large publicly owned rented stock. With this has come a degree of rent pooling and cross-subsidization not found in the other countries. The potential benefits of this were set out in Chapters 3 and 4. The benefits of rent pooling are however being dissipated as the emphasis on housing associations increases.

We are not advancing an argument that everything is better elsewhere. We have pointed to many continuing housing problems throughout Europe. The experience of other countries sometimes suggests ways of doing things differently. It has pointed to pitfalls as well as advantages in doing things differently.

11.4 INVESTMENT AND DISTRIBUTION

Two questions might be asked of any housing policy instrument:

1. What does it do for investment?
2. To what extent does it redistribute resources in favour of those suffering inadequate housing conditions?

If the answer to both questions is 'little or nothing' there is a *prima facie* case for doubting the usefulness of the instrument as a means of improving housing standards.

If housing problems were only problems of physical shortages, supply-side measures might suffice. If they were only problems of distribution then redistribution generally, without any special supply-side housing policies, might suffice. Redistribution would influence supply and more demand would bring forth more supply. In practice housing problems are a complex interaction of both demand-side and supply-side problems. Housing policies in Europe will continue to require both supply- and demand-side components which influence both the efficiency and the equity of markets.

Fresh housing initiatives by governments across Europe are likely to require new institutional arrangements which promote a more effective inter-action between political and market processes. If governments continue to work with the market place they must, if they are to promote worthwhile housing policies, accept the importance of their roles in converting need into demand and ensuring that there are efficient institutional arrangements for making that demand effective in stimulating supply.

References

Acosta, R. and Renard, V. (1993) *Urban Land and Property Markets in France*, UCL Press, London.

Alegre, J. (1990) The housing issue at European level, in *COFACE European Housing Conference Proceedings*, (eds L. Laurent and M. Jacques), COFACE, Brussels, pp. 73–82.

Alonso, W. (1964) *Location and Land Use*, Harvard University Press, Cambridge, MA.

Arblaster, L. and Hawtin, M. (1994) *Health, Housing and Social Policy: Homes for Wealth or Health*, Socialist Health Association, London.

Audit Commission (1992) *Developing Local Authority Housing Strategies*, HMSO, London.

Aughton, H. and Malpass, P. (1994) *Housing Finance: A Basic Guide*, Shelter, London.

Ball, M. J. (1985) The urban rent question. *Environment and Planning A*, **17**, 503–525.

Ball, M., Harloe, M. and Martens, M. (1988) *Housing and Social Change in Europe and the USA*, Routledge, London.

Barclays Bank (1994a) *Greece Country Report*, Barclays Bank Economics Department, Poole.

Barclays Bank (1994b) *Portugal Country Report*, Barclays Bank Economics Department, Poole.

Barclays Bank (1995) *Economic Review*, Barclays Bank Economics Department, Poole.

Barlow, J. (1993) Controlling the housing land market: some examples from Europe. *Urban Studies*, **30**(7), 1129–1149.

Barlow, J. (1994) Affordable housing – unaffordable mistakes?, paper presented to *Housing Studies Association Conference*, Bristol, September 1994.

Barlow, J. and Chambers, D. (1992) *Planning Agreements and Affordable Housing Provision*, Centre for Urban and Regional Research, University of Sussex.

Barlow, J. and Duncan, S. (1988) The use and abuse of housing tenure. *Housing Studies*, **3**, 219–231.

Barlow, J., Cocks, R. and Parker, M. (1994) *Planning for Affordable Housing*, HMSO, London.

Barr, N. (1987) *The Economics of the Welfare State*, Weidenfeld and Nicolson, London.

Barre, R. (1975) *Étude d'une réforme du financement du logement*, La Documentation Française, Paris.

Begg, D., Fischer, S. and Dornbusch, R. (1994) *Economics*, 4th edn, McGraw-Hill, London.

Bessy, P. (1992) Un menage sur six percoit une aide au logement. *Economique et Statistique*, **251**.

Best, R., Kemp, P., Coleman, D., Merrett, S. and Crook, T. (1992) *The Future of Private Renting, Consensus and Action*, Joseph Rowntree Foundation, York.

BIPE (1991) *Les Aides Publiques au Logement en Europe*, Direction de la Construction, Ministère de l'Equipement, du Logement, des Transports et de l'Espace, Paris.

Birch, J., Dwelly, T. and Kemp, P. (1993) The point of low return. *Roof*, March/April, 22–25.

Boelhouwer, P. and Priemus, H. (1990) Dutch housing policy realigned. *Netherlands Journal of Housing and Environmental Research*, **5**(1), 105–119.

Boelhouwer, P.J. and van der Heijden, H.M.H. (1992) *Housing Systems in Europe, Part I, A Comparative Study of Housing Policy*, Delft University Press, Delft.

Boucher, F. (1988) France, in *Between Owner Occupation and the Rented Sector: Housing in Ten European Countries*, (eds H. Kroes, F. Ymkers and A. Mulder), NCIV, De Bilt, pp. 287–349.

Bramley, G. (1990) *Bridging the Affordability Gap*, School of Advanced Urban Studies, University of Bristol, Bristol.

Bramley, G. (1991) *Bridging the Affordability Gap in 1990*, Association of District Councils/Housebuilders Federation, London.

Bramley, G. (1993) The enabling role for local authorities: a preliminary evaluation, in *Implementing Housing Policy*, (eds P. Malpass and R. Means), Open University Press, Buckingham, pp. 127–149.

Brenner, J.F. and Franklin, H.M. (1977) *Rent Control in North America and Four European Countries*, The Potomac Institute, Washington, DC.

Brown, C.V. and Jackson, P.M. (1990) *Public Sector Economics*, 4th edn, Basil Blackwell, London.

Bundesministerium (1979) *Current Trends and Policies in the Field of Housing, Building and Planning*, Federal Ministry for Regional Planning Building and Urban Development, Bonn.

Bundesministerium (1990) *Wohnungspolitik nach dem 2. Weltkrieg*, Bundesministerium für Raumordnung, Bauwesen und Städtebau, Bonn.

Bundesministerium (1992a) *Wohngeld und Mietbericht, 1991*, Bundesministerium für Raumordnung, Bauwesen und Städtebau, Bonn.

Bundesministerium (1992b) *'So hilft der staat beim bauen'*, Bundesministerium für Raumordnung, Bauwesen und Städtebau, Bonn.

Burrows, L., Phelps, L. and Walentowicz, P. (1993) *For Whose Benefit? The Housing Benefit Scheme Reviewed*, Shelter, London.

CDC (1993a) *Le secteur locatif dans l'économie du logement*, Cahiers Epargne et Habitat, Caisse des Dépôts et Consignations, Paris.

CDC (1993b) *Rapport Annual 1992, Groupe Caisse des Dépôts*, Caisse des Dépôts et Consignations, Paris.

CES (1993) *Évaluation de l'efficacité économique et sociale des aides publiques au logement*, Conseil Economique et Sociale, Direction des Journaux Officiels, Paris.

Chapman, M., McIntosh, S., Murie, A. and Whitting, G. (1994) *Scottish Housing and Europe*, Scottish Homes, Edinburgh.

COFACE (1989a) *Social Housing Policy, The Netherlands*, Housing Commission Report, COFACE, Brussels.

COFACE (1989b) *Social Housing Policy, France*, Housing Commission Report, COFACE, Brussels.

COFACE (1989c) *Social Housing Policy, Federal Republic of Germany*, Housing Commission Report, COFACE, Brussels.

COFACE (1990) *La Politique Sociale du Logement, Portugal*, Housing Commission Report, COFACE, Brussels.

Committee of Enquiry into Housing in Greater London (1965) *The Milner Holland Report*, HMSO, London.

Conijn, J. (1993) Dynamic cost principle in the rented sector: the debacle with an innovative financial instrument, paper presented at *European Housing Finance Seminar*, University of Bristol, Bristol.

Crook, A.D.H. (1988) Deregulation of private rented housing in Britain: investors' responses to government housing policy in the 1980s. *Built Environment*, **14**(314), 155–167.

Crook, A.D.H., Hughes, J. and Kemp, P. (1995) *The Supply of Privately Rented Homes: Today and Tomorrow*, Joseph Rowntree Foundation, York.

Crook, T. (1992) The revival of private rented housing: A comparison and commentary on recent proposals, in *The Future of Private Rented Housing: Consensus and Action*, (eds R. Best, P. Kemp, D. Coleman, S. Merrett and T. Crook), Joseph Rowntree Foundation, York, pp. 58–76.

CSO (1990) *Report on the 1990 Family Expenditure Survey*, HMSO, London.

CSO (1991) *Report on the 1991 Family Expenditure Survey*, HMSO, London.

Curci, G. and Taffin, C. (1991) Les Écarts de Loyer. *Economie et Statistique*, **240**, 29–36.

Daly, M. (1994) *The Right to a Home, the Right to a Future, Third Report of the European Observatory on Homelessness*, FEANTSA, Brussels.

Danish Ministry of Housing and Ministry of the Environment (1977) *Current Trends and Policies in the Field of Housing, Building and Planning*, Ministry of Housing, Copenhagen.

Danish Ministry of Housing and Building (1984) *Financing of Housing in Denmark*, Ministry of Housing and Building, Copenhagen.

de Gans, H.A. and Oskamp, A. (1992) Future housing need in the Randstad Holland: a matter of continuing individuation? *Netherlands Journal of Housing and the Built Environment*, **7**(2), 157–178.

Dienemann, O. (1990) Das Wohnungsproblem – der desolate zustand vieler Städte und Gemeinden-Ergebnisse eines ehrgeizigen Programmes zur Lösung der Wohnungsfrage in der DDR bis 1990, Bauakademie, Berlin.

Dienemann, O. (1993) Housing problems in the former German Democratic Republic and the 'New German States', in *The New Housing Shortage: Housing affordability in Europe and the USA*, (ed. G. Hallett), Routledge, London, pp. 128–150.

Dieterich, H., Dransfeld, E. and Voβ, W. (1993) *Urban Land and Property Markets in Germany*, UCL Press, London.

DIW (1986) Zur Entwicklung der Mietbelastung privater Haushalte, *Wochenbericht 4/86*, Deutsches Institut für Wirtschaftsforschung, Berlin.

DIW (1989) Lage und Perspektiven am Wohnungsmarkt, *Wochenbericht 24/89*, Deutsches Institut für Wirtschaftsforschung, Berlin.

DIW (1990) Wohnungsbau 1989 und 1990: Förderung nicht ausreichend, *Wochenbericht 3/90*, Deutsches Institut für Wirtschaftsforschung, Berlin.

DIW (1991) Aktuelle Tendenzen im Wohnungsbau und bei der Wohnungsbaufinanzierung, *Wochenbericht 45/91*, Deutsches Institut für Wirtschaftsforschung, Berlin.

DIW (1992) Aktuelle Tendenzen im Wohnungsbau und Wohnungsbaufinanzierung, *Wochenbericht 49/92*, Deutsches Institut für Wirtschaftsforschung, Berlin.

DOE (1982) *Housing and Construction Statistics 1971–1981, Great Britain*, HMSO, London.

DOE (1992) *Planning Policy Guidance Note 3*, March 1992.

DOE (1993a) *Housing and Construction Statistics in Great Britain*, HMSO, London.

DOE (1993b) *English House Condition Survey 1991*, HMSO, London.

DOE (1994) *Housing and Construction Statistics 1983–1993, Great Britain*, HMSO, London.

DOE (Ireland) (1978) *Current Trends and Policies in the Field of Housing, Building and Planning*, An Roinn Comhshaoil, Dublin.

DOE (Ireland) (1991) *A Plan for Social Housing*, An Roinn Comhshaoil, Dublin.

DOE (Ireland) (1993) *Developments in Housing Policy*, An Roinn Comhshaoil, Dublin.

Down, D., Holmans, A. and Small, H. (1994) Trends in the size of the private rented sector in England. *Housing Finance*, **22**(5), 7–11.

Drake, M. (1991) *Housing Associations and 1992 the Impact of the Single European Market*, National Federation of Housing Associations, London.

Drake, M. (1992) *Europe and 1992: A Handbook for Local Housing Authorities*, Institute of Housing, Coventry.

Duclaud-Williams, R. (1978) *The Politics of Housing in Britain and France*, Heinemann, London.

Dunmore, K. (1992) *Planning for Affordable Housing: A Practical Guide*, Institute of Housing, Coventry.

Eekhoff, J. (1989) Wohnungspolitik für die neunziger Jahre: Muss der Staat wieder Verstärkt eingreifen? *Gemeinnütziges Wohnungswesen*, **7**, 371–378.

Emms, P. (1990) *Social Housing: A European Dilemma?*, SAUS, University of Bristol.

ENH (1993) *Livro Branco sobre a Politica da Habitacäo em Portugal*, ENH, Lisbon.

Ermisch, J. (ed.) (1990) *Housing and The National Economy*, Avebury, Aldershot, England.

European Commission (1993) *Statistics on Housing in the European Community*, EC, Brussels.

European Commission (1994) *Statistics on Housing in the European Union*, EC, Brussels.

European Commission (1994a) *A Legal Analysis of the Impact of EC Legislation on the Housing Sector*, EC, Brussels.

European Commission (1994b) *Who is Who in Housing in the European Community*, EC, Brussels.

Eurostat (1986) *Social Indicators for the European Community*, Statistical Office for the European Community, Luxembourg.

Ford, J. and Wilcox, S. (1994) *Affordable Housing, Low Incomes and the Flexible Labour Market*, Research Report 22, NFHA, London.

Forrest, R. and Murie, A. (1988) *Selling the Welfare State: The Privatization of Public Housing*, Routledge, London.

French Housing Ministry (1992) *Les aides publiques au logement*, information sheets, Paris.

French Housing Ministry (1993) *Le Logement en France*, Direction de l'Habitat et de la Construction, Ministère du Logement, Paris.

French Housing Ministry (1994a) *Le compte du logement: Tableaux statistiques, 1984–1992*, Direction de L'Habitat et de la Construction, Ministère du Logement, Paris.

French Housing Ministry (1994b) *Le compte du logement: Rapport à la Commission des Comptes du Logement*, Direction des Affaires Economiques et Internationales, Ministère du Logement, Paris.

Garnett, D., Reid, B. and Riley, H. (1991) *Housing Finance*, IOH, Longman, Coventry/Harlow.

GdW (1992) *GdW Bericht 1991/92*, GdW, Köln.

GdW (1993) *GdW Bericht 1992/93*, GdW, Köln.

Geindre, F. (1993a) *Le Logement: Une Priorité pour Le XIe Plan, Rapport au Premier ministre*, La Documentation Française, Paris.

Geindre, F. (1993b) Les difficultés du secteur du logement, in *Villes, démocratie, solidarité: le pari d'une politique*, (eds F. Geindre and G. de la Gorce), La Documentation Française, Paris, pp. 133–147.

German Ministry for Regional Planning, Building and Urban Development and Federal Ministry for Economics (1979) *Current Trends and Policies in the Field of Housing, Building and Planning*, Federal Ministry for Regional Planning Building and Urban Development, Bonn.

Ghékiere, L. (1993) Patrimoines locatifs sociaux: politiques de vente comparées des Etats de la CEE, in *Maastricht: Enjeux pour le mouvement HLM*, Report from 54th HLM Congress, June 1993, UNFOHLM, Paris, pp. 31–37.

Ghékiere, L (1994) *Observatory on European Social Housing, report 1st Quarter 1994*, UNFOHLM, Paris.

Ghékiere, L. and Quilliot, R. (1991) *Marchés et Politiques du Logement dans La CEE*, La Documentation Française, Paris.

Golland, A (1995) House Prices, Land Prices and Building Costs in the UK, Netherlands and Germany, Working Paper, De Montfort University.

Grant, C. (ed.) (1992) Built to last? Reflections on British housing policy. Shelter, London.

Gyourko, J. (1990) Controlling and assisting privately rented housing. *Urban Studies*, **27**(6), 785–793.

Haffner, M.E.A. (1993) Fiscal treatment of owner-occupiers in six EC countries: A description. *Scandinavian Housing and Planning Research*, **10**(1), 49–54.

Hallett, G. (1977) *Housing and Land Policies in West Germany and Britain*, Macmillan, London.

Hallett, G. (1993) *The New Housing Shortage: Housing Affordability in Europe and the USA*, Routledge, London.

Hallett, G. (1994) *Housing Needs in Western and Eastern Germany*, Anglo-German Foundation for the Study of Industrialised Society, London.

Hancock, K. (1993) Can't pay? won't pay? or economic principles of affordability. *Urban Studies*, **30**(1), 127–145.

Harloe, M. (1985) *Private Rented Housing in the United States and Europe*, Croom Helm, London.

Harloe, M. (1988) Housing and social change in Europe and the USA, in *The Changing Role of Social Rented Housing*, (eds M. Ball, M. Harloe and M. Martens), Routledge, London, pp. 41–86.

Hills, J., Hubert, F., Tomann, H. and Whitehead, C. (1990) Shifting subsidies from bricks and mortar to people: experiences in Britain and West Germany. *Housing Studies*, 5(3), 147–167.

Hills, J. (1992) *Unravelling Housing Finance: Subsidies, Benefits and Taxation*, Clarendon Press, Oxford.

HLM Aujourd'hui (1991) *Habitat en Chiffres*, no. 22, HLM, Paris.

HMSO (1977) *Housing Policy a Consultative Document*, Cmnd 6851, HMSO, London.

HMSO (1987) *Housing: The Government's Proposals*, Cmnd 214, HMSO, London.

HMSO (1982) *The Private Rented Housing Sector*, Volume 1, Report to The House of Commons Environment Committee, HMSO, London.

Housing Research Foundation (1989) *The Future of Private Renting*, HRF, London.

Howenstine, E.J. (1981) *Private Rental Housing in Industrialized Countries*, Department of Housing and Urban Development, Washington, DC.

Howenstine, E.J. (1986) *Housing Vouchers A Comparative International Analysis*, New Brunswick Center for Urban and Policy Research, Rutgers University.

Hubert, F. (1992) *Risk and Incentives in German Social Housing Finance*, Free University of Berlin, Berlin.

Hubert, F. (1993) *Private Rented Housing in Germany*, report to Scottish Homes, Free University of Berlin, Berlin.

Ineichen, B. (1993) *Homes and Health*, E & FN Spon, London.

INSEE (1992) Le Logement Locatif de 1984 à 1989, *INSEE Resultats 203–204*, Consommation-Mode de Vie, Paris.

Jacques, M. (1990) The Housing Issue in the Twelve EC Member States, in *COFACE European Housing Conference Proceedings*, (eds L. Laurent and M. Jacques), COFACE, Brussels, pp. 31–71.

Joseph Rowntree Foundation (1991) The impact of the Business Expansion Scheme on the provision of rented housing, *Housing Research Findings*, **29**.

Joseph Rowntree Foundation (1993a) Local housing companies: the opportunities for council housing, *Housing Research Findings*, **82.**

Joseph Rowntree Foundation (1993b) The state of the private rented sector, *Housing Research Findings*, **90**.

Joseph Rowntree Foundation (1994a) *Inquiry into Planning for Housing*. Joseph Rowntree Foundation, York.

Joseph Rowntree Foundation (1994b) Housing support and poverty traps: lessons from abroad, *Housing Research Findings*, **131**.

Kearns, A. (1992) Affordability for housing association tenants: a key issue for British social housing policy. *Journal of Social Policy*, **21**(4), 525–549.

Kemeny, J. (1995) *From Public Housing to the Social Market: Rental Policy Strategies in Comparative Perspective*, Routledge, London.

Kemp, P. (1988) *The Private Provision of Rented Housing*, Avebury, Aldershot.

Kemp, P. (1990) Income-related assistance with housing costs: a cross-national comparison. *Urban Studies*, **27**(6), 795–908.

Kemp, P. (1992) The ghost of Rachman, in *Built to Last? Reflections on British housing policy*, (ed. C. Grant), Shelter, London, pp. 110–121.

Kleinman, M. (1995) Meeting housing needs through the market: an assessment of housing policies and the supply/demand balance in France and Great Britain. *Housing Studies*, **10**(1), 17–38.

Kornek, M. (1990) The housing management system in East Germany. *Housing Finance International*, August, 46–47.

Krätke, S. (1989) The future of social housing – problems and prospects of 'social ownership': the case of West Germany. *International Journal of Urban and Regional Research*, **1989**, 282–303.

Kroes, H., Ymkers, F. and Mulder, A. (1988) *Between Owner Occupation and the Rented Sector, Housing in 10 European Countries*, NCIV, De Bilt.

Landes, A. (1994) *Property: Spain – Flemings Research Report 21 January 1994*, Robert Fleming Spain, AV SA, Madrid.

Laurent, L. and Jacques, M. (eds) (1990) *Proceedings European Housing Conference*, COFACE, Brussels.

Lefebvre, B. (1992) Housing in France: the consequences of 10 years of deregulation, paper presented at *ENHR Housing Finance Group Meeting*, The Hague.

Leutner, B. (1987) *Housing Taxation in the Federal Republic of Germany*, GEWOS, Hamburg.

Leutner, B. and Jensen, D. (1988) German Federal Republic, in *Between Owner Occupation and the Rented Sector: Housing in Ten European Countries*, (eds H. Kroes, F. Ymkers and A. Mulder), NCIV, De Bilt, pp. 145–181.

Lloyds Bank (1995) *Lloyds Bank Economic Bulletin*, **1**, February 1995.

London Research Centre (1995) LRC Housing Update 10. January 1995. *Roof*, January/February (insert).

Louvot, C. (1992) De la location à la propriété: le parc de logements se redistribue. *Economie et Statistique*, **251**, 15–27.

Maclennan, D. (1988) Private rental housing: Britain viewed from abroad, in *The Private Provision of Rented Housing*, (ed. P. Kemp), Avebury, Aldershot, pp. 147–174.

Maclennan, D. and Williams, R. (1990) *Affordable Housing in Britain and America*, Joseph Rowntree Foundation Housing Finance Series, York.

Maclennan, D., Gibb, K. and More, A. (1991) *Fairer Subsidies, Faster Growth*, Joseph Rowntree Foundation, York.

Magalhäes, F. (1995) *Housing in Portugal, Treaty of Windsor Research Paper*, Instituto Superior Téchnico, Lisbon.

Malpass, P. and Murie, A. (1990) *Housing Policy and Practice*, 3rd edn, Macmillan, Basingstoke.

Marcuse, P. and Schumann, W. (1992) Housing in the colours of the GDR, in *The Reform of Housing in Eastern Europe and the Soviet Union*, (eds B. Turner, J. Hegedüs and I. Tosics), Routledge, London, pp. 74–144.

Matznetter, W. (1994) *Levels of Home-ownership across Europe: Economic, Political, Demographic and Architectural Factors at Work*, ENHR Conference Paper, Glasgow.

Menkveld, A. (1991) Comparing housing costs to income ratios among seven West European Countries: framework for analysis and the macro-level, paper presented at *Housing Policy as a Strategy for Change Conference*, Oslo.

Menkveld, A. (1993) An international comparison of housing consumption in the National Accounts in various OECD countries. *Scandinavian Housing and Planning Research*, **10**, Research Note, 43–48.

Minford, P., Peel, M. and Ashton, P. (1987) *The Housing Morass*, The Institute of Economic Affairs, London.

Muellbauer, J. (1990) *The Great British Housing Disaster and Economic Policy*, Institute for Public Policy Research, London.

Nath, S.K. (1969) *A Reappraisal of Welfare Economics*, Routledge and Kegan, London.

Nationale Woningraad (1993) *Some Facts about Housing*, Information Leaflet, NWR, Almere.

Nationale Woningraad (1994) *Report on Social Housing*, NWR, Almere.

Nederlandse Woonbund (1995) Dure armoede huren in de particuliere sector. *Woonbondig*, February.

Needham, B. (1992) A theory of land prices when land is supplied publicly: the case of the Netherlands. *Urban Studies*, **29**(5), 669–686.

Needham, B., Koenders, P. and Kruijt, B. (1993) *Urban Land and Property Markets in the Netherlands*, UCL Press, London.

Netherlands Central Bureau of Statistics (1992) *Statistical Yearbook, 1992*, CBS, The Hague.

Netherlands Ministry of Housing and Physical Planning (1975) *Current Trends and Policy in Housing and Building*, Netherlands Ministry of Housing and Physical Planning, The Hague.

Netherlands Ministry of Housing and Physical Planning (1977) *Current Trends and Policy in Housing and Building*, Netherlands Ministry of Housing and Physical Planning, The Hague.

Netherlands Ministry of Housing, Physical Planning and the Environment (1989) *Summary of Policy Document on Housing in the Nineties*, Netherlands Ministry of Housing, Physical Planning and the Environment, The Hague.

Netherlands Ministry of Housing, Physical Planning and the Environment (1992a) *Statistics on Housing in the European Community*, Netherlands Ministry of Housing, Physical Planning and the Environment, The Hague.

Netherlands Ministry of Housing, Physical Planning and the Environment (1992b) *A Description of Key Areas of Housing in the European Member States*, Netherlands Ministry of Housing, Physical Planning and the Environment, The Hague.

Netherlands Ministry of Housing, Physical Planning and Environment (1993) *Housing in the Netherlands, Country Monograph*, Netherlands Ministry of Housing, Physical Planning and the Environment, The Hague.

NFHA (1990) *Paying for Rented Housing*, Research Report 12, NFHA, London.

NFHA (1993) *CORE Annual Statistics 1991/1992*, Research Report 19, NFHA, London.

Nora, S. and Eveno, B. (1975) *L'amélioration de l'habitat ancien*, La Documentation Française, Paris.

Norton, A. and Novy, K. (1991) *Low Income Housing in Britain and Germany*, Anglo-German Foundation for the Study of Industrial Society, London.

Observatory on European Social Housing (1994) Germany: draft reform of subsidy to social housing, *News Bulletin 1*, UNFOHLM, Paris.

OECD (1983) *National Accounts Detailed Tables*, OECD, Paris.

OECD (1991) *National Accounts Detailed Tables*, OECD, Paris.

Oosterhaven, J. and Klunder, M.E. (1988) Dutch rent control and its far reaching consequences, paper for the *International Conference on Housing, Policy and Urban Innovation*, Amsterdam.

Oxley, M.J. (1975) Economic theory and urban planning. *Environment and Planning A*, **7**(5), 497–508.

Oxley, M.J. (1984) Owner occupation in various European countries, in *Land Management: New Directions*, (eds D. Chiddick and A. Millington), E & FN Spon, London, pp. 144–151.

Oxley, M.J. (1987) The aims and effects of housing allowances in Western Europe, in *Housing Markets and Policies under Fiscal Austerity*, (ed. W. Van Vliet), Greenwood Press, Westport, pp. 165–178.

Oxley, M.J. (1991a) The aims and methods of comparative housing research. *Scandinavian Housing and Planning Research*, **8**, 67–77.

Oxley, M.J. (1991b) Housing subsidies in Western Europe, in *Management, Quality and Economics in Building*, (eds A. Bezelga and P. Brandon), E & FN Spon, London, pp. 1783–1792.

Oxley, M.J. (1995) Private and social rented housing in Europe: distinctions, comparisons and resource allocation. *Scandinavian Journal of Housing and Planning Research*, **12**(2), 59–72.

Oxley, M.J. and Smith, J. (1993) *Social Rented Housing in the European Community*, European Housing Research Working Paper Series, Number 2, De Montfort University, Milton Keynes.

Oxley, M.J. and Smith, J. (1994) Investing in private rented housing: a European perspective. *Property Review*, **3**(3), 98–99.

Papa, O. (1992) *Housing Systems in Europe Part II: A Comparative Study of Housing Finance*, Delft University Press, Delft.

Power, A. (1993) *Hovels to High Rise: State Housing in Europe since 1850*, Routledge, London.

Priemus, H. (1988) Economic and demographic stagnation: housing and housing policy: the case of the Netherlands 1974–1984. *Housing Studies*, **2**(1), 17–27.

Priemus, H. (1990) Changes in the social rented sector in The Netherlands and the role of housing policy, paper presented at *ENHR Conference on Housing Debates and Urban Challenges*, Paris.

Priemus, H., Kleinman, M., Maclennan, D. and Turner, B. (1994) Maastricht Treaty: consequences for national housing policies. *Housing Studies*, **9**(2), 163–182.

Priemus, H. (1995) How to abolish social housing? The Dutch case. *International Journal of Urban and Regional Research*, **19**(1), 145–155.

Pryke, M. and Whitehead, C.M.E. (1991) *An Overview of Recent Change in the Provision of Private Finance for Social Housing*, Discussion Paper 28, University of Cambridge.

Quintet, D. (1988) *Les HLM: Approches Sociales, Économique et Juridiques*, ADELS, Paris.

Richardson, H.W. (1978) *Regional and Urban Economics*, Penguin, London.

Ricketts, M. (1987) Public policy and the private rented sector of the housing market. *Property Management*, **5**(2), 108–113.

Robinson, R. (1979) *Housing Economics and Public Policy*, Macmillan, London.

Rowley, C.K. and Peacock, A.T. (1975) *Welfare Economics*, Martin Robertson, London.

Ruonavaara, H. (1993) Types and forms of housing tenure: towards solving the comparison/translation problem. *Scandinavian Housing and Planning Research*, **8**, 67–77.

Samuelson, P.A. and Nordhaus, W.D. (1992) *Economics*, 14th edn, McGraw-Hill, London.

Schuler-Wallner, G. and Wullkopf, U. (1991) *Housing shortage and homelessness in the Federal Republic of Germany*, report for Expert Committee on 'Housing' of the International Federation for Housing and Planning, IWU, Darmstadt.

Scottish Homes (1994) *The Public Sector in Scotland*, Scottish Homes Working Paper, Scottish Homes, Edinburgh.

Siksiö, O. (1990) Learning from tenure: an international comparison on the meaning of tenure in nine European countries – East and West, in *Housing Evaluation*, CIB (Conseil International du Bâtiment pour la recherche l'etude et la documentation) proceedings, Publication 118, Rotterdam, pp. 151–73.

Smith, J. (1994) Social housing provision and investment: the role of the state, paper presented at *ENHR Conference*, Glasgow.

Social Housing (1991) Dutch social housing funding body emerges as model for potential UK agency. *Social Housing*, March, 4–5.

Stafford, D.C. (1978) *The Economics of Housing Policy*, Croom Helm, London.

Tomann, H. (1990) Housing in West Germany, in *Affordable Housing in Europe*, (eds D. Maclennan and R. Williams), Joseph Rowntree Foundation, York, pp. 55–73.

Ulbrich, R. (1992) *Verteilungswirkungen wohnungspolitischer Instrumente*, Institut Wohnen and Umwelt, Darmstadt.

UNFOHLM (1993) *Introductory Report for the HLM Congress 1993*, UNFOHLM, Paris.

United Nations Economic Commission for Europe (1990) *Rent policy in ECE Countries*, United Nations, Geneva.

United Nations Economic Commission for Europe (1993) *Annual Bulletin of Housing and Construction Statistics*, United Nations, Geneva.

Van Weesep, J. and Van Kempen, R. (1992a) *Housing in the Dutch Welfare State*, STEPRO Working Papers, University of Utrecht.

Van Weesep, J. and Van Kempen, R. (1992b) Economic change, income differentiation and housing: urban response in the Netherlands. *Urban Studies*, **29**(6), 979–990.

Van Vliet, W. (1990) *International Handbook of Housing Policies and Practices*, Greenwood, London.

Von Gluch, E. (1992) *Baubedarf in den neuen Bundesländern bis 2005*, ifo Institut für Wirtschaftsforschung, Munich.

Whitehead, C. and Kleinman, M. (1986) *Private Rented Housing in the 1980s and 1990s*, Department of Land Economy, University of Cambridge/Granta Editions, Cambridge.

Whitehead, C.M.E. (1991) From need to affordability: an analysis of UK housing objectives. *Urban Studies*, **28**(6), 871–887.

Wilcox, S. (1990) *The Need for Social Rented Housing in England in the 1990s*, Institute of Housing, London.

Wilcox, S. (1993) *Housing Finance Review, 1993*, Joseph Rowntree Foundation, York.

Williams, P. (1994) The housing market in Northern Ireland in 1993. *Housing Finance*, **22**(5), 30–37.

Williams, R.H. and Wood, B. (1994) *Urban Land and Property Markets in the UK*, UCL Press, London.

Willmott, P. and Murie, A. (1988) *Polarisation and Social Housing: The British and French Experience*, Policy Studies Institute, London.

Wood, G.A. (1990) The tax treatment of housing: economic issues and reform measures. *Urban Studies*, **27**(6), 809–830.

Ymkers, F. and Kroes, H. (1988) The Netherlands, in *Between Owner Occupation and the Rented Sector: Housing in Ten European Countries*, (eds H. Kroes, F. Ymkers and A. Mulder), NCIV, De Bilt, pp. 183–241

Author index

Subject index

Page numbers appearing in **bold** refer to figures and page numbers appearing in *italic* refer to tables.